The Best AMERICAN ESSAYS 1998

GUEST EDITORS OF
THE BEST AMERICAN ESSAYS

1986 ELIZABETH HARDWICK
1987 GAY TALESE
1988 ANNIE DILLARD
1989 GEOFFREY WOLFF
1990 JUSTIN KAPLAN
1991 JOYCE CAROL OATES
1992 SUSAN SONTAG
1993 JOSEPH EPSTEIN
1994 TRACY KIDDER
1995 JAMAICA KINCAID
1996 GEOFFREY C. WARD
1997 IAN FRAZIER
1998 CYNTHIA OZICK

The Best AMERICAN ESSAYS 1998

Edited and with an Introduction
by CYNTHIA OZICK

ROBERT ATWAN
Series Editor

HOUGHTON MIFFLIN COMPANY
BOSTON • NEW YORK

ISSN 0888-3742
ISBN 0-395-86051-2
ISBN 0-395-86052-0 (pbk.)

Printed in the United States of America

QUM 10 9 8 7 6 5 4

"Portrait of the Essay as a Warm Body." First published in *The Atlantic Monthly*. Copyright © 1998 by Cynthia Ozick.

"The Telephone" by Anwar F. Accawi. First published in *The Sun*. Copyright © 1997 by Anwar F. Accawi. Reprinted by permission of the author.

"Shadow Cities" by André Aciman. First published in *The New York Review of Books*. Copyright © 1997 by André Aciman. Reprinted by permission of the author.

"How I Learned to Speak Italian" by Helen Barolini. First published in *The Southwest Review*. Copyright © 1997 by Helen Barolini. Reprinted by permission of the author.

"Graven Images" by Saul Bellow. First published in *News from the Republic of Letters*. Copyright © 1997 by *News from the Republic of Letters*. Reprinted by permission of the author.

"The Merely Very Good" by Jeremy Bernstein. First published in *The American Scholar*. Copyright © 1997 by Jeremy Bernstein. Reprinted by permission of the author.

"States of Reading" by Sven Birkerts. First published in *The Gettysburg Review*. Copyright © 1997 by Sven Birkerts. Reprinted by permission of the author.

"What Is Realism?" by J. M. Coetzee. First published in *Salmagundi*. Copyright © 1997 by J. M. Coetzee. Reprinted by permission of the author.

"Altar Boy" by Brian Doyle. First published in *The American Scholar*. Copyright © 1997 by Brian Doyle. Reprinted by permission of the author.

"Witness" by Andre Dubus. From *Meditations from a Movable Chair* by Andre Dubus. Copyright © 1998 by Andre Dubus. Reprinted by permission of Alfred A. Knopf, Inc.

"Will You Still Feed Me?" by Joseph Epstein. First published in *The American Scholar*. Copyright © 1997 by Joseph Epstein. Reprinted by permission of the author.

Contents

Contents

Foreword

I'VE GROWN so accustomed to being asked what makes a good essay that I was taken by surprise recently when someone asked me what I considered a poor essay.

Years ago, when I was instructing college freshmen in the humble craft of writing essays — or "themes," as we called them — I noticed that many students had already been taught how to manufacture the Perfect Theme. It began with an introductory paragraph that contained a "thesis statement" and often cited someone named Webster; it then pursued its expository path through three paragraphs that "developed the main idea" until it finally reached a "concluding" paragraph that diligently summarized all three previous paragraphs. The conclusion usually began "Thus we see that . . ." If the theme told a personal story, it usually concluded with the narrative cliché "Suddenly I realized that . . ." Epiphanies abounded.

What was especially maddening about the typical five-paragraph theme had less to do with its tedious structure than with its implicit message that writing should be the end product of thought and not the enactment of its process. My students seemed unaware that writing could be an act of discovery, an opportunity to say something they had never before thought of saying. The worst themes were largely the products of premature conclusions, of unearned assurances, of minds made up. As Robert Frost once put it, for many people thinking merely means voting. Why go through the trouble of writing papers on an issue when all that's required is an opinion poll? So perhaps it did make more sense to call these productions themes and not essays, since what was being written had almost no connection with the original sense of "essaying" — trying out ideas and attitudes, writing out of a condition of uncertainty, of not-knowing. "Sleep lingers all our lifetime about our eyes," says Emerson, "as night hovers all day in the boughs of the fir-tree."

The five-paragraph theme was also a charade. It not only paraded relentlessly to its conclusion; it began with its conclusion. It was all about its conclusion. Its structure permitted no change of direction, no reconsideration, no wrestling with ideas. It was — and still is — the perfect vehicle for the sort of reader who likes to ask: "And your point is . . . ?"

The most talented essayists have aims other than merely getting a point across or a position announced or an identity established. It may help to imagine an essay as a Cubist rendition of an idea: the essayist would rather you see all sides and aspects of a thought. Some essayists — Montaigne was the first — seem literally to be turning ideas over in their minds. The intellectual essay is nothing if not ruminative; the autobiographical essay may continually lose its sense of direction. Both kinds of essays, like Samuel Johnson's unforgettable *Rasselas,* will often reach a "conclusion in which nothing is concluded."

You will find few tidy conclusions in this collection. To capture the essayistic spirit of this volume you might try reading the brief concluding essay first. After seeing a performance of *A Doll's House,* the literary critic James Wood explains why he thinks Chekhov is a far more satisfying writer than Ibsen. It has to do with something all of us at one time or another have called "real life." Unlike Ibsen, Chekhov is "not hustling life into comprehensibility." His characters think aimlessly, their remarks aren't conveniently underlined for the reader, they rarely make a "dramatic 'point.'" In contrast, Ibsen "is always tying the moral shoelaces of his characters, making everything neat, presentable, knowable." Like the five-paragraph theme.

But wait. There's a small problem here, one that prevents a neat conclusion. Wood reminds us of how often in Chekhov's fiction "we encounter the formulation 'And suddenly he realized that . . .'" Is this, then, actually "real life" or are we back to literary convention? Are Chekhov's stories responsible for the formulaic epiphanies that ritually conclude so many personal essays? Is it artistically risky for the essay to imitate fiction? Or is "real life" so elusive that all a writer can do to pretend to capture it is substitute a fresh formula for one that's gone stale? These are questions that will surface throughout this collection, whether, like Andre Dubus's "Witness," the essay is hauntingly private, or, like J. M. Coetzee's "What Is Realism?," it crosses so many literary boundaries at once that the reader may wonder whether "real life" exists at all — with or without quotation marks.

The Best American Essays features a selection of the year's outstanding essays, essays of literary achievement that show an awareness of craft and a forcefulness of thought. Hundreds of essays are gathered annually from a wide variety of national and regional publications. These essays are then screened and approximately one hundred are turned over to a distinguished guest editor, who may add a few personal discoveries and who makes the final selections.

To qualify for selection, the essays must be works of respectable literary quality, intended as fully developed, independent essays on subjects of general interest (not specialized scholarship), originally written in English (or translated by the author) for publication in an American periodical during the calendar year. Periodicals that want to make sure their contributors will be considered each year should include the series on their complimentary subscription list (Robert Atwan, Series Editor, *The Best American Essays*, P.O. Box 220, Readville, MA 02137).

This year, I'd again like to thank my friend Matthew Howard at *The Boston Review* for his generous advice and assistance. It was a pleasure, as always, to work with the Houghton Mifflin staff, especially Janet Silver, Heidi Pitlor, and Larry Cooper. And it was a singular delight to work on this year's collection with Cynthia Ozick. In her splendid introductory essay on the essay, she says that "true essayists rarely write novels." It may be rare, but there are some noted exceptions, and she is one of them. Known for her award-winning fiction, she is also the author of three outstanding essay collections: *Art & Ardor, Metaphor & Memory,* and *Fame & Folly.* A truer essayist would be hard to find.

R.A.

Introduction: Portrait of the Essay as a Warm Body

AN ESSAY is a thing of the imagination. If there is information in an essay, it is by-the-by, and if there is an opinion in it, you need not trust it for the long run. A genuine essay has no educational, polemical, or sociopolitical use; it is the movement of a free mind at play. Though it is written in prose, it is closer in kind to poetry than to any other form. Like a poem, a genuine essay is made out of language and character and mood and temperament and pluck and chance.

And if I speak of a genuine essay, it is because fakes abound. Here the old-fashioned term poetaster may apply, if only obliquely. As the poetaster is to the poet — a lesser aspirant — so the article is to the essay: a look-alike knockoff guaranteed not to wear well. An article is gossip. An essay is reflection and insight. An article has the temporary advantage of social heat — what's hot out there right now. An essay's heat is interior. An article is timely, topical, engaged in the issues and personalities of the moment; it is likely to be stale within the month. In five years it will have acquired the quaint aura of a rotary phone. An article is Siamese-twinned to its date of birth. An essay defies its date of birth, and ours too.

A small historical experiment. Who are the classical essayists who come at once to mind? Montaigne, obviously. Among the nineteenth-century English masters, the long row of Hazlitt, Lamb, De Quincey, Stevenson, Carlyle, Ruskin, Newman, Martineau, Arnold. Of the Americans, Emerson. It may be argued that nowadays these are read only by specialists and literature majors, and by the

latter only when they are compelled to. However accurate the
claim, it is irrelevant to the experiment, which has to do with
beginnings and their disclosures. Here, then, are some introductory passages:

> One of the pleasantest things in the world is going on a journey; but I
> like to go by myself. I can enjoy society in a room; but out of doors,
> nature is company enough for me. I am then never less alone than
> when alone.   — William Hazlitt, "On Going a Journey"

> To go into solitude, a man needs to retire as much from his chamber
> as from society. I am not solitary whilst I read and write, though nobody
> is with me. But if a man would be alone, let him look at the stars.
>   — Ralph Waldo Emerson, "Nature"

> I have often been asked how I first came to be a regular opium eater;
> and have suffered, very unjustly, in the opinion of my acquaintance,
> from being reputed to have brought upon myself all the sufferings
> which I shall have to record, by a long course of indulgence in this
> practice purely for the sake of creating an artificial state of pleasur-
> able excitement. This, however, is a misrepresentation of my case.
>   — Thomas De Quincey, "Confessions of an English Opium Eater"

> The human species, according to the best theory I can form of it, is
> composed of two distinct races, the men who borrow, and the men who
> lend.   — Charles Lamb, "The Two Races of Men"

> I saw two hareems in the East; and it would be wrong to pass them over
> in an account of my travels; though the subject is as little agreeable as
> any I can have to treat. I cannot now think of the two mornings thus
> employed without a heaviness of heart greater than I have ever brought
> away from Deaf and Dumb Schools, Lunatic Asylums, or even Prisons.
>   — Harriet Martineau, "From Eastern Life"

> The future of poetry is immense, because in poetry, where it is worthy
> of its high destinies, our race, as times goes on, will find an ever and
> surer stay. There is not a creed which is not shaken, not an accredited
> dogma which is not shown to be questionable, not a received tradition
> which does not threaten to dissolve. . . . But for poetry the idea is
> everything; the rest is a world of illusion, of divine illusion.
>   — Matthew Arnold, "The Study of Poetry"

> The changes wrought by death are in themselves so sharp and final,
> and so terrible and melancholy in their consequences, that the thing
> stands alone in man's experience, and has no parallel upon earth. It
> outdoes all other accidents because it is the last of them. Sometimes it

leaps suddenly upon its victims, like a Thug; sometimes it lays a regular siege and creeps upon their citadel during a score of years. And when the business is done, there is a sore havoc made in other people's lives, and a pin knocked out by which many subsidiary friendships hung together. — Robert Louis Stevenson, "Aes Triplex"

It is recorded of some people, as of Alexander the Great, that their sweat, in consequence of some rare and extraordinary constitution, emitted a sweet odor, the cause of which Plutarch and others investigated. But the nature of most bodies is the opposite, and at their best they are free from smell. Even the purest breath has nothing more excellent than to be without offensive odor, like that of very healthy children. — Michel de Montaigne, "Of Smells"

What might such a little anthology of opening sentences reveal? First, that language differs from one era to the next: there are touches of archaism here, if only in punctuation and cadence. Second, that splendid minds may contradict each other (outdoors, Hazlitt never feels alone; Emerson urges the opposite). Third, that the theme of an essay can be anything under the sun, however trivial (the smell of sweat) or crushing (the thought that we must die). Fourth, that the essay is a consistently recognizable and venerable — or call it ancient — form. In English: Addison and Steele in the eighteenth century, Bacon and Browne in the seventeenth, Lyly in the sixteenth, Bede in the seventh. And what of the biblical Koheleth — Ecclesiastes — who may be the oldest essayist reflecting on one of the oldest subjects: world-weariness?

So the essay is ancient and various: but this is a commonplace. There is something else, and it is more striking yet — the essay's power. By "power" I mean precisely the capacity to do what force always does: coerce assent. Never mind that the shape and intent of any essay is against coercion or suasion, or that the essay neither proposes nor purposes to get you to think like its author. A genuine essay is not a doctrinaire tract or a propaganda effort or a broadside. Thomas Paine's "Common Sense" and Emile Zola's "J'Accuse" are heroic landmark writings; but to call them essays, though they may resemble the form, is to misunderstand. The essay is not meant for the barricades; it is a stroll through someone's mazy mind. All the same, the essay turns out to be a force for agreement. It co-opts agreement; it courts agreement; it seduces agreement. For the brief hour we give to it, we are sure to fall into surrender and conviction. And this will occur even if we are intrinsically roused to resistance.

To illustrate: I may not be persuaded by Emersonianism as an ideology, but Emerson — his voice, his language, his music — persuades me. When we look for superlatives, not for nothing do we speak of "commanding" or "compelling" prose. If I am a skeptical rationalist or an advanced biochemist, I may regard (or discard) the idea of the soul as no better than a puff of warm vapor. But here is Emerson on the soul: "when it breathes through [man's] intellect, it is genius; when it breathes through his will, it is virtue; when it flows through his affection, it is love." And then — well, I am in thrall, I am possessed; I believe.

The novel has its own claims on surrender. It suspends our participation in the society we ordinarily live in, so that — for the time we are reading — we forget it utterly. But the essay does not allow us to forget our usual sensations and opinions; it does something even more potent: it makes us deny them. The authority of a masterly essayist — the authority of sublime language and intimate observation — is absolute. When I am with Hazlitt, I know no greater companion than nature. When I am with Emerson, I know no greater solitude than nature.

And what is most odd about the essay's power to lure us into its lair is how it goes about this work. We feel it when a political journalist comes after us with a point of view — we feel it the way the cat is wary of the dog. A polemic is a herald, complete with feathered hat and trumpet. A tract can be a trap. A magazine article generally has the scent of so-much-per-word. What is certain is that all of these are more or less in the position of a lepidopterist with his net: they mean to catch and skewer. They are focused on prey — i.e., us. The genuine essay, by contrast, never thinks of us; the genuine essay may be the most self-centered (the politer word would be subjective) arena for human thought ever devised.

Or else, though still not having you and me in mind (unless as an exemplum of common folly), it is not self-centered at all. When I was a child, I discovered in the public library a book that enchanted me then, and the idea of which has enchanted me for life. I have no recollection either of the title or of the writer — and anyhow very young readers rarely take note of authors; stories are simply and magically *there*. The characters included, as I remember them, three or four children and a delightful relation who is a storyteller, and the scheme was this: each child calls out a story element — most often an object — and the storyteller gathers up whatever is supplied (blue boots, a river, a fairy, a pencil box) and makes out of these random, unlikely, and disparate offerings a tale both logical and surprising. An essay, it seems to me, may be similarly constructed — if so deliberate a term applies. The essayist, let us say, unexpectedly stumbles over a pair of old blue boots in a corner of the garage, and this reminds her of when she last wore them — twenty years ago, on a trip to Paris, where on the banks of the Seine she stopped to watch an old fellow sketching, with a box of colored pencils at his side. The pencil wiggling over his sheet is a grayish pink, which reflects the threads of sunset pulling westward in the sky, like the reins of a fairy cart . . . and so on. The mind meanders, slipping from one impression to another, from reality to memory to dreamscape and back again.

In the same way Montaigne, in our sample, when contemplating the unpleasantness of sweat, ends with the pure breath of children. Or Stevenson, starting out with mortality, speaks first of ambush, then of war, and finally of a displaced pin. No one is freer than the essayist — free to leap out in any direction, to hop from thought to thought, to begin with the finish and finish with the middle, or to eschew beginning and end and keep only a middle. The marvel of it is that out of this apparent causelessness, out of this scattering of idiosyncratic seeing and telling, a coherent world is made. It is coherent because, after all, an essayist must be an artist, and every artist, whatever the means, arrives at a sound and singular imaginative frame — or call it, on a minor scale, a cosmogony.

And it is into this frame, this work of art, that we tumble like tar babies, and are held fast. What holds us there? The authority of a voice, yes; the pleasure — sometimes the anxiety — of a new idea, an untried angle, a snatch of reminiscence, bliss displayed or shock conveyed. An essay can be the product of intellect or memory, lightheartedness or gloom, well-being or disgruntlement. But always there is a certain quietude, on occasion a kind of detachment. Rage and revenge, I think, belong to fiction. The essay is cooler than that. Because it so often engages in acts of memory, and despite its gladder or more antic incarnations, the essay is by and large a serene or melancholic form. It mimics that low electric hum, sometimes rising to resemble actual speech, that all human beings carry inside their heads — a vibration, garrulous if somewhat indistinct, that never leaves us while we wake. It is the hum of perpetual noticing: the configuration of someone's eyelid or tooth, the veins on a hand, a wisp of string caught on a twig, some words your fourth-grade teacher said, so long ago, about the rain, the look of an awning, a sidewalk, a bit of cheese left on a plate. All day long this inescapable hum drums on, recalling one thing and another, and pointing out this and this and this. Legend has it that Titus, emperor of Rome, went mad because of the buzzing of a gnat that made its home in his ear; and presumably the gnat, flying out into the great world and then returning to her nest, whispered what she had seen and felt and learned there. But an essayist is more resourceful than an emperor, and can be relieved of this interior noise, if only for the time it takes to record its murmurings. To seize the hum and set it down for others to hear is the essayist's genius.

It is a genius bound to leisure, and even to luxury, if luxury is measured in hours. The essay's limits can be found in its own reflective nature. Poems have been wrested from the inferno of catastrophe or war, and battlefield letters too: these are the spontaneous bursts and burnings that danger excites. But the meditative temperateness of an essay requires a desk and a chair, a musing and a mooning, a connection to a civilized surround; even when the subject itself is a wilderness of lions and tigers, mulling is the way of it. An essay is a fireside thing, not a conflagration or a safari.

This may be why, when we ask who the essayists are, it turns out — though novelists may now and then write essays — that true essayists rarely write novels. Essayists are a species of metaphysician: they are inquisitive — also analytic — about the least grain of being. Novelists go about the strenuous business of marrying and burying their people, or else they send them to sea, or to Africa, or (at the least) out of town. Essayists in their stillness ponder love and death. It is probably an illusion that men are essayists more often than women (especially since women's essays have in the past frequently assumed the form of unpublished correspondence). And here I should, I suppose, add a note about maleness and femaleness as a literary issue — what is popularly termed "gender," as if men and women were French or German tables and sofas. I *should* add such a note; it is the fashion, or, rather, the current expectation or obligation — but there is nothing to say about any of it. Essays are written by men. Essays are written by women. That is the long and the short of it. John Updike, in a genially confident discourse on maleness ("The Disposable Rocket"), takes the view — though he admits to admixture — that the "male sense of space must differ from that of the female, who has such an interesting, active, and significant inner space. The space that interests men is outer." Except, let it be observed, when men write essays: since it is only inner space — interesting, active, significant — that can conceive and nourish the contemplative essay. The "ideal female body," Updike adds, "curves around the centers of repose," and no phrase could better describe the shape of the ideal essay — yet women are no fitter as essayists than men. In promoting the felt salience of sex, Updike nevertheless drives home an essayist's point. Essays, unlike novels, emerge from the sensations of the self. Fiction creeps into foreign bodies; the novelist can inhabit not only a sex not his own, but also beetles and noses and hunger artists and nomads and beasts; while the essay is, as we say, personal.

And here is an irony. Though I have been intent on distinguishing the marrow of the essay from the marrow of fiction, I confess I have been trying all along, in a subliminal way, to speak of the essay as if it — or she — were a character in a novel or a play: moody, fickle, given on a whim to changing her clothes, or the subject; sometimes obstinate, with a mind of her own; or hazy and light; never predictable. I mean for her to be dressed — and addressed — as we would Becky Sharp, or Ophelia, or Elizabeth Bennet, or Mrs. Ramsay, or Mrs. Wilcox, or even Hester Prynne. Put it that it is pointless to say (as I have done repeatedly, disliking it every moment) "the essay," "an essay." The essay — an essay — is not an abstraction; she may have recognizable contours, but she is highly colored and individuated; she is not a type. She is too fluid, too elusive, to be a category. She may be bold, she may be diffident, she may rely on beauty, or on cleverness, on eros or exotica. Whatever her story, she is the protagonist, the secret self's personification. When we knock on her door, she opens to us, she is a presence in the doorway, she leads us from room to room; then why should we not call her "she"? She may be privately indifferent to us, but she is anything but unwelcoming. Above all, she is not a hidden principle or a thesis or a construct: she is *there*, a living voice. She takes us in.

CYNTHIA OZICK

The Best
AMERICAN
ESSAYS
1998

ANWAR F. ACCAWI

The Telephone

FROM THE SUN

WHEN I WAS growing up in Magdaluna, a small Lebanese village in the terraced, rocky mountains east of Sidon, time didn't mean much to anybody, except maybe to those who were dying, or those waiting to appear in court because they had tampered with the boundary markers on their land. In those days, there was no real need for a calendar or a watch to keep track of the hours, days, months, and years. We knew what to do and when to do it, just as the Iraqi geese knew when to fly north, driven by the hot wind that blew in from the desert, and the ewes knew when to give birth to wet lambs that stood on long, shaky legs in the chilly March wind and baaed hesitantly, because they were small and cold and did not know where they were or what to do now that they were here. The only timepiece we had need of then was the sun. It rose and set, and the seasons rolled by, and we sowed seed and harvested and ate and played and married our cousins and had babies who got whooping cough and chickenpox — and those children who survived grew up and married *their* cousins and had babies who got whooping cough and chickenpox. We lived and loved and toiled and died without ever needing to know what year it was, or even the time of day.

It wasn't that we had no system for keeping track of time and of the important events in our lives. But ours was a natural — or, rather, a divine — calendar, because it was framed by acts of God. Allah himself set down the milestones with earthquakes and droughts and floods and locusts and pestilences. Simple as our calendar was, it worked just fine for us.

Take, for example, the birth date of Teta Im Khalil, the oldest woman in Magdaluna and all the surrounding villages. When I first met her, we had just returned home from Syria at the end of the Big War and were living with Grandma Mariam. Im Khalil came by to welcome my father home and to take a long, myopic look at his foreign-born wife, my mother. Im Khalil was so old that the skin of her cheeks looked like my father's grimy tobacco pouch, and when I kissed her (because Grandma insisted that I show her old friend affection), it was like kissing a soft suede glove that had been soaked with sweat and then left in a dark closet for a season. Im Khalil's face got me to wondering how old one had to be to look and taste the way she did. So, as soon as she had hobbled off on her cane, I asked Grandma, "How old is Teta Im Khalil?"

Grandma had to think for a moment; then she said, "I've been told that Teta was born shortly after the big snow that caused the roof on the mayor's house to cave in."

"And when was that?" I asked.

"Oh, about the time we had the big earthquake that cracked the wall in the east room."

Well, that was enough for me. You couldn't be more accurate than that, now, could you? Satisfied with her answer, I went back to playing with a ball made from an old sock stuffed with other, much older socks.

And that's the way it was in our little village for as far back as anybody could remember: people were born so many years before or after an earthquake or a flood; they got married or died so many years before or after a long drought or a big snow or some other disaster. One of the most unusual of these dates was when Antoinette the seamstress and Saeed the barber (and tooth puller) got married. That was the year of the whirlwind during which fish and oranges fell from the sky. Incredible as it may sound, the story of the fish and oranges was true, because men — respectable men, like Abu George the blacksmith and Abu Asaad the mule skinner, men who would not lie even to save their own souls — told and retold that story until it was incorporated into Magdaluna's calendar, just like the year of the black moon and the year of the locusts before it. My father, too, confirmed the story for me. He told me that he had been a small boy himself when it had rained fish and oranges from heaven. He'd gotten up one morning after a stormy night and walked out into the yard to find fish as long as his forearm still flopping here and there among the wet navel oranges.

The year of the fish-bearing twister, however, was not the last remarkable year. Many others followed in which strange and wonderful things happened: milestones added by the hand of Allah to Magdaluna's calendar. There was, for instance, the year of the drought, when the heavens were shut for months and the spring from which the entire village got its drinking water slowed to a trickle. The spring was about a mile from the village, in a ravine that opened at one end into a small, flat clearing covered with fine gray dust and hard, marble-sized goat droppings, because every afternoon the goatherds brought their flocks there to water them. In the year of the drought, that little clearing was always packed full of noisy kids with big brown eyes and sticky hands, and their mothers — sinewy, overworked young women with protruding collarbones and cracked, callused brown heels. The children ran around playing tag or hide-and-seek while the women talked, shooed flies, and awaited their turns to fill up their jars with drinking water to bring home to their napping men and wet babies. There were days when we had to wait from sunup until late afternoon just to fill a small clay jar with precious, cool water.

Sometimes, amid the long wait and the heat and the flies and the smell of goat dung, tempers flared, and the younger women, anxious about their babies, argued over whose turn it was to fill up her jar. And sometimes the arguments escalated into full-blown, knockdown-dragout fights; the women would grab each other by the hair and curse and scream and spit and call each other names that made my ears tingle. We little brown boys who went with our mothers to fetch water loved these fights, because we got to see the women's legs and their colored panties as they grappled and rolled around in the dust. Once in a while, we got lucky and saw much more, because some of the women wore nothing at all under their long dresses. God, how I used to look forward to those fights. I remember the rush, the excitement, the sun dancing on the dust clouds as a dress ripped and a young white breast was revealed, then quickly hidden. In my calendar, that year of drought will always be one of the best years of my childhood, because it was then, in a dusty clearing by a trickling mountain spring, I got my first glimpses of the wonders, the mysteries, and the promises

hidden beneath the folds of a woman's dress. Fish and oranges
from heaven . . . you can get over that.

But, in another way, the year of the drought was also one of the
worst of my life, because that was the year that Abu Raja, the retired
cook who used to entertain us kids by cracking walnuts on his
forehead, decided it was time Magdaluna got its own telephone.
Every civilized village needed a telephone, he said, and Magdaluna
was not going to get anywhere until it had one. A telephone would
link us with the outside world. At the time, I was too young to
understand the debate, but a few men — like Shukri, the retired
Turkish-army drill sergeant, and Abu Hanna the vineyard keeper
— did all they could to talk Abu Raja out of having a telephone
brought to the village. But they were outshouted and ignored and
finally shunned by the other villagers for resisting progress and
trying to keep a good thing from coming to Magdaluna.

One warm day in early fall, many of the villagers were out in
their fields repairing walls or gathering wood for the winter when
the shout went out that the telephone-company truck had arrived
at Abu Raja's *dikkan*, or country store. There were no roads in
those days, only footpaths and dry streambeds, so it took the
telephone-company truck almost a day to work its way up the rocky
terrain from Sidon — about the same time it took to walk. When
the truck came into view, Abu George, who had a huge voice and,
before the telephone, was Magdaluna's only long-distance commu-
nication system, bellowed the news from his front porch. Everybody dropped what they were doing and ran to Abu Raja's house
to see what was happening. Some of the more dignified villagers,
however, like Abu Habeeb and Abu Nazim, who had been to big
cities like Beirut and Damascus and had seen things like tele-
phones and telegraphs, did not run the way the rest did; they
walked with their canes hanging from the crooks of their arms, as
if on a Sunday afternoon stroll.

It did not take long for the whole village to assemble at Abu
Raja's *dikkan*. Some of the rich villagers, like the widow Farha and
the gendarme Abu Nadeem, walked right into the store and stood
at the elbows of the two important-looking men from the telephone company, who proceeded with utmost gravity, like priests at
Communion, to wire up the telephone. The poorer villagers stood
outside and listened carefully to the details relayed to them by the
not-so-poor people who stood in the doorway and could see inside.

"The bald man is cutting the blue wire," someone said.

"He is sticking the wire into the hole in the bottom of the black box," someone else added.

"The telephone man with the mustache is connecting two pieces of wire. Now he is twisting the ends together," a third voice chimed in.

Because I was small and unaware that I should have stood outside with the other poor folk to give the rich people inside more room (they seemed to need more of it than poor people did), I wriggled my way through the dense forest of legs to get a first-hand look at the action. I felt like the barefoot Moses, sandals in hand, staring at the burning bush on Mount Sinai. Breathless, I watched as the men in blue, their shirt pockets adorned with fancy lettering in a foreign language, put together a black machine that supposedly would make it possible to talk with uncles, aunts, and cousins who lived more than two days' ride away.

It was shortly after sunset when the man with the mustache announced that the telephone was ready to use. He explained that all Abu Raja had to do was lift the receiver, turn the crank on the black box a few times, and wait for an operator to take his call. Abu Raja, who had once lived and worked in Sidon, was impatient with the telephone man for assuming that he was ignorant. He grabbed the receiver and turned the crank forcefully, as if trying to start a Model T Ford. Everybody was impressed that he knew what to do. He even called the operator by her first name: "Centralist." Within moments, Abu Raja was talking with his brother, a concierge in Beirut. He didn't even have to raise his voice or shout to be heard.

If I hadn't seen it with my own two eyes and heard it with my own two ears, I would not have believed it — and my friend Kameel didn't. He was away that day watching his father's goats, and when he came back to the village that evening, his cousin Habeeb and I told him about the telephone and how Abu Raja had used it to speak with his brother in Beirut. After he heard our report, Kameel made the sign of the cross, kissed his thumbnail, and warned us that lying was a bad sin and would surely land us in purgatory. Kameel believed in Jesus and Mary, and wanted to be a priest when he grew up. He always crossed himself when Habeeb, who was irreverent, and I, who was Presbyterian, were around, even when we were not bearing bad news.

And the telephone, as it turned out, was bad news. With its coming, the face of the village began to change. One of the first effects was the shifting of the village's center. Before the telephone's arrival, the men of the village used to gather regularly at the house of Im Kaleem, a short, middle-aged widow with jet-black hair and a raspy voice that could be heard all over the village, even when she was only whispering. She was a devout Catholic and also the village *shlikki* — whore. The men met at her house to argue about politics and drink coffee and play cards or backgammon. Im Kaleem was not a true prostitute, however, because she did not charge for her services — not even for the coffee and tea (and, occasionally, the strong liquor called arrack) that she served the men. She did not need the money; her son, who was overseas in Africa, sent her money regularly. (I knew this because my father used to read her son's letters to her and take down her replies, as Im Kaleem could not read and write.) Im Kaleem was no slut either — unlike some women in the village — because she loved all the men she entertained, and they loved her, every one of them. In a way, she was married to all the men in the village. Everybody knew it — the wives knew it; the itinerant Catholic priest knew it; the Presbyterian minister knew it — but nobody objected. Actually, I suspect the women (my mother included) did not mind their husbands' visits to Im Kaleem. Oh, they wrung their hands and complained to one another about their men's unfaithfulness, but secretly they were relieved, because Im Kaleem took some of the pressure off them and kept the men out of their hair while they attended to their endless chores. Im Kaleem was also a kind of confessor and troubleshooter, talking sense to those men who were having family problems, especially the younger ones.

Before the telephone came to Magdaluna, Im Kaleem's house was bustling at just about any time of day, especially at night, when its windows were brightly lit with three large oil lamps, and the loud voices of the men talking, laughing, and arguing could be heard in the street below — a reassuring, homey sound. Her house was an island of comfort, an oasis for the weary village men, exhausted from having so little to do.

But it wasn't long before many of those men — the younger ones especially — started spending more of their days and evenings at Abu Raja's *dikkan*. There, they would eat and drink and

talk and play checkers and backgammon, and then lean their
chairs back against the wall — the signal that they were ready to
toss back and forth, like a ball, the latest rumors going around the
village. And they were always looking up from their games and
drinks and talk to glance at the phone in the corner, as if expecting
it to ring any minute and bring news that would change their
lives and deliver them from their aimless existence. In the mean-
time, they smoked cheap, hand-rolled cigarettes, dug dirt out from
under their fingernails with big pocketknives, and drank lukewarm
sodas that they called Kacula, Seffen-Ub, and Bebsi. Sometimes,
especially when it was hot, the days dragged on so slowly that the
men turned on Abu Saeed, a confirmed bachelor who practically
lived in Abu Raja's *dikkan,* and teased him for going around barefoot and unshaven since the Virgin had appeared to him behind
the olive press.

The telephone was also bad news for me personally. It took away
my lucrative business — a source of much-needed income. Before
the telephone came to Magdaluna, I used to hang around Im
Kaleem's courtyard and play marbles with the other kids, waiting
for some man to call down from a window and ask me to run to
the store for cigarettes or arrack, or to deliver a message to his
wife, such as what he wanted for supper. There was always something in it for me: a ten- or even a twenty-five-piaster piece. On a
good day, I ran nine or ten of those errands, which assured a steady
supply of marbles that I usually lost to Sami or his cousin Hani,
the basket weaver's boy. But as the days went by, fewer and fewer
men came to Im Kaleem's, and more and more congregated at
Abu Raja's to wait by the telephone. In the evenings, no light fell
from her window onto the street below, and the laughter and noise
of the men trailed off and finally stopped. Only Shukri, the retired
Turkish-army drill sergeant, remained faithful to Im Kaleem after
all the other men had deserted her; he was still seen going into or
leaving her house from time to time. Early that winter, Im Kaleem's
hair suddenly turned gray, and she got sick and old. Her legs
started giving her trouble, making it hard for her to walk. By spring
she hardly left her house anymore.

At Abu Raja's *dikkan,* the calls did eventually come, as expected,
and men and women started leaving the village the way a hailstorm
begins: first one, then two, then bunches. The army took them.

Jobs in the cities lured them. And ships and airplanes carried them to such faraway places as Australia and Brazil and New Zealand. My friend Kameel, his cousin Habeeb, and their cousins and my cousins all went away to become ditch diggers and mechanics and butcher-shop boys and deli owners who wore dirty aprons sixteen hours a day, all looking for a better life than the one they had left behind. Within a year, only the sick, the old, and the maimed were left in the village. Magdaluna became a skeleton of its former self, desolate and forsaken, like the tombs, a place to get away from.

Finally, the telephone took my family away, too. My father got a call from an old army buddy who told him that an oil company in southern Lebanon was hiring interpreters and instructors. My father applied for a job and got it, and we moved to Sidon, where I went to a Presbyterian missionary school and graduated in 1962. Three years later, having won a scholarship, I left Lebanon for the United States. Like the others who left Magdaluna before me, I am still looking for that better life.

ANDRÉ ACIMAN

Shadow Cities

FROM THE NEW YORK REVIEW OF BOOKS

ON A LATE spring morning almost two years ago, while walking
on Broadway, I suddenly noticed that something terrible had happened to Straus Park. The small park, located just where Broadway
intersects West End Avenue on West 106th Street, was being fenced
off. A group of workers wearing orange reflector shins were man-
ning all kinds of equipment, and next to what must have been
some sort of portable comfort station was a large electrical gener-
ator. Straus Park was being dismantled, demolished.

Not that Straus Park was such a wonderful place to begin with.
Its wooden benches were dirty, rotting, and perennially littered
with pigeon droppings. You'd think twice before sitting, and if you
did sit you'd want to leave immediately. It too had become a
favorite hangout for the homeless, the drunk, and the addict. Over
the years the old cobblestone pavement had turned into an undu-
lating terrain of dents and bulges, mostly cracked, with missing
pieces sporadically replaced by tar or cement, the whole thing
blanketed by a deep, drab, dirty gray. Finally, the emptied basin of
what used to be a fountain had turned into something resembling
a septic sandbox. Unlike the fountains of Rome, this one, like the
park itself, was a down-and-out affair. Never a drop. The fountain
had been turned off decades ago.

Straus Park was, like so many tiny, grubby parks one hardly ever
notices on the Lower East Side, relegated to a past that wasn't
ancient enough to have its blemishes forgiven or to feel nostalgic
about. One could say the same of the Art Nouveau–style statue of
what I mistook for a reclining Greek nymph lost in silent contem-

plation, looking inward, as it were, to avoid looking at what was around her. She looked very innocent, very Old World, and very out of place, almost pleading to be rescued from this ugly shrub that dubbed itself a park. In fact, the statue wasn't even there that day. She had disappeared, no doubt sold.

The thing I liked most about the square was gone. The way so many other things are gone today from around Straus Park: the Olympia Deli, the Blue Rose, Ideal Restaurant, Mr. Kay's Barbershop, the Pomander Bookshop, the Siam Spice Rack, Chelsea Two, and the old Olympia Theater, drawn and quartered, as all the theaters are these days, plus the liquor store that moved across the street but really disappeared when it changed owners, the flower store that went high tech, and La Rosita, which went from being down-and-under to up-and-coming.

Why should anybody care? And why should I, a foreigner, of all people, care? This wasn't even my city. Yet I had come here, an exile from Alexandria, doing what all exiles do on impulse, which is to look for their homeland abroad, to bridge the things here to things there, to rewrite the present so as not to write off the past. I wanted to rescue things everywhere, as though by restoring them here I might restore them elsewhere as well. In seeing one Greek restaurant disappear, or an old Italian cobbler's turn into a bodega, I was once again reminded that something was being taken away from the city and, therefore, from me — that even if I don't disappear from a place, places disappear from me.

I wanted everything to remain the same. Because this too is typical of people who have lost everything, including their roots or their ability to grow new ones. They may be mobile, scattered, nomadic, dislodged, but in their jittery state of transience they are thoroughly stationary. It is precisely because you have no roots that you don't budge, that you fear change, that you'll build on anything, rather than look for land. An exile is not just someone who has lost his home; it is someone who can't find another, who can't think of another. Some no longer even know what home means. They reinvent the concept with what they've got, the way we reinvent love with what's left of it each time. Some people bring exile with them the way they bring it upon themselves wherever they go.

I hate it when stores change names, the way I hate any change of season, not because I like winter more than spring, or because I like old store X better than new store Y, but because, like all foreigners who settle here and who always have the sense that their time warp is not perfectly aligned to the city's, and that they've docked, as it were, a few minutes ahead or a few minutes behind Earth time, any change reminds me of how imperfectly I've connected to it. It reminds me of the thing I fear most: that my feet are never quite solidly on the ground, but also that the soil under me is equally weak, that the graft didn't take. In the disappearance of small things, I read the tokens of my own dislocation, of my own transiency. An exile reads change the way he reads time, memory, self, love, fear, beauty: in the key of loss.

I remembered that on summer days many years earlier when I was doing research on my dissertation, I would sometimes leave the gloomy stacks of Butler Library at Columbia and walk out into the sun down to 106th Street, where I'd find a secluded shaded bench away from the drunks and sit there awhile, eat a sandwich, a pizza, occasionally smiling at some of the elderly ladies who sat, not in the park, but along the benches outside, the way they did on Saturday afternoons around Verdi Square on 72nd Street and had probably learned to do on sunny, windy summer days in central Europe, and as they still do in those mock-England spots in Paris that the French call *petits squares,* where people chat while their children play. Some of these ladies spoke with thick accents. I pictured their homes to myself, lots of lace, many doilies, Old World silverware, mannered Austro-Hungarian everything, down to the old gramophone, the black-and-white pictures on the wall, and *de rigueur* schnapps and slivovitz.

They made me think of old 1950s pictures of New York, where it seems to grow darker much sooner in the evening than it does nowadays, where everyone wears long gray overcoats because winters were always colder then, and when the Upper West Side teemed with people who had come before the war and then stayed on, building small, cluttered lives, turning this neighborhood into a reliquary of Frankfurt-am-Main — their Frankfurt-away-from-home, Frankfurt-on-the Hudson, as the old joke goes, but not an inappropriate name for a city that, in Germany today,

dubs itself "Mainhattan," and which is, ironically enough, a far
stranger city to them, now that it imitates Manhattan, than their
adopted Manhattan imitating old Frankfurt. There I met old Mrs.
Danziger with the tattoo on her arm. Eighty-three-year-old Kurt
Appelbaum, a concert pianist in his day, was sitting at such a bench;
we spoke; we became friendly; one night, without my asking, he
offered to play the *Waldstein* and *Rhapsody in Blue* for me, "But do
not tape," he said, perhaps because he wished I would, and now
that I think of it, I wish I had, as I sat and listened on a broken
chair he said had been given to him by Hannah Arendt, who had
inherited it from an old German colleague at the New School who
had since died as well.

This was the year I rediscovered the Busch Quartet's 1930s
recordings of Beethoven, and I imagined its members playing
everywhere in those Old World, prewar living rooms around Straus
Park. And by force of visualizing them here, I had projected them
onto the park as well, so that its benches and the statue and the
surrounding buildings and stores were, like holy men, stigmatized
by Beethoven's music as it was played by a group of exiles from
Hitler's Reich.

I would come every noon, for the statue mostly, because she was,
like me, willing to stand by in this halfway station called Straus
Park. She reminded me of those statues one finds everywhere in
Rome, springing on you from their niches in the evening when
you least expect them.

It is difficult to explain what seclusion means when you find it on
an island in the middle of Broadway, amid the roar of midday
traffic. What I was looking for, and had indeed found quite by
accident, was something that reminded me of an oasis — in the
metaphorical sense, since this was a "dry" fountain — but an oasis
of the soul, a place where, for no apparent reason, people stop on
their various journeys elsewhere. Straus Park, it seemed, was created precisely for this, for contemplation, for restoration — in
both its meanings — for retrospection, for finding oneself, for
finding the center of things.

And indeed there was something physically central about Straus
Park. This, after all, was where Broadway and West End Avenue
intersected, and the park seemed almost like a raised hub on West

106th Street, leading to Riverside Park on one side and to Central Park on the other. Straus Park was not on one street but at the intersection of four. Suddenly, before I knew why, I felt quite at home. I was in one place that had at least four addresses.

Here you could come, sit, and let your mind drift in four different directions: Broadway, which at this height had an unspecified northern European cast; West End, decidedly Londonish; 107th, very quiet, very narrow, tucked away around the corner, reminded me of those deceptively humble alleys where one finds stately homes along the canals of Amsterdam. And 106th, as it descended toward Central Park, looked like the main alley of small towns on the Italian Riviera, where, after much trundling in the blinding light at noon and the stagnant odor of fuel from the train station where you just got off, you finally approach a sort of cove, which you can't make out yet, but which you know is there, hidden behind a thick row of Mediterranean pines, over which, if you really strain your eyes, you'll catch the tops of striped beach umbrellas jutting beyond the trees, and beyond these, if you could just take a few steps closer, the sudden, spectacular blue of the sea.

To the west of Straus Park, however, the slice of Riverside and 106th had acquired a character that was strikingly Parisian, and with the fresh breeze that seemed to swell and subside all afternoon long, you sensed that behind the trees of Riverside Park, serene and silent flowed an elusive Seine, and beyond it, past the bridges that were to take you across, though you couldn't see any of it yet, was not the Hudson, not New Jersey, but the Left Bank — not the end of Manhattan, but the beginning of a whole bustling city awaiting beyond the trees — as it awaited so many decades ago, when as a boy, dreaming of Paris, I would go to the window and looking out to the sea at night would think that this was not North Africa at all, but the Île de la Cité. Perhaps what lay beyond the trees was not the end of Manhattan, or even Paris, but the beginning of another, unknown city, the real city, the one that always beckons, the one we invent each time and may never see and fear we've begun to forget.

There were moments when, despite the buses and the trucks and the noise of people with boom boxes, the traffic light would change and everything came to a standstill and people weren't speaking, and the unrelenting sun beat strong on the pavement,

and then you could almost swear this was an early summer afternoon in Italy, and that if I really thought about it, what lay behind
Riverside Park was not just my imaginary Seine, but that it could
be the Tiber as well. What made me think of Rome was that
everything here reminded me of the kind of place all tourists know
so well when, thirsty and tired with too much walking all day, you
arrive at a tiny empty piazza with a little fountain, douse your face,
then unbuckle your sandals, sit on the scalding marble edge of a
Baroque fountain, and simply let your feet rest awhile in what is
always exquisitely clear, nondrinkable water.

Depending on where I sat, or on which corner I moved to within
the park, I could be in any of four to five countries and never for
a second be in the one I couldn't avoid hearing, seeing, and
smelling. This, I think, is when I started to love, if love is the word
for it, New York. I would return to Straus Park every day, because
returning was itself now part of the ritual of remembering the
shadow cities hidden here — so that I, who had put myself there,
the way squatters put themselves somewhere and start to build on
nothing, with nothing, would return for no reason other than
perhaps to run into my own footprints. This became my habit, and
ultimately my habitat. Sometimes finding you are lost where you
were lost last year can be oddly reassuring, almost familiar. You
may never find yourself, but you do remember looking for yourself.
That too can be reassuring, comforting.

On a hot summer day I came looking for water in a place where
no water exists, the way dowsers do when they search for trapped,
underground places, seeking out the ghost of water, its remanence.
But the kind of water I was really looking for was not fountain
water at all, Roman or otherwise. I remembered my disappoint-
ment in Rome years ago when, dunking my feet in the turtle
fountain early one afternoon, it occurred to me that these surrep-
titious footbaths in the middle of an emptied Rome in August and
all this yearning for sunlight, heat, and water amounted to nothing
more than a poor man's simulated swim at the beaches of my
childhood, where water was indeed plentiful, and where all of your
body could bathe, not just your toes.

At Straus Park, I had discovered the memory of water. Here I
would come to remember not so much the beauty of the past as

the beauty of remembering, realizing that just because we love to look back doesn't mean we love the things we look back on.

There is a large fountain in Rome at Piazza Navona, where the four rivers of the world are represented: the Ganges, the Nile, the Plate, and the Danube. I knew it well, because it stood not far from a small bookstore where, years ago, as a teenager, I would go to purchase one Penguin book a week — a small, muggy, and sultry shop, from which I recall the sense of bliss on first coming out into the sun with a new book in my hand. As I surveyed these four rivers, which, was the question, do I splash my face in?

There is no frigate like a book, says Emily Dickinson. There was nothing I have loved more than to take a good book and sit somewhere in a quiet open spot in Rome with so many old things around me, open up to any page, and begin traveling back sometimes, as when I read Lawrence Durrell and Cavafy, thinking of time — of all that retrospection, to quote Whitman — or eagerly looked forward to the New World, as when I learned to love Eliot and Pound. Does a place become one's home because this is where one read the greatest number of books about other places? Can I long for Rome when I am finally standing where I yearned to stand when I was once a young man in Rome?

All this, if it hasn't already, begins to acquire absurd proportions when I realize that, during that dissertation summer of many years ago, I had applied for and gotten a job to teach in an American high school in Rome. So that as I sat here in Straus Park, going through my usual pickup sticks and cat's cradle of memories, I had discovered something unique: I didn't want to go to Rome, not for a year, not for half a year, not even for a month, because it finally dawned on me that I didn't very much like Rome, nor did I really want to be in France, or Egypt for that matter — and though I certainly did not like New York any better, I rather enjoyed my Straus-Park-Italy and my Straus-Park-Paris much more, the way sometimes I like postcards and travel books better than the places they remind me of, art books better than paintings, recordings better than live performances, and fantasies more than the people I fantasize about — some of whom are not only destined to disappoint, but can't even be forgiven for standing in the way of the pictures we originally had of them. Once in Rome, I would most certainly long to be in Straus Park remembering the Rome where I'd once remembered the beaches of my childhood. Italy was just my way of grafting myself to New York.

I could never understand or appreciate New York unless I could make it the mirror — call it the mnemonic correlate — of other cities I've known or imagined. No Mediterranean can look at a sunset in Manhattan and not think of another sunset thousands of miles away. No Mediterranean can stand looking at the tiny lights speckling the New Jersey cliffs at night and not remember a galaxy of little fishing boats that go out to sea at night, dotting the water with their tiny lights till dawn, when they come back to shore. But it is not New Jersey I see when I watch the sun set from Riverside Drive.

The real New York I never see either. I see only the New York that either sits in for other places or helps me summon them up. New York is the stand-in, the ersatz of all the things I can remember and cannot have, and may not even want, much less love, but continue to look for, because finding parallels can be more compelling than finding a home, because without parallels there can't be a home, even if, in the end, it is comparing we like, not the objects we compare. Outside of comparing, we cannot feel. One may falsify New York to make it more habitable, but by making it more habitable in that way, one also makes it certain it remains a falsehood, a figment.

New York is my home precisely because it is a place from where I can begin to be elsewhere — an analogue city, a surrogate city, a shadow city that allows me to naturalize and neutralize this terrifying, devastating, unlivable megalopolis by letting me think it is something else, somewhere else, that it is indeed far smaller, quainter than I feared, the way some cities on the Mediterranean are forever small and quaint, with just about the right number of places where people can go, sit, and, like Narcissus leaning over a pool of water, find themselves at every bend, every store window, every sculptured forefront. Straus Park allowed me to place more than one film over the entire city of New York, the way certain guidebooks of Rome do. For each photograph of an ancient ruin comes a series of colored transparencies. When you place the transparency over the picture of a ruin, the missing or fallen parts suddenly reappear, showing you how the Forum and the Colosseum must have looked in their heyday, or how Rome looked in the Middle Ages, and then in the late Renaissance, and so on. But when you lift all the plastic sheets, all you see are today's ruins.

I didn't want to see the real New York. I'd go backward in time and uncover an older New York, as though New York, like so many other cities on the Mediterranean, had an ancient side that was less menacing, that was not so difficult to restore, that had more past than present, and that corresponded to the old-fashioned world I think I come from. Hence, my obsession with things that are old and defunct and that seep through like ancient cobblestones and buried rails from under renewed coats of asphalt and tar. Sealed-off ancient firehouses, ancient stables turned into garages, ghost buildings awaiting demolition, old movie theaters converted into Baptist churches, old marketplaces that are now lost, subway stops that are ghost stations today — these are the ruins I dream of restoring, if only to date the whole world back a bit to my time, the way Herr Appelbaum and Frau Danziger belonged to my time. Going to Straus Park was like traveling elsewhere in time. *How frugal is the chariot that bears the human soul.*

How uncannily appropriate, therefore, to find out fifteen years later that the statue that helped me step back in time was not that of a nymph, but of Memory herself. In Greek her name is Mnemosyne, Zeus' mistress, mother of the Muses. I had, without knowing it, been coming to the right place after all. This is why I was so disturbed by the imminent demolition of the park: my house of memories would become a ghost park. If part of the city goes, part of us dies as well.

Of course, I had panicked too soon. Straus Park was marvelously restored. After spending more than a year in a foundry, a resurrected statue of Memory remembered her appointed place in the park and resumed her old position. Her fountain is the joy of children and of all people who lean over to splash their faces on a warm summer day. I go there very often, sometimes to have coffee in the morning after dropping my children off at school. I have now forgotten what the old Straus Park looked like. I do not miss it, but somehow part of me is locked there too, so that I come here sometimes to remember my summer of fifteen years ago as well, though I am glad those days are gone.

My repeated returns to Straus Park make of New York not only the shadow city of so many other cities I've known, but a shadow city of itself, reminding me of an earlier New York in my own life, and before that of a New York which existed before I was born and which has nothing to do with me but which I need to see — in old photographs, for example — because, as an exile without a past, I like to peek at others' foundations to imagine what mine might look like had I been born here, where mine might be if I were to build here. I like to know that Straus Park was once called Schuyler Square, and before that it was known as Bloomingdale Square, and that these are places where everything about me and the city claims a long, continuous, call it a common, ancestral, imaginary past, where nothing ever bolts into sudden being, but where nothing ever disappears, not those I love today, nor those I've loved in the past, that Old World people like Herr Appelbaum, who played Gershwin for me on 105th Street one night when he could have played Schubert instead, and Mrs. Danziger, who never escaped the Nazis and brought them with her in her dreams at night, might still sit side by side with Ida Straus, who refused to board the life-boats when the *Titanic* sank and stayed on with her husband — that all these people and all these layers upon layers of histories, warmed-over memories, and overdrawn fantasies should forever go into letting my Straus Park, with its Parisian Frankfurts and Roman Londons, remain forever a tiny, artificial speck on the map of the world that is my center of gravity, from which radiates every road I've traveled, and to which I always long to return when I am away.

But perhaps I should spell the mystery out and say what lies at the bottom of all this. Straus Park, this crossroad of the world, this capital of memory, this place where the four fountains of the world and the four quarters within me meet one another, is not Paris, is not Rome, could not be London or Amsterdam, Frankfurt or New York. It is, of course, Alexandria.

I come to Straus Park to remember Alexandria, be it an unreal Alexandria, an Alexandria that does not exist, that I've invented, or learned to cultivate in Rome as in Paris, so that in the end the Paris and the Rome I retrieve here are really the shadow of the shadow of Alexandria, versions of Alexandria, the remanence of Alexandria, infusing Straus Park itself now, reminding me of something that is not just elsewhere but that is perhaps more in me than it was ever out there, that it is, after all, perhaps just me, a me that is no less a figment of time than this city is a figment of space.

HELEN BAROLINI

How I Learned to Speak Italian

FROM THE SOUTHWEST REVIEW

HE WAS A patient man. His sloping shoulders curved with a bearing that spoke more of resistance and steadfastness than of resignation; his ruffled hair was graying, his eyes were mild and gray behind the glasses that were the badge of his work — he set type and proofread for *La Gazzetta*. It was because of his job at that weekly Italian-language newspaper in Syracuse that I met Mr. de Mascoli. In my last year at the university I determined it wasn't Spanish that interested me after all, but Italian. However, at that point I couldn't switch my language requirement; I would have to keep Spanish and do Italian on my own. I went to the *Gazzetta* to put in a want ad for a tutor. Instead, I found Mr. de Mascoli willing to teach me.

And why Italian? Because during that last year before graduation I had met an Italian student who had come over on a Fulbright grant to study at Syracuse University. Knowing him awakened in me unsuspected longings for that Mediterranean world of his, which I suddenly, belatedly realized could also be mine. I became conscious of an Italian background that had been left deliberately vague and in abeyance by my parents, who, though children of Italian immigrants, had so homogenized into standard American that their only trace of identity was an Italian surname, often misspelled and always mispronounced.

I knew nothing of Italian. It was not a popular subject at home. We had just come out of World War II, in which Italy had been our enemy, and my father was at once scornful and touchy about Italy's role in that conflict. And even before that we had never been part of the Italian community of the North Side, my parents having selected their first, then second home on James Street, a thoroughfare of great mansions receding eastward into large, comfortable homes, then more modest two-families until, finally, it became the commercial area of Eastwood. I would not learn until recently that I had grown up on the street named for Henry James's grandfather, an early developer of the barren tracts from which Syracuse grew and from which Henry enjoyed his income.

My parents' aspirations were away from the old Italian neighborhoods and into something better. My father made a significant leap into the American mainstream when he became a member of both the Rotary Club and the Syracuse Yacht and Country Club, where he and my mother golfed and I spent aimless summers.

It never occurred to my father to speak his own father's language to my two brothers or to me, and so we grew up never conversing with our only two living grandparents, my father's father and my mother's mother, and so never knowing them. My grandfather came to call each Christmas, my father's birthday; he sat uneasily in the sunroom with his overcoat on, took the shot of Scotch he was offered, and addressed the same phrase to me each year: "Youa gooda gehl?" Then he'd hand me a nickel. There was a feeling of strain in the performance. My father was a man of substance; he was not.

With my grandmother there was a brief ritual phrase in her dialect mouthed by us children when we went to the old Queen Anne–style house in Utica where my mother and all her brothers and sisters grew up. My grandmother was always in the kitchen, dressed in black, standing at a large black coal range stirring soup or something. My brothers and I, awkward in the presence of her foreignness, would be pushed in her direction by our mother during those holiday visits and told, "Go say hello to Gramma."

We'd go to the strange old woman, who didn't look like any of the grandmothers of our friends or like any of those on the covers of the *Saturday Evening Post* around Thanksgiving time. Gramma didn't stuff a turkey or make candied sweet potatoes and pumpkin pies. She made chicken soup filled with tiny pale meatballs and a bitter green she grew in her backyard along with broad beans and basil, things that were definitely un-American in those days. Her smell was like that of the cedar closet in our attic. She spoke strange words with a raspy sound.

When we stepped into her kitchen to greet her, she smiled broadly and tweaked our cheeks. We said in a rush the phrase our mother taught us. We didn't know what it meant. I think we never asked. And if we were to know it meant "How are you?" what difference would it have made? What further knowledge would we have had of the old woman in the shapeless black garment, with her wisps of gray hair falling out of the thick knob crammed with large old-fashioned tortoiseshell hairpins? None. We were strangers.

When, on a visit upstate, I had occasion to drive through Cazenovia, a village on the shores of Lake Cazenovia, it appeared to me as if in a dream. I saw again the lakeshore meadow that has always remained indelibly imprinted on my mind from childhood, but that I had thought must, by now, have vanished from the real world. That meadow, now called Gypsy Bay Park, was the site of family picnics to which we and Aunt Mary's family proceeded from Syracuse, while the other contingent (which was by far the greater number — my mother's three brothers, two other sisters, and all their families plus our grandmother) came from Utica. Cazenovia was the approximate halfway point, and there in the meadow on the lake, the cars would all pull up and baskets of food would be unloaded for the great summer reunion.

My father drove a car that had a front fold-up seat that I was allowed to stand at and hold on to while looking straight out the window at the roadway, pretending that I was the driver guiding us all to the lake. I always made it, and the weather was always fine.

And so we met in a landscape that, today, I would never have expected to glimpse again in its original state. Whenever, over the years, I would think back to the picnics in Cazenovia, I would imagine the locale filled with new housing developments or fast-food chains on the lakeshore. But no, the meadow was still green with grass, still fringed with trees bending toward the water, still free of picnic tables, barbecue grills on metal stands, and overflowing trash cans. It was the same as when I was five years old and the gathering took on the mythic quality that it still retains for me.

It was Gramma who had decreed this annual outing. When two of her daughters married and moved from Utica, she had made known her wish: that the family should meet each summer, when travel was easier, and eat together al fresco. It was her pleasure to have all her children, and their children, convene in the meadow and spend the day eating, singing, playing cards, gossiping, throwing balls, making jokes and toasts. It was a celebration of her progeny, of which she, long widowed, was the visible head, the venerable ancestor, the symbol of the strong-willed adventurer who had come from the Old World to make a new life and to prosper.

She was monumental. I can see her still, an imposing figure, dressed in black although it was summer, seated on a folding camp chair (just for her) under the shade of a large, leafy elm tree. She sat there as silently as a Sioux chief and was served food, given babies to kiss, and paid homage to all day. The others spread around her, sitting on blankets on the grass, or on the running boards of their Oldsmobiles and Buicks. What made my grandmother so intriguing was the mystery of her. For, despite its gaiety, the family picnic was also a time of puzzlement for me. Who was this stranger in black with whom I could not speak? What was her story? What did she know?

What I knew of my grandmother I heard from my mother: she believed in good food on the table and good linen on the bed. Everything else was fripperies, and she had the greatest scorn for those who dieted or got their nourishment through pills and potions. She knew you are what you eat, and she loved America for the great range of foods that it provided to people like her, used to so little, used to making do. She could not tolerate stinginess; she lived with her eldest son and his family of eleven and did all the gardening and cooking, providing a generous table.

She founded the family's well-being on food. She had gotten up early, baked bread, or used the dough for a crusty white pizza, sprinkled with oil, oregano, and red pepper, or with onions and potatoes, olives and anchovies — but never with tomato sauce, for that disguised the taste of good bread dough and made it soggy and soft. She provided these pizzas, or panini, to the mill workers whose wives were too lazy or too improvident to do it themselves. She kept the men's orders all in her mind; she had great powers of concentration, and her memory took the place of jotted-down notes. She never got an order wrong. From workers' lunches, she expanded into a small grocery store. Soon she was importing foodstuffs from Italy. Eventually, what she turned over to her sons was one of the largest wholesale food companies in central New York.

At those picnics my cousins were older than I, mostly young people in their teens and twenties. The boys wore knickerbockers and played banjos or ukuleles, and the girls wore white stockings and sleeveless frocks. My uncles played cards and joked among themselves; the women arranged and served endless platters of food. Somebody was always taking snapshots, and I have many of them in a large album that has survived a dozen moves.

My grandmother stayed regally under her tree like a tribal queen, and mounds of food were placed around her like offerings. Her daughters and daughters-in-law kept up a steady parade of passing the foods they had been preparing all week: fried chicken, salamis, prosciutto, roasted sweet peppers, fresh tomatoes sliced with mozzarella and basil, eggplant fritters, zucchini imbottiti, platters of corn, huge tubs of fresh salad greens, caciotto cheese, rounds of fresh crusty bread, every kind of fruit, and biscotti galore. It was as if my grandmother's Thanksgiving took place not in bleak November but on a summer day when there would be sun on her shoulders, flowers blooming and cool breezes off the lake, blue skies above and the produce of her backyard garden abundantly present. She lived with the memory of the picnic through the long upstate winter, and by the time spring had come, she would go out to plant the salad greens and put in the stakes for the broad beans and tomatoes, planting and planning for the coming picnic.

We were about fifty kin gathered in that meadow, living proof of the family progress. Gramma's sons and daughters vied to offer her their services, goods, and offspring — all that food, those cars, the well-dressed young men who would go to college. And Butch, an older cousin, would take me by the hand to the water's edge and I'd be allowed to wade in Cazenovia's waters, which were always tingling cold and made me squeal with delicious shock.

And yet with all that, for all the good times and good food and the happy chattering people who fussed over me and my brothers, I still felt a sense of strangeness, a sense of my parents' tolerating with an edge of disdain this Old World *festa* only for the sake of the old lady. When I asked my mother why Gramma looked so strange and never spoke to us, I was told she came from the old country, she doesn't speak our language. She might as well have been from Mars.

I never remember hearing our own mother speak to her mother, although she must have, however briefly. I only recall my astonishment at Mother's grief when Gramma died and we went to Utica for the funeral. How could Mother really feel so bad about someone she had never really talked to? Was it just because she was expected to cry? Or was she crying for the silence that had lain like a chasm between them?

Mother was a smartly dressed, very American lady who played golf and bridge and went to dances. She seemed to us to have nothing to do with the old woman in a kitchen where, at one time, a dozen and more people had sat around the long, linoleum-covered table. Nor did my father, with his downtown meetings and busy manner, seem to have any connection with his own father, who was called the Old Man and wore baggy pants and shuffled like a movie comedian.

There was no reason for me or my brothers to think, as we were growing up, that we were missing anything by not speaking Italian. We knew that our father spoke it, because at Christmas when the Old Man came to call, we'd overhear long streams of it and laugh at the queerness of it in our home. My mother, no, could never have been said to speak or know Italian, only some dialect phrases. But in my father reposed the tongue of his fathers, and it hadn't been important to him (or to us) that we have it.

Once, in my convent school history class, Sister Matilda asked me to pronounce Marconi's first name for her. I should know, she said, because I was Italian. No, I don't know, I answered proudly (even though I could correctly picture it, written out, in my mind). I was not Italian, I was American. And I flushed with shame at the nun's having singled me out like that.

What had I to do with Marconi or Mussolini or any of those funny types I'd see on the North Side the few times I accompanied my mother there for shopping? We didn't speak or eat Italian at home, with the exception of the loaf of Italian bread my father brought home every day from the Columbus Bakery. Occasionally my mother would prepare an Italian dinner for her mostly Irish friends, and then she'd have to go to the North Side, where the Italians lived and had their own pungent grocery stores, to find the pasta or the imported cheese and oil she needed. I hated to accompany her; the smell from barrels of dried and salted baccalà or of ripe provolone hanging by cords from the ceiling was as great an affront to my nose as the sound of the raspy Italian dialect spoken in the store was to my ears. That it all seemed crude and degrading was something I had absorbed from my parents in their zeal to advance themselves. It was the rather touching snobbery of second-generation Italian Americans toward those who were, in their view, "just off the boat."

But it was on the North Side that the *Gazzetta* offices were located, so I had to go there. And there I met Mr. de Mascoli. I could have grown up in Syracuse and lived there all my life without ever knowing that the *Gazzetta* existed. It took an Italian student to make me aware of the Italian paper, the beauty of Italian, and a lot of other things, too.

My father, as a Rotary project, had invited the Italian student (and a Colombian and a Venezuelan also) home for Thanksgiving dinner, to give them a taste of real America. What happened during that curious cultural exchange was not so much a forging of ties with America for the Italian and the South Americans as an awareness in myself of my own Latin bloodline and a longing to see from where and what I had originated. At Thanksgiving dinner it wasn't pilgrims and Plymouth I thought of but Catullus. The Latin poets I read in my college courses connected to the Italian student, who was already a *dottore* from an Italian university and was saying things in a sharply funny, ironic way — a way no American spoke. It was strange that my awakening came at an all-American celebration through the medium of a tall, lean-faced student of forestry who was relating to my father, in good English, his experiences during the war as an interpreter for the British troops pushing up through the Gothic Line to Florence.

Florence! I had never given thought to that fabled place, but in that instant I longed to see it. In my immediate conversion, I, who knew nothing of Italy or Italians, not even how to pronounce Marconi's first name, became aligned forever with the Italianness that had lain unplumbed and inert in me. My die was cast, over crammed turkey *gigante,* Yankee creamed onions and Hubbard squash, across from parents who would have been horrified to know it.

I was attracted to the Italian student, and he to me. When we started seeing each other, he was critical of my not knowing his language. "I know French and Spanish," I said. He was not impressed.

"Your language should have been Italian," he said sternly.

"I've had Latin, so it shouldn't be so hard to learn," I replied.

"Try this." He handed me his copy of the *Gazzetta.* It was the first time I had seen the paper, seen Italian. I couldn't make any sense of unfamiliar formations like *gli* and *sgombero,* the double *z*'s and the verb endings. I was filled with dismay, but I decided to learn and I thought it could be done easily, right at home. After all, my father knew Italian.

"No use in learning a language like that," my father said dismissively when I approached him. "Spanish is more useful. Even Portuguese will get you further than Italian."

Further where? Toward the foreign service in Brazil? But that was not my direction.

Learning Italian became something stronger than just pleasing the Italian student. I began to recall things, like my mother saying that just before her death Gramma had called for a sip of the mountain spring water near her Calabrian village. That was her last wish, her last memory; she had left Calabria at the age of seventeen with a husband of almost forty and had never gone back. But sixty years later, as she lay dying in Utica, it was only the water of her native hills that she wanted and called for.

I wanted to go see where she came from. I wanted to be able to talk to the Old Man, who still came each Christmas, and to tell him who I really was besides a gooda gehl, and to find out who he was.

I went deliberately to the *Gazzetta,* on the North Side, to find an Italian teacher rather than go to the university's Italian department because, when I called the department, I was answered by a professor who said, giving his name twice, "Pah-chay or Pace speaking." As if one could choose between the Italian name and the Anglicized version. For me, even then, there was only one way he could have said his name, and if he didn't understand that, he was not the teacher I wanted. Mr. de Mascoli was.

He was like Pinocchio's stepfather, a gentle Geppetto. And he was genuinely pleased that I should want to learn Italian. He would give me lessons in his home each evening after supper, he said. He wanted no payment. He had come from the hard, mountainous central part of Italy called the Abruzzo. He arrived in America in the late 1920s, not as an illiterate laborer, but as an idealist, a political émigré out of sympathy with the fascist regime. And he had been educated. He had a profound love for his homeland, and it was that love that made him want to give me its language.

I accepted his offer. And I thought of all the fine things I would send him in return when I got to Italy — the finest olive oil and Parmesan cheese for his wife; the nougat candy called *torrone* for his children; and for him an elegantly bound volume of Dante. I would send him copies of Italian newspapers and magazines, because he had told me confidentially that, yes, *La Gazzetta* was really the *porcheria* everyone said it was. But bad as it was, it kept the language alive among the people on the North Side. When it was gone, what would they have?

I went to Mr. de Mascoli's home each night in the faded old Chevy my father had passed on to me for getting to the university. The first night I arrived for my lessons I wore a full-skirted, almost ankle-length Black Watch tartan skirt my father had brought me from a trip to Chicago. It was topped by a wasp-waisted, buttoned-to-the-neck lime-green jacket. It was the New Look that Dior had just introduced to signal the end of wartime restrictions on fabric and style, and I felt very elegant, then too elegant, as Mr. de Mascoli led me down a hall to his kitchen. We sat at the table in the clean white kitchen that showed no sign of the meal he and his wife and children had just eaten. Mrs. de Mascoli, a short, pudgy, youngish woman, made a brief appearance and greeted me cordially. I could hear she was American, but she had neither the education nor the ascetic and dedicated air of her husband. She spoke the kind of rough-hewn English one heard on the North Side. In her simple, friendly way, she too was pleased that I was coming for Italian lessons.

In their clean white kitchen I spent a whole winter conjugating verbs, learning the impure *s* and the polite form of address. I began to speak Mr. de Mascoli's native language. I learned with a startled discomfit that my surname had a meaning and could be declined. Mollica was not only a family name but a noun of the feminine gender, meaning crumb, or the soft inner part of the loaf as distinct from the good, hard outer crust. The name had been a bane to me, since teachers, salesgirls, and camp counselors were

never able to say it. I would always have to repeat it and spell it as
they stuttered and stumbled, mangling and mouthing it in ludi-
crous ways. It was my cross, and then I learned it meant crumb.

I began to fantasize: what if, like the draught that changed
Alice's size, I could find a DRINK ME! that would switch me from
a hard-to-pronounce crumb to something fine like Miller? Daisy
Miller, Maud Miller. Even Henry. I'd be a different person immediately. In fact, for the first time I'd be a person in my own right,
not just a target for discriminatory labels and jokes.

From years of Latin I could see how my name was related to all
those words meaning soft: mollify, mollescent (the downside of
tumescent), mollusk. (A moll, as in Moll Flanders, was something
else!)

The Italian minces no meanings: *mollare*, the verb, means to
slacken; from that, the adjective *molle* means not only soft or lim-
ber, but flabby, pliant, even wanton. From *molle* comes *mollica*, and
then *mollezza*, that intriguing word meaning effeminancy and suggesting its counterpart, *malizia*, which signifies cunning, malice.
But I was marked from the start by softness, not cunning.

My mother could have been Mrs. Mollifiable, so thoroughly had
she taken on the meaning of her married name. Her maiden
name, Cardamone, derived either from an Eastern spice plant
called *kardamon* in Greek (the Calabria of her family origins had
been the ancient Greek-dominated Magna Graecia) or from one
who cards wool — and, if the latter, in Italian one who is a carder
is a tease (a *card!*) and, worse, a backbiter. This meaning derives
from the Latin *cardus*, thistle, whose prickles were used to card
wool; then, figuratively, the meaning extends to include the prickles of a verbal barb, as in badmouthing. Which might have given
my mother a certain luster that her soft Mollica weepiness did not
possess.

And what must have been the lewd cracks my father was party
to, with a name from which so many allusions to soft and limp
could be made?

A molleton, or *mollettone* in Italian, is literally a swanskin, or a
soft skin. Is this, I asked myself, why I was hypersensitive and thin-
skinned? Because I come from a genetic line that was so incon-
gruously delicate among the smoldering emotions of southern
Italy that it became identified forever after by a surname that told

all? Were my forebears a soft touch, too soft for their own good
in a place where basic fiber and guts would have been more
pressingly urgent than skin like a swan?

What if I had been not Miss Softbread but, say, Sally Smith of
the hard edge, a name evoking the manly English smithy at his
forge, with all the honorable tradition and advantage *that* en-
tailed? How my life might have advanced! I wondered about trans-
lating my name to Krumm; being female had an advantage — I
could marry a right-sounding name. But then I'd have to abandon
my Italian lessons and the plan to go to Italy and the Italian
student.

I continued my lessons. At home I practiced singing in Italian
with my opera records as I followed words in the libretti. In the
highflown phrases of operatic lingo I began to form myself a
language as remote as could be from my grandmother's dialect or
the North Side, but, I thought with satisfaction, very grand and
eloquent.

"Ardo per voi, forestiero innamorato," I sang in the sunroom along
with Ezio Pinza. *"Ma perchè così straziarmi,"* I said to Mr. de Mascoli
one night, right out of Rossini's *Mosè,* when he plied me with verbs.
Or, rhetorically, *"O! Qual portento è questo!"* I expressed no every-
day thought but something compounded of extreme yearning,
sacrifice, tribulation, or joy. In the speech of grand opera everything becomes grander, and I felt so, too, as I sang all the roles.
It was as if I were learning Elizabethan or Chaucerian English to
visit contemporary London as I memorized my lines prepara-
tory to leaving for Italy. I had worked and saved for a year to get
there.

When I went to say goodbye to Mr. de Mascoli, he seemed sad
and stooped. We had often spoken of the harshness many Italians
had suffered in their own land and how they had had to emigrate,
leaving with nothing, not even a proper language to bolster them.
I told him I would write to him in Italian and send him news of
his country. He said, "My country is a poor and beautiful place. I
do not hate her."

"And I never will!" I answered.

I went to Italy thinking to rejoin the Italian student, who had
already returned to his country, but that is another story: he
turned out always to have been married. It wasn't the end of

the world for me. I was in Italy and everything else was just beginning.

I studied in Perugia, I wrote articles for the *Syracuse Herald-Jour-
nal,* I saw Italy. I surpassed my initial Italian lessons and acquired
a Veneto accent when I met and married an Italian poet and
journalist, Antonio Barolini. He had courted me reading from a
book of his poetry that included an ode to Catullus with the lovely
lines (to be put on my grave marker):

> ora la fanciulla è sogno,
> sogno il poeta e l'amore . . .

Thus I acquired another Italian surname. Like the wine? some
people inquire at introductions. Yes, I say, even though they're
confusing me with Bardolino. But having been born bread, I like
that union with wine.

We lived some years in Italy before Antonio was sent to New York
as the U.S. correspondent for *La Stampa.* We found a house outside
the city, and it was there, finally, that I thought again of Mr. de
Mascoli. The unlikely link to the printer was a May Day pageant
given at my children's country day school. As the children frol-
icked on the lush green lawn, they sang a medley of spring songs,
ending with an English May Day carol whose refrain was:

> For the Lord knows when we shall meet again
> To be Maying another year.

It struck me with great sadness. I thought of the Italian student,
of my grandmother and the mountain spring she had never returned to, of Mr. de Mascoli and his gentle patience, of all the lost
opportunities and combinations of all our lives.

I had never written to Mr. de Mascoli from Italy or sent him the
fine gifts I promised. That night I made a package of the Italian
papers and magazines we had at home, along with some of my
husband's books that I had translated from Italian, and sent them
to the printer in Syracuse with a letter expressing my regret for
the delay and an explanation of what had happened in my life
since I last saw him more than ten years before.

The answer came from his wife. On a floral thank-you note
(which I still have) with`the printed message *It was so thoughtful of
you,* she had written: "It is almost three years that I lost my husband

and a son a year later which I think I will never get over it. I miss
them very much . . . It was our wish to go back to Italy for a trip
but all in vain. The books you sent will be read by my sister-in-law
who reads very good Italian, not like me, I'm trying hard to read
but don't understand it as well as her, but she explains to me. Like
my husband to you . . ."

I thought of time that passed and the actions that remained
forever stopped, undone. The May Day carol kept coming back
to me:

> For the Lord knows when we shall meet again
> To be Maying another year.

And if not Maying, all the other things we'd planned to do for
ourselves, for others. And then the others are no longer here. A
few years after that May Day, Antonio died suddenly in Rome. He
is buried far away in his Vicenza birthplace while I continue to live
outside New York, alone now, since our daughters are married and
gone. Life does not permit unrelenting sadness. May goes but
comes back each year. And though some shadow of regret remains
for all the words left unsaid and acts left undone, there will be
other words, other acts . . .

I often think of how my life, my husband's, and the lives of our
three daughters were so entwined with the language that Mr. de
Mascoli set out to give me so long ago. Despite his efforts and my
opera records, I still speak Italian with an upstate tonality; my
daughters do much better. Though Italian couldn't root perfectly
in me, it did in them: the eldest is chair of the Italian department
at an Ivy League university; the middle one lives and teaches in
Italy, a perfect signora; and the youngest has brought up her own
two American daughters to speak Italian from birth.

Occasionally I visit Susanna in Italy, but it's long between trips
and each visit is short. The country has changed: Mr. de Mascoli's
Italy is no longer a poor country of peasants pushed into war and
ruinous defeat by a dictator, but a prosperous industrial nation.
Susi married an Italian artist from Urbino and they have two sons,
Beniamino and Anselmo, with whom I speak Italian, for they speak
no English.

Now I am called Nonna. I never knew the word to address my
own grandmother when I was a child standing mute and embar-

rassed in front of her. Now, if it weren't too late, I would call her
Nonna, too. We could speak to each other and I'd hear of the
spring in Calabria.

   How unexpected it all turned out . . . how long a progress as
the seed of a long-ago infatuation found its right ground and produced its fruit. None of it did I foresee when I sat in his tidied
white kitchen and learned to speak Italian with Mr. de Mascoli.

SAUL BELLOW

Graven Images

FROM NEWS FROM THE REPUBLIC OF LETTERS

HARRY S. TRUMAN liked to say that as president of this country
he was its most powerful citizen — but sometimes he added, smiling, the photographers were even more powerful. They could tell
the commander in chief where to go, make him move his chair,
cross his legs, hold up a letter, order him to smile or to look stern.
He acknowledged their power and, as a political matter, deferred
to their judgment. What the people thought of their chief execu-
tive would to some extent be decided by the photographers and
the picture editors. Photographers may claim to be a priesthood
interpreting the laws of light, and light is a universal mystery that
the picture takers measure with their light meters. "In nature's
book of infinite mystery, a little I can read," says the Egyptian
soothsayer in *Antony and Cleopatra*. Pictures taken in the light must
be developed in the shallow mystery of darkrooms. But photographers have nothing in common with soothsayers. Their interests,
apart from the technical one, are social and political. To some
extent, it is they who decide how you are to be publicly seen. Your
"visual record" is in their hands.

Broadly speaking, your *amour propre* is the territory invaded by
the picture takers. You may wish or not wish to be in public life.
Some people have not the slightest desire to be in the papers or
on TV. Others feel that papers and TV screens confer immortality.
TV crews on a city street immediately attract big crowds. The arrival
of television cameras offers people the opportunity each and every
one of them has dreamt of — a shot at eternity. Not by deeds, not
by prayers, but solely by their faces, grinning and mugging.

But this aspect of modern image-making or idolatry is not, for me, the most interesting one. What I discover when I search my soul is that I have formed a picture of myself as I wish to be seen, and that while photographers are setting up their lights and cameras I am summoning up and fortifying that picture. My intent is to triumph over the photographers' vision of me — their judgment as to what my place in photographic reality is to be. They have *technics* — Science — on their side. On my side there is vanity and deceit — there is, as I have already said, *amour propre;* there is, moreover, a nagging sense that my powers of candor are weakening and sagging, and that my face betrays how heavily it is mortgaged to death. *Amour propre,* with all its hypocritical tricks, is the product of your bourgeois outlook. Your aim is to gain general acceptance for your false self, to make propaganda, concealing your real motives — motives of personal advantage. You persuade people to view you as you need to be viewed if you are to put it over on them. We all are, insofar as we live for our *amour propre,* loyal to nothing except our secret, crippled objectives — the objectives of every "civilized" man.

Et cetera.

Yes, we're all too familiar with *amour propre,* thanks to the great romantic writers of the nineteenth century. But give clever people something to understand and you can count on them to understand it. So in facing the photographers it's not the exposure of my *amour propre* that concerns me. What I feel in making innumerable last-minute ego arrangements is that the real me will decide to withhold itself. I know that the best picture instruments of Germany or "state-of-the-art" Japan are constructed for ends very different from mine. What need is there to bring these powerful lenses up to the very tip of my nose? They will meaninglessly enlarge the pores of my skin. You will supply them with shots that remind viewers of the leg of a mosquito photographed through a microscope. The truth about you is that you have lost more hair than you thought and that your scalp is shining through — the truth is that you have huge paisley-shaped bruises under your eyes and that your bridgework when you smile is far from "photogenic." You are not simply shown — you are exposed. This exposure cannot be prevented. One can only submit to the merciless cruelty of "pure objectivity," which is so hard on your illusions.

Then, too, from a contemporary point of view, the daily and

weekly papers — to say nothing of television — do not feel that they are honoring the truth if they do not tear away the tatters of vanity that cover our imperfections. No one is safe from exposure except the owners, the main stockholders, and the leading advertisers of the great national papers. Things weren't always like this. The "gentlemen" described by Aristotle are immune to shame — they are made that way; nothing shameful can touch these aristocrats. But Adam and Eve, when they had eaten the apple of self-consciousness, sewed fig leaves together to cover their nakedness.

It is the (not always conscious) premise of the photographer that his is the art of penetrating your private defenses. We, his subjects, can learn not to care. But we are not by any means an Aristotelian class, trained in the virtues. We are democrats and lead our petty lives in the shadow of shame. And for this as for all our weaknesses and vices there arise, in all civilized countries, entire classes of people, categories of specialists who specialize in *discovery* and exposure.

Their slogan is: Let the Record Show. And what the record shows is, of course, change and decay, instability, weakness and infirmity, darkness as endless and winding as the Malabar Caves as E. M. Forster years ago described them in *A Passage to India*.

A photograph that made me look worse than the Ruins of Athens was published by *Time* together with a line from William Blake: "The lineaments of gratified desire." Nowhere in the novel *Time* was reviewing had I so much as hinted that my face, with its lineaments, was anything like the faces Blake had in mind (faces of prostitutes, as his text explicitly tells us). But there was my dreary, sullen, tired, and aging mug. I was brought low by Blake's blazing words. But it is the prerogative of the mass media to bring you down when they think that you have gotten ahead of yourself — when they suspect you of flying too high. It doesn't damage us to be exposed, to appear in distorted shapes on film or slick paper or newsprint. I often remember how at the age of ninety-nine Freud's grandmother complained that in the paper "they made me look a hundred years old."

But picture editors and journalists often seem to feel that they are the public representatives of truth, and even that they are conferring some sort of immortality on you by singling you out. But you had better be prepared for rough treatment. Often your "privacy" is to them a cover for the lies and manipulations of *amour propre.*

Who would have thought that minor vanities might lead to such vexations. Your secrets will die in the glare of publicity. When the police strip Dimitri Karamazov to his foul underpants, he says to them, "Gentlemen, you have sullied my soul."

But the world has undergone a revolutionary transformation. Such simple, romantic standards of personal dignity and of the respect due to privacy are to be found today only in remote corners of backward countries. Maybe in the Pyrenees or in the forgotten backlands of Corsica — places where I shouldn't care to live. Everywhere else, the forces of insight are on the lookout. The function of their insights is to make your secrets public, for the public has a right to know, and it is the duty of journalists to deliver the secrets of people "in the news" to their readers. For every story has a story behind it — which is to say that your face, in its own way a story, the story that you present, has another, sometimes very different story underlying it, and it is through the skill of the photographer that these layers of story are revealed.

Painters and sculptors, whose publics are smaller, also approach our heads and faces with insight. They class themselves as artists and are more intellectually sophisticated — better educated than photographers. They have generally absorbed a certain amount of twentieth-century psychology, and their portraits may be filled or formed by their ideas and they may have a diagnostic intent. Do you want to know whether X, our subject, is a violent narcissist? Or whether his is a real, a human face, not a false ideological mask or disguise.

The photograph — to narrow it down — reduces us to two dimensions and it makes us small enough to be represented on a piece of paper or a frame of film. We have been trained by the camera to see the external world. We look *at* and not *into,* as one philosopher has put it. We do not allow ourselves to be *drawn* into what we see. We have been trained to go by the externals. The camera shows us only those, and it is we who do the rest. What we do this *with* is the imagination. What photographs have to show us is the external appearance of objects or beings in the real world, and this is only a portion of their reality. It is after all a convention.

I have known — and still know — many excellent photographers whose work I respect. There are demonic, sadistic camera technicians, too. All trades are like that. But neither the kindly nor the wicked ones can show us the realities we so hope — or long — to see.

Finally, there is the ancient Jewish rule forbidding graven images. My maternal grandfather refused to have his picture taken. But when he was dying my mother brought in a photographer and hid him behind the bushes.

This faded picture is one of my Old World legacies. I also inherited the brass family samovar and my mother's silver change purse. In this purse I now carry Betapace, Hytrin, and Coumadin tablets.

My grandfather's picture was taken in the late 1890s. He is sitting, dying in an apple orchard, his beard is spread over his upper body. His elbow rests on the top of his walking stick and his hand supports his head. His big eyes tell you that he is absorbed in *olam ha-bo* — the world to come, the next life. My mother used to say, "He would have been very angry with me. To make pictures was sinful [an *averah*], but I took the *averah* on myself."

When we were very young, my parents told us that until we came of age they would be responsible for our transgressions. But that is an altogether different matter. What I am saying here is that nowadays not even the nobs have their portraits painted, and the masses preserve the faces of ancestors in daguerreotypes and Kodaks. The critical mind sees an insignificant photographer hidden in the bushes, inserting a plate and pulling the cloth over his head. Perhaps the old man knew perfectly well that his picture was being taken. My mother was then old enough to bear the burden of this sin. She committed it because she loved him and was afraid of forgetting what he had looked like.

In any case, I have been not only photographed but cast in bronze and also painted. Since I am too impatient to sit still, painters and sculptors have worked from photographs. The Chicago Public Library exhibits the busts of bookish local boys. The artist who did my head was obliged to measure it while I was watching the Chicago Bulls on television. It was an important game and I didn't intend to miss it.

Considering the bronze head on display in the Harold Washington Library, I think that Pablo Picasso would have done it better. He might perhaps have given me a third eye and two noses. I'd have loved two noses.

But for a one-nose job, the bust in the Chicago library isn't at all bad.

JEREMY BERNSTEIN

The Merely Very Good

FROM THE AMERICAN SCHOLAR

EARLY IN 1981 I received an invitation to give a lecture at a
writers' conference that was being held someplace on the Delaware
River in Pennsylvania, just across from New Jersey. I don't remember the exact location, but a study of the map convinces me that
it was probably New Hope. My first inclination was to say no. There
were several reasons. I was living in New York City and teaching
full time. My weekends were precious and the idea of getting up
before dawn on a Saturday, renting a car, and driving across the
entire state of New Jersey to deliver a lecture was repellent. As I
recall, the honorarium offered would have barely covered the expense. Furthermore, a subject had been suggested for my lecture
that, in truth, no longer interested me. Since I both wrote and
did physics, I had often been asked to discuss the connection, if
any, between these two activities. When this first came up, I felt
obligated to say something, but after twenty years, about the only
thing that I felt like saying was that both physics and writing,
especially if one wanted to do them well, were extremely difficult.

The conference seemed to be centered on poetry, and one of
the things that came to mind was an anecdote that Robert Oppenheimer used to tell about himself. Since Oppenheimer will play a
significant role in what follows, I will elaborate. After Oppenheimer graduated from Harvard in 1925 — in three years, summa
cum laude — he was awarded a fellowship to study in Europe.
Following a very unhappy time in England, where he seems to have
had a sort of nervous breakdown — he physically attacked an old
friend, Francis Fergusson, apparently following an intimate discus-

sion he and Fergusson had been having about Oppenheimer's
feelings of sexual inadequacy — he went to Germany to get his
Ph.D. He studied with the distinguished German theoretical physicist Max Born in Göttingen and took his degree there in 1927 at
the age of twenty-three. Born's recollections of Oppenheimer,
which were published posthumously in 1975, were not sympathetic. Oppenheimer, he wrote, "was a man of great talent and he
was conscious of his superiority in a way which was embarrassing
and led to trouble. In my ordinary seminar on quantum mechanics, he used to interrupt the speaker, whoever it was, not excluding
myself, and to step to the blackboard, taking the chalk and declar-
ing: 'This can be done much better in the following manner.'" In
fact, it got so bad that Oppenheimer's fellow students in the
seminar petitioned Born to put a stop to it.

Quantum mechanics had been invented in the year before by
Erwin Schrödinger, Werner Heisenberg — also a Born disciple —
and Paul A. M. Dirac. The next year, Dirac came as a visitor to
Göttingen and, as it happened, roomed in the large house of a
physician named Cario where Oppenheimer also had a room.
Dirac was twenty-five. The two young men became friends — insofar as one could have a friendship with Dirac. As young as he was,
Dirac was already a great physicist, and I am sure he knew it. He
probably just took it for granted. However, he was, and remained,
an enigma. He rarely spoke, but when he did, it was always with
extraordinary precision and often with devastating effect. This
must have had a profound effect on Oppenheimer. While Oppenheimer was interrupting Born's seminars, announcing that he
could do calculations better in the quantum theory, Dirac, only
two years older, had *invented* the subject. In any case, in the course
of things the two of them often went for walks. In the version of
the story that I heard Oppenheimer tell, they were walking one
evening on the walls that surrounded Göttingen and got to discussing Oppenheimer's poetry. He had published, and continued
to publish, poems in such places as *Hound and Horn*. I would
imagine that the "discussion" was more like an Oppenheimer
monologue, which was abruptly interrupted by Dirac, who asked,
"How can you do both poetry and physics? In physics we try to
give people an understanding of something that nobody knew
before, whereas in poetry . . ." Oppenheimer allowed one to fill

in the rest of the sentence. As interesting as it might have been to hear the responses, this did not seem to be the sort of anecdote that would go over especially well at a conference devoted to poetry.

Pitted against these excellent reasons for my not going to the conference were two others that finally carried the day. In the first place, I was in the beginning stages of a love affair with a young woman who wanted very much to write. She wanted to write so much that she had resigned a lucrative job with an advertising agency and was giving herself a year in which, living on her savings, she was going to do nothing but write. It was a gutsy thing to do, but like many people — most, no doubt — who try it, she was finding it pretty rough going. In fact, she was rather discouraged. So, to cheer her up, I suggested attending this conference, where she might have a chance to talk with other people who were in the same boat. This aside, I had read in the tentative program of the conference that one of the other tutors was to be Stephen Spender. This, for reasons I will now explain, was decisive. I should begin by saying right off that I am not a great admirer of Spender's poetry. He is, for me, one of those people whose writing about their writing is more interesting than their writing itself. But I had read with great interest Spender's autobiography — *World Within World* — especially for what it revealed about the poet who did mean the most to me — namely, W. H. Auden. Auden's Dirac-like lucidity, the sheer wonder of the language, and the sense of fun about serious things — "At least my modern pieces shall be cheery / Like English bishops on the Quantum Theory" — were to me irresistible. I became fascinated by Spender's obsession with Auden. Auden must have been to Spender what Dirac was for Oppenheimer, a constant reminder of the difference between being "great" and being "merely" very good. I was also struck by the fact that, like Oppenheimer, Spender seemed "unfocused." Partly Jewish, partly homosexual, partly Communist, partly a British establishment figure, one wondered when he got time to write poetry. By being profoundly eccentric, both Auden and Dirac, probably not by accident, insulated themselves. They focused like laser beams. What I did not know in 1981 — I learned it only after Spender's journals were published in 1986 — was that Spender had paid a brief visit to the Institute for Advanced Study in Princeton in November of 1956, the year before I got there and two years before Dirac came on one of his perennial visits.

Spender's journal entry on his visit is fascinating both for what it says and for what it does not say. He begins by noting that "Oppenheimer lives in a beautiful house, the interior of which is painted almost entirely white." This was the director's mansion. Spender did not notice that, because of Oppenheimer's western connections, there was also the odd horse on the grounds. He continues: "He has beautiful paintings. As soon as we came in, he said: 'Now is the time to look at the van Gogh.' We went into his sitting room and saw a very fine van Gogh of a sun above a field almost entirely enclosed in shadows." At the end of my first interview with Oppenheimer, immediately after I had driven cross-country from Los Alamos in a convertible with a large hole in the roof and had been summoned to the interview while still covered in grime, he said to me that he and his wife had some pictures I might like to look at sometime. I wondered what he was talking about. Some months later I was invited to a party at the Oppenheimers' and realized that he was talking about a van Gogh. Some years later, I learned that this was part of a small collection he had inherited from his father to which he had never added.

A few days after Oppenheimer's funeral in 1967, I was at the Pilates gymnasium in New York, where George Balanchine was also a client. I had noticed that Balanchine was listed on the funeral program as having selected the music for it. I said to Balanchine that I didn't realize that he was a friend of Oppenheimer's. Balanchine said that he wasn't, but that a few days before Oppenheimer's death he had been invited to Princeton, where he and Oppenheimer, who knew that he was dying, discussed the music to be played — *Requiem Canticles* by Stravinsky and the String Quartet in C Sharp Minor, opus 131, by Beethoven — at the funeral. Balanchine was at a loss to explain this incident. I recall telling him about the van Gogh.

In his journal entry, Spender describes Oppenheimer's physical appearance: "Robert Oppenheimer is one of the most extraordinary-looking men I have ever seen. He has a head like that of a very small intelligent boy, with a long back to it, reminding one of those skulls which were specially elongated by the Egyptians. His skull gives an almost egg-shell impression of fragility, and is supported by a very thin neck. His expression is radiant and at the same time ascetic." Much of this description seems right to me except that it leaves out the fact that Oppenheimer did have the sun-wrinkled look of someone who had spent a great deal of time outdoors, which he had. Spender also does not seem to have remarked on Oppenheimer's eyes, which had a kind of wary luminescence. Siamese cats make a similar impression. But more important, Oppenheimer appears in Spender's journal as a disembodied figure with no contextual relevance to Spender's own life.

There is no comment about the fact that, three years earlier, Oppenheimer had been "tried" for disloyalty to this country and that his clearance had been taken away. One of the charges brought against him was that his wife, Katherine Puening Oppenheimer, was the former wife of Joseph Dallet, who had been a member of the Communist Party and who had been killed in 1937 fighting for the Spanish Republican Army. In 1937, Spender was also a member of the Communist Party in Britain and had also spent time in Spain. Did Oppenheimer know this? He usually knew most things about the people who interested him. Did "Kitty" Oppenheimer know it? Did this have anything to do with the fact that, during Spender's visit, she was upstairs "ill"? Spender offers no comment. What was he thinking? There were so many things the two of them might have said to each other, but didn't. They talked about the invasion of the Suez Canal.

The next year, my first year at the Institute for Advanced Study, Auden also came for a brief visit. There was a small lunch in the institute's cafeteria — no van Gogh for Auden — at which Oppenheimer presided. I have an indelible memory of Oppenheimer's telling Auden some fairly pointless anecdote about learning Sanskrit. Auden's unkempt face had a look of inscrutable bemusement.

In the fall of my second year at the institute, Dirac came for a visit. We all knew that he was coming, but no one had actually encountered him, despite rumored sightings. By this time, Dirac, who was in his mid-fifties, had a somewhat curious role in physics. Unlike Einstein, he had kept up with many of the developments and indeed from time to time commented on them. But, like Einstein, he had no school or following and had produced very few students. He had essentially no collaborators. Once, when asked about this, he remarked that "the really good ideas in physics are had by only one person." That seems to apply to poetry as well. He taught his classes in the quantum theory at Cambridge University, where he held Newton's Lucasian chair, by, literally, reading in his precise, clipped way from his great text on the subject. When this was remarked on, he replied that he had given the subject a good deal of thought and that there was no better way to present it.

At the institute we had a weekly physics seminar over which Oppenheimer presided, often interrupting the speaker. Early in the fall we were in the midst of one of these — there were about forty people in attendance in a rather small room — when the door opened. In walked Dirac. I had never seen him before, but I had often seen pictures of him. The real thing was much better. He wore much of a blue suit — trousers, shirt, tie, and, as I recall, a sweater — but what made an indelible impression were the thigh-length muddy rubber boots. It turned out that he was spending a good deal of time in the woods near the institute with an ax, chopping a path in the general direction of Trenton. Some years later, when I had begun writing for *The New Yorker* and attempted a profile of Dirac, he suggested that we might conduct some of the sessions while clearing this path. He was apparently still working on it.

The profile was never written, since eventually Dirac decided that he didn't want to be bothered, but one thing remains with me. He told me that his habit of silence began in his childhood, when his father insisted that the family speak French at table. Since Dirac did not know much French, he remained silent and continued to do so. But here he was, muddy boots and all, in the middle of our seminar, his graying hair somewhat tousled by his efforts in the woods. Oppenheimer found him a seat. He sat down and looked around at all of us with a faint smile. A colleague sitting next to me whispered in my ear, in an imitation of Dirac's voice, a variant of that line from the old British joke, "Is this what the common people call physics?" I think we all felt a little silly. I don't know how Oppenheimer felt.

Now it is some twenty-five years later. The sun has not yet come up, and I am driving across the state of New Jersey with my companion. We have left New York at about 5 A.M. so that I will arrive in time for a midmorning lecture. I have cobbled something together about physics and writing. Neither of us has had a proper breakfast. As we go through the Lincoln Tunnel I recall an anecdote my Nobelist colleague T. D. Lee once told me about Dirac. He was driving him from New York to Princeton through this same tunnel. Sometime after they had passed it, Dirac interrupted his silence to remark that, on the average, about as much money would be collected in tolls if they doubled the toll and had tollbooths only at one end. A few years later the Port Authority seems to have made the same analysis and halved the number of tollbooths. We pass the turnoff that would have taken us to Princeton. It is tempting to pay a visit. But Oppenheimer is by then dead and Dirac living in Florida with his wife, the sister of fellow physicist Eugene Wigner. Dirac used to introduce her to people as Wigner's sister, as in "I would like you to meet Wigner's sister." Dirac died in Florida in 1984.

We arrived at the conference center a few minutes before my lecture was scheduled to begin. There was no one, or almost no one, in the lecture room. However, in midroom, there was Spender. I recognized him at once from his pictures. Christopher Isherwood once described Spender's eyes as having the "violent color of blue-bells." Spender was wearing a dark blue suit and one of those striped British shirts — Turnbull and Asser? — the mere wearing of which makes one feel instantly better. He had on a club tie of some sort. He said nothing during my lecture and left as soon as it was over, along with the minuscule audience that I had traveled five hours by car to address. My companion and I then had a mediocre lunch in one of the local coffee shops. There seemed to be no official lunch. I was now thoroughly out of sorts and was ready to return to New York, but she wanted very much to stay for at least part of Spender's poetry workshop, and so we did.

I had never been to a poetry workshop and couldn't imagine what one would consist of. I had been to plenty of physics workshops and knew only too well what *they* consisted of: six physicists in a room with a blackboard shouting at one another. The room where Spender was to conduct his workshop was full, containing perhaps thirty people. One probably should not read too much into appearances, but these people — mostly women — looked to

me as if they were clinging to poetry as if it were some sort of life
raft. If I had had access to Spender's journals (they came out a few
years later), I would have realized that he was very used to all of
this. In fact, he had been earning his living since his retirement
from University College in London a decade earlier by doing lec-
tures and classes for groups like this. I would also have realized
that by 1981 he was pretty tired of it, and pretty tired of being an
avatar for his now dead friends — Auden, C. Day Lewis, and the
rest. He had outlived them all, but was still under their shadow,
especially that of Auden, whom he had first met at Oxford at about
the same age and same time that Oppenheimer had met Dirac.

Spender walked in with a stack of poems written by the workshop
members. He gave no opening statement, but began reading student poems. I was surprised by how awful they were. Most seemed
to be lists: "sky, sex, sea, earth, red, green, blue," and so forth.
Spender gave no clue about what he thought of them. Every once
in a while he would interrupt his reading and seek out the author
and ask such a question as, "Why did you choose red there rather
than green? What does red mean to you?" He seemed to be on
autopilot.

It is a pity that there are no entries in Spender's *Journals* for this
precise period. But it is clear that he was leading a rich social life
at the time: dinner with Jacqueline Onassis one day, the Roth-
schilds' at Mouton a week later — the works. My feeling was that
whatever he was thinking of had little to do with this workshop.
Somehow, I was getting increasingly annoyed. It was none of my
business, I guess, but I had put in a long day, and I felt that Spender
owed us more. I didn't know what — but more.

My companion must have sensed that I was about to do something because she began writing furiously in a large notebook that
she had brought along. Finally, after one particularly egregious
"list," I raised my hand. Spender looked surprised, but he called
on me. "Why was that a poem?" I asked. In reading his *Journals*
years later, I saw that this was a question that he had been asked
by students several times and had never come up with an answer
that really satisfied him. In 1935, Auden wrote an introduction for
an anthology of poetry for schoolchildren in which he defined
poetry as "memorable speech." That sounds good until one asks,
Memorable to whom? Doesn't it matter? If not, why a workshop?

I can't remember what Spender answered, but I then told him that, when I was a student, I had heard T. S. Eliot lecture. After the lecture one of the students in the audience asked Eliot what he thought the most beautiful line in the English language was — an insane question, really, like asking for the largest number. Much to my amazement Eliot answered without the slightest hesitation, "'But look, the morn in russet mantle clad / Walks o'er the dew of yon high eastward hill.'" I asked Spender what he thought the most beautiful line in the English language was. He got up from his chair and in a firm hand wrote a line of Auden's on the blackboard. He looked at it with an expression that I have never forgotten — sadness, wonder, regret, perhaps envy. He recited it slowly and then sat back down. There was total silence in the room. I thanked him, and my companion and I left the class.

I had not thought of all of this for many years, but recently, for some reason, it all came back to me, nearly. I remembered everything except the line that Spender wrote on the blackboard. All that I could remember for certain was that it had to do with the moon — somehow the moon. My companion of fifteen years ago is my companion no longer, so I could not ask her. I am a compulsive collector of data from my past, mostly in the form of items that were once useful for tax preparation. Perhaps I had saved the program of the conference with the line written down on it. I looked in the envelopes for 1981 and could find no trace of this trip. Then I had an idea — lunatic, lunar, perhaps. I would look through Auden's collected poems and seek out every line having to do with the moon, to see if it jogged my memory. One thing that struck me, once I started this task, was that there are surprisingly few references to the moon in these poems. In a collection of eight hundred and ninety-seven pages, I doubt if there are twenty. From *Moon Landing*, there is "Unsmudged, thank God, my Moon still queens the Heavens as she ebbs and fulls . . ." Or from *The Age of Anxiety*, "Mild, unmilitant, as the moon rose / And reeds rustled . . ." Or from "Nocturne," "Appearing unannounced, the moon / Avoids a mountain's jagged prongs / And sweeps into the open sky / Like one who knows where she belongs" — all wonderful lines, but not what I remembered. The closest was "White hangs the waning moon / A scruple in the sky . . . ," also from *The Age of Anxiety*. This still didn't seem right.

Then I got an idea. I would reread Spender's *Journals* to see if he mentions a line in Auden's poetry that refers to the moon. In the entry for the sixth of February 1975, I found this: "It would not be very difficult to imitate the late Auden. [He had died in 1973.] For in his late poetry there is a rather crotchety persona into whose carpet slippers some ambitious young man with a technique as accomplished could slip. But it would be very difficult to imitate the early Auden. 'This lunar beauty / Has no history, / Is complete and early . . .'" This, I am sure of it now, is the line that Spender wrote on the blackboard that afternoon in 1981.

Poor Stephen Spender, poor Robert Oppenheimer, each limited, if not relegated, to the category of the merely very good, and each inevitably saddened by his knowledge of what was truly superior. "Being a minor poet is like being a minor royalty," Spender wrote in his *Journals*, "and no one, as a former lady-in-waiting to Princess Margaret once explained to me, is happy as that." As for Oppenheimer, I recall Isidor Rabi once telling me that "if he had studied the Talmud and Hebrew, rather than Sanskrit, he [Oppenheimer] would have been a much greater physicist. I never ran into anyone who was brighter than he was. But to be more original and profound I think you have to be more focused."

As Spender says, W. H. Auden's poetry cannot be imitated, any more than Paul Dirac's physics can be. That is what great poetry and great physics have in common: both are swept along by the tide of unanticipated genius as it rushes past the merely very good.

States of Reading

FROM THE GETTYSBURG REVIEW

IN THE opening pages of his coy and crafty novel *If on a Winter's Night a Traveler,* Italo Calvino performs what for any true reader has to feel like a striptease. Or maybe the beginning overtures of what will turn into a full-out seduction. In any event, there is a sense of excited approach, an almost titillating enumeration of the stages by which a reader gets ready to engage a book. "Adjust the light so you won't strain your eyes," he croons. "Do it now, because once you're absorbed in reading there will be no budging you." And: "Try to foresee now everything that might make you interrupt your reading. Cigarettes within reach, if you smoke, and the ashtray. Anything else? Do you have to pee? All right, you know best."

Calvino continues, building tension now by tracking back to the moments just after the reader's purchase of the book in question. Familiar sensations: "You are at the wheel of your car, waiting at a traffic light, you take the book out of the bag, rip off the transparent wrapping, start reading the first lines. A storm of honking breaks over you . . ."

Then: "Yes, you are in your room, calm; you open the book to page one, no, to the last page, first you want to see how long it is."

And: "You turn the book over in your hands, you scan the sentences on the back of the jacket . . . Of course, this circling of the book, too, this reading around it before reading inside it, is part of the pleasure in a new book, but like all preliminary pleasures, it has its optimal duration if you want it to serve as a thrust toward the more substantial pleasure of the consummation of the act, namely, the reading of the book." So Calvino guides his chapter to conclusion, the conclusion being, in effect, the reader's excited haste to turn the page to begin. The paradox is suddenly evident: we are reading about getting ready to read, taking part in the tensions of deferral, even as we breached our own deferral pages ago. All of this is clever and could be shown to be more deeply intriguing, but what interests me is not metafictional self-reflexiveness, but something else: simply that all of this tantalization, this spirited foreplay, is possible only where there exists a shared assumption — that the state we achieve when immersed in a novel is powerful, pleasure-inducing, and very nearly hypnotic. ("Adjust the light," he coaxes, "because once you're absorbed in reading there will be no budging you.")

As striptease can work its thrills only on the understanding that the forbidden fruit, the corpora delectable, is right there, under the shimmer of coverings, so Calvino can toy with us in this way only because we know what a transformation of consciousness a successful — that is, *immersed* — reading act accomplishes.

Reading — and I will speak of it here in its realized mode — is *not* a continuation of the daily by other means. It is not simply another thing one does, like gathering up the laundry, pondering a recipe, checking the tire pressure, or even talking to a friend on the telephone. Reading is a change of state, a change of state of a very particular sort. And while this can be talked about, it seldom is. Who knows why?

Several things happen when we move via the first string of words from our quotidian world into the realm of the written. We experience almost immediately a transposition — perhaps an expansion, perhaps a condensation — of our customary perception of reality. We shift our sense of time from our ordinary, sequential, clockface awareness to a quasi-timeless sense of suspension, that sublime forgetting of the grid sometimes called duration. Finally, and no less significantly, we find ourselves instantly and implicitly changing our apprehension of the meaning structure of the world.

I would like to explore this transition by looking at the opening passage of Saul Bellow's novel *Humboldt's Gift:*

> The book of ballads published by Von Humboldt Fleisher in the Thirties was an immediate hit. Humboldt was just what everyone had been

waiting for. Out in the Midwest I had certainly been waiting eagerly, I can tell you that. An avant-garde writer, the first of a new generation, he was handsome, fair, large, serious, witty, he was learned. The guy had it all. All the papers reviewed his book. His picture appeared in *Time* without insult and in *Newsweek* with praise. I read *Harlequin Ballads* enthusiastically. I was a student at the University of Wisconsin and thought about nothing but literature day and night. Humboldt revealed to me new ways of doing things. I was ecstatic. I envied his luck, his talent, and his fame, and I went east in May to have a look at him — perhaps to get next to him. The Greyhound bus, taking the Scranton route, made the trip in about fifty hours. That didn't matter. The bus windows were open. I had never seen real mountains before. Trees were budding. It was like Beethoven's *Pastorale*. I felt showered by the green, within.

Bellow's Charlie Citrine goes on for nearly five hundred pages, but I will stop here — not to make any point about the novel, its characters, or conflicts, but to ask: How is my inwardness, my consciousness, different while I'm reading from whatever it was the instant before I began?

Most obviously, the formerly dissipated field of my awareness has been suddenly and dramatically channeled. My attention is significantly, then almost entirely, captured by the voice and what it is telling me. Charlie's confidential tone immediately captures me, replacing whatever cadences I had been thinking in. "An avant-garde writer, the first of a new generation, he was handsome, fair, large, serious, witty, he was learned. The guy had it all." My thought becomes Citrine's, my rhythms and instincts his — I change.

With the shift in momentum and focus comes an alteration in time frame. All the divisions and chronologies of the daily present are submerged beneath the timeless awareness of events unfolding as they must. Reading even a few of Bellow's sentences, we feel ourselves entering the duration world of the tale, the same world that fireside listeners stepped into when the tribal teller began to summon up the other place of the narrative.

Along with this altered sense of time — bound up with it — comes a condensation of reality. Things are linked each to each through association, not physical or chronological proximity. Months, never mind days, are elided in the space of a breath: "I envied his luck, his talent, and his fame, and I went east in May to have a look at him — perhaps to get next to him. The Greyhound bus, taking the Scranton route . . ." Reality — dull, obstacle-laden reality, which moves all too often at the pace of an intravenous dripper — is reconfigured by the imagination — speeded up, harmonized, made efficient — and served back to us in a far more palatable state, appealing in the extreme.

Finally — and my categories are necessarily imprecise — the words, even in so small an excerpt as I cited, change what I call the meaning structure of the world. To follow Citrine fully, as we long to do, we agree to the core requirement of any work of creative literature that we put ourselves in the hands of a self, a sensibility, that will front life with an original and uncorrected passion, that we will allow this self to dictate its understanding of the world to us. We must adopt Citrine's worldview as our own for the duration of the novel. This acceptance on our part is, I believe, the most important and profound consequence of the literary encounter.

The meaning structure of the world is, for most of us, experienced as an imprecise and mainly unfocused mingling of thoughts and perceptions. Strands of meaning are as if woven through expanses of seemingly unconnected elements — things observed carefully or obliquely, fitfully attended to or ignored. The upshot, unless we feel a powerful call to something higher and possess the discipline to strive constantly toward it, is that we greet the world outside of our immediate sphere of concern as a chaos essentially beyond our grasp, as an event the meaning of which will be disclosed to us later, if ever. The constant deferral of significance is the operative principle of most lives: tomorrow, next week — I'll think about it, I'll figure it out — not right now.

The meaning structure of a novel is absolutely different. Using condensation, moving in an altogether different medium of time, the author creates an artifact that is, in certain striking ways, a semblance of life, but with this exception: *everything* in the novel points toward *meaning*. Every sentence, every meaning observation, every turn of events serves an aesthetic and intellectual purpose. The novel smelts contingency and returns it as meaning.

We can see this distinction, between the outer world of reality and the inner world of the text, even in the act of reading, the way we read. In one of the most famous passages in his *Confessions*, Saint Augustine professes his astonishment at seeing Saint Ambrose reading a text without moving his lips. Augustine lived from A.D. 354 to 430, and his simple observation suggests something essential about the evolution of reading. It has gone inward. Reading aloud is common practice these days mainly with children, illiterate adults, or those who cannot, owing to some infirmity, read for themselves. To accompany your reading with silent lip motions is to signal that you may have only the most tenuous grasp on vocabulary and syntax.

This transition from exterior vocalizing to silent but perceptible lip movement to an interiority indicated outwardly only by the back and forth shuttling of the eyes signifies a considerable augmentation of the power of the reading act. So long as there are still lip motions, there exists a bridge between the world conjured on the page and the exterior realm. But when those motions cease, then the reader simultaneously represents two opposed kinds of presence. One is the physical, the actual — that which occupies space and can be located; the other is the invisible, the unreal — that which happens vividly in the imagination and cannot be fathomed or legislated by any other person. Silent reading, then, is the very signature — the emblem — of subjectivity. The act of reading creates for us a world within a world — indeed, a world within a hollow sphere, the two of them moving not only at different rates, but also, perhaps, counter to one another.

The tension between outer and inner is sharpened by the fact that when readers are fully absorbed in a book and the ulterior world it presents, their awareness of solid reality is supplanted by awareness of what the imagination is experiencing. Then, truly, the stubborn surfaces we live among become figments — a paradoxical transformation, since most of the people who discredit the practice of reading, particularly of novels, do so because the contents of the books are seen to be not-real, mere figments. These reading skeptics mistakenly assume that reading attempts to carry on the business of living by other — suspiciously intangible — means. They seldom consider that reading involves a change of state, that it is a sudden, and at times overwhelming, modification of the quotidian.

Changes of state. I believe increasingly that this, and mainly this, is the core mission of artistic writing. We go to such writing, engage it, not because it is an adjunct or a supplement to our daily living, but because it allows us the illusion of departure from it. I am not talking merely about bored commuters losing themselves in books by Tom Clancy or John Grisham, but of the somewhat more exalted pattern of departure and return effected by more serious novels. A work of art has done its deeper work when it starts to feel like arrival.

Everyone knows that Plato, in the tenth book of his *Republic*, proposed to banish the poets from the ideal State he was envisaging. At the conclusion of his argument he has Socrates say to Glaucon:

> we must remain firm in our conviction that hymns to the gods and praises of famous men are the only poetry which ought to be admitted into our State. For if you go beyond this and allow the honeyed muse to enter, either in epic or lyric verse, not law and the reason of mankind, which by common consent have ever been deemed best, but pleasure and pain will be the rulers in our State.

I would agree, I think, that the poet — the artist/writer — poses a threat to the State, at least to the State as Plato thinks of it — which is as a Republic, or "res publica," or "thing of the people" — but not on account of emotional persuasiveness. Rather, the artist is a threat because the effect of art, no matter what its ostensible subject might be, is to alter the relation to experience, to affect a change of state — and the main point of the new relation is not to clarify concrete matters in the here and now, but to propose an understanding that transcends the here and now. The experience is fundamentally asocial, for it directs preoccupation away from the *what* and *how* of daily business toward the *why*, the mere asking of which marks separation from the quotidian, if not yet transcendence. A social order founded on the question *why*, and the relation to things it implies, would not sustain the headlong consumerism we think of as the only possible option these days.

No matter how I try to come at it, my conception of the aesthetic experience — the reading experience — involves, at its core, a transfer between subjectivities; not a simple passing of contents from one subjective "I" to another. Writers are artists precisely to the extent that they use the transformative agency of imagination to surpass personality — the contingent attributes of identity — in order to get at what can be said to exist behind the jumble of appearances: some version of truth that results when the artist has disinterestedly reckoned the forces that underlie psychological, social, or other kinds of relationships.

I realize that the critical orthodoxy of our era repudiates this possibility of underlying universals, upholding instead the relativism, the constructedness, of all experience. Yet the reader's self — dare I say, *soul* — and the fact of his engagement with the literary work refutes this version of things. Whether that reader is immersed in Jane Austen, Joseph Conrad, Jane Smiley, or Saul Bellow, the immersion is attained only in part by stylistic power and the presentation of specific situational elements. The true bond is the reader's conviction that beyond all particulars, standing as the very ground and air of the work, is the writer's willing of a supporting world in its entirety. And this willing, which is at the same time an understanding, is achieved only through a complete and possessive act of imagination. It is finally this ability — and determination — to internalize a world that marks the literary artist. Never mind whether it is the world stretching away behind Samuel Beckett's Molloy, Vladimir Nabokov's Pnin, Jane Austen's Emma, or Bellow's Charlie Citrine.

When we begin reading *Humboldt's Gift*, or most any other novel, we expend an enormous energy. Only part of this goes toward understanding character, setting, and the details of situation. The rest represents an energy of erasure, of self-silencing. We suspend our sense of the world at large, bracket it off, in order that the author's implicit world may declare itself: "The book of ballads published by Von Humboldt Fleisher in the Thirties was an immediate hit. Humboldt was just what everyone had been waiting for. Out in the Midwest I had certainly been waiting eagerly, I can tell you that." Already it begins. The words make a voice, and the voice begins to sound in our auditory imagination, and as we enter the book we move from hearing the voice to listening to it. And to listen is to surrender self-thoughts, impinging awarenesses, and judgments; to listen is to admit a stance, a vantage, a world other than our own. Of course we do not succeed entirely. Of course the author's world bears a number of features that we project from our own irrepressible sense of things. But the interior transfer is profound nonetheless.

Reading, in this very idealized portrayal, is not simply an inscribing of the author's personal subjectivity upon a reader's receptivity. Rather, it is the collaborative bringing forth of an entire world, a world complete with a meaning structure. For hearing completes itself in listening, and listening happens only where there is some subjective basis for recognition. The work is not merely the bridge between author and reader; it is an enabling entity. The text is a pretext. The writer needs the idea of audition — of readers — in order to begin the creative process that gets him beyond the immediate, daily perception of things. In this one sense, the writer does not bring forth the work so much as the work, the idea of it, brings the writer to imaginative readiness. The finished work, the whole of it, then enables the reader to project a sensible and meaningful order of reality, one that might be initially at odds with the habitual relation to things. Writer and reader make a circuit — complete — outside the entanglements of the social contract.

This account of reading is not the majority view. Nor is it in any way self-evident. I don't know if it ever was, but certainly we have trouble thinking this way now. In our time the artistic experience has been compromised on all fronts. For one thing, there is not the belief in art — in literature especially — that existed in previous epochs. We don't, most of us, trust in the transformative power of artistic vision. And lacking the trust, we not only seek it out less, but we are less apt to open ourselves to it when there is a chance.

Then, too, there are fewer strong creations — true works of art that arrive on the page for the right reasons, that have not been deformed by the pressures of the marketplace. One can advance all sorts of reasons for this, including prominently the sheer difficulty of creating a world implicitly coherent when our own is so evidently incoherent. True artists — regardless of their subject or its epoch — are still required to grasp the forms and forces that make the reality of the present.

Third — and there are many other factors — is the climate of distractedness that envelops us. The world is too much here, too complex, is transected by too many competing signals. We don't believe in sense, in explanatory meaning, in the same way we once did. We are losing our purchase on time — not just the serene leisure required for reading, but also our vestigial awareness of that other time — unstructured duration time — that is the sustaining element of all art. For it is only in the durational mode that we can grasp that noncontingent relation to experience, the perception that used to be called "under the aspect of eternity" — the seeing of life in a way that acknowledges as its foundation the mystery of the *fact* of existence.

Then there is the effect that electronic technologies are having on writing and reading. This, while indirect, may be the chief one: that these technologies are, in their capacity as mediating tools, dissolving a sense of time that was until quite recently the human norm. Screen transactions not only make possible a fractured and layered and accelerated relation to time, they *require* it. They train us to a new set of expectations, even as the various complex demands of our living remove us further from the naturally contoured day. Reading of the kind that I have been describing cannot survive in such a climate as we are manufacturing for ourselves. The one hope is that reading will, instead of withering away in the glare of a hundred million screens, establish itself as a kind of preserve, a figurative place where we can go when the self needs to make contact with its sources.

It could be, then, that we are just starting to appreciate the potency that reading possesses. It is an interesting speculation: that the cultural threats to reading may be, paradoxically, revealing to us its deeper saving powers. I use the word "saving" intentionally here, not because I want to ascribe to reading some great function of salvation, but because I want to emphasize one last time the ideas of transformation and change of state. The movement from quotidian consciousness into the consciousness irradiated by artistic vision is analogous to the awakening to spirituality. The reader's aesthetic experience is, necessarily, lowercase, at least when set beside the truly spiritual. But it is marked by similar recognitions, including a changed relation to time, a condensation of the sense of significance, an awareness of a system or structure of meaning, and — most difficult to account for — a feeling of being enfolded by something larger, more profound.

Working through these thoughts, I happened upon an essay called "First Person Singular" by Joseph Epstein, wherein he cites Goethe as saying, "A fact of our existence is of value not insofar as it is true, but insofar as it has something to signify." To this Epstein adds concisely, "Only in art do all facts signify." He communicates in seven short words much of what I have been belaboring here: facts signify whenever one believes that existence is intended, that there are reasons that, as Pascal wrote, reason knows nothing of.

My depiction of the exalted potential of the text and the no less exalted transformation of the reader by the text draws its main energy from spiritual analogy. But I will end by remarking one way in which the analogy breaks down. In religion there is generally a provision made for the afterlife — that is part of its implicit assurance of purpose, the bait on the hook that would capture the frightened soul. Literature extends no such promise. Quite the reverse. With literature we are always at least subliminally aware of the mocking fact that only the work has a claim to living on, and then most likely through others. Within its borders it achieves the poignant eternity that John Keats accords to one of the figures in his "Ode on a Grecian Urn":

> Fair youth, beneath the trees, thou canst not leave
> Thy song, nor ever can those trees be bare;
> Bold Lover, never, never canst thou kiss,
> Though winning near the goal — yet, do not grieve;
> She cannot fade, though thou hast not thy bliss,
> For ever wilt thou love, and she be fair!

This is how it is with literary art: though it can give us no afterlife, within its realm of departure we are made plain to ourselves in a way that feels strangely lasting.

J. M. COETZEE

What Is Realism?

FROM SALMAGUNDI

THERE IS first of all the problem of the opening, namely, how to get us from where we are, which is, as yet, nowhere, to the far bank. It is a simple bridging problem, a problem of knocking together a bridge. People solve such problems every day. They solve them, and having solved them make a start.

So let us assume that, however it may be done, it is done. Let us take it that the bridge is built, that we have crossed it, we can leave it behind, forget it. We have left behind the territory in which we were. We are in the far territory, where we want to be.

Elizabeth Costello is a writer, born in 1927, which makes her sixty-nine years old, going on seventy. She has written nine novels, two books of poems, a book on the bird life of Queensland, and a body of journalism. By birth she is Australian. She was born in Melbourne and lives there today, but spent the years 1950 to 1962 abroad, in England and France. She has been married twice. She has two children, one by each marriage. Her son, John, who figures in this narrative, teaches in the Department of Astronomy at the Australian National University.

Elizabeth Costello made her name with her fourth novel, *The House on Eccles Street* (1969), whose main character is Marion Bloom, wife of Leopold Bloom, the principal character of another novel, *Ulysses* (1922), by James Joyce. She has been widely honored, at home and abroad. There has even come into existence an Elizabeth Costello Society, based in Albuquerque, New Mexico, which puts out a quarterly *Elizabeth Costello Newsletter.*

In October of 1995 Elizabeth Costello traveled, or travels (present tense henceforth), to Waltham, Massachusetts, to Appleton College, to receive the Appleton Award. This award is made biennially to a major world writer, selected by a jury of eminent critics and writers. It consists of a purse of $100,000, funded by a bequest from the Stowe estate, and a gold medal. It is one of the larger literary prizes in the United States.

On her visit to Massachusetts Elizabeth Costello (Costello is her maiden name) is accompanied by her son. She has become a little frail: without him she would not undertake this taxing trip across half the world and across two seasons.

We skip. They have reached Waltham and have been conveyed to their hotel, a surprisingly large building for a small city, a tall hexagon, all dark marble outside and crystal and mirrors inside. In her room a dialogue takes place.

"Will you be comfortable?" asks the son.

"I'm sure I will," she replies. Her room is on the twelfth floor, with a prospect over a golf course. Beyond are wooded hills.

"Then why not have a rest? They are fetching us at six-thirty. I'll give you a call a few minutes beforehand."

He is about to leave. She speaks.

"John, what do they want from me?"

"Tonight? Nothing. It's just a dinner with the jury. We won't let it turn into a long evening. I'll remind them you are tired."

"And tomorrow?"

"Tomorrow is a different story. You'll have to gird your loins for tomorrow, I'm afraid."

"I've forgotten why I agreed to come. It seems a great ordeal to put oneself through, for no good reason. I should have told them to forget the ceremony and send the check in the mail."

After the long flight, she is looking her age. She has never taken care of her appearance; she used to be able to get away with it; now it shows. Old and tired.

"It doesn't work that way, I'm afraid, Mother. If you want the money, you must go through with the show."

She shakes her head. She is still wearing the old blue raincoat she wore from the airport. Her hair has a greasy, lifeless look. She has made no move to unpack. If he leaves her now, what will she do? Lie down in her raincoat and shoes?

He is here, with her, out of love. He cannot imagine her getting through this trial without him at her side. He stands by her because he is her son, her loving son. But he is also on the point of becoming — distasteful word — her trainer.

He thinks of her as a seal, an old, tired circus seal. One more time she must heave herself up onto the tub, one more time show that she can balance the ball on her nose. Up to him to coax her, put heart in her, get her through the performance.

At six-thirty he knocks. She is ready, waiting, full of doubts but prepared to face the foe. She wears her blue costume and silk jacket, her lady novelist's uniform, and the white shoes with which there is nothing wrong yet which somehow make her look like Daisy Duck. She has washed her hair and brushed it back. It still looks greasy, but honorably greasy, like a navvy's or a mechanic's. Already on her face a passive look that, if you saw it in a young girl, you would call withdrawn. A face without personality, the kind that photographers have to work on to lend distinction. Like Keats, he thinks, the great advocate of blank receptiveness.

The blue costume, the greasy hair, these are details, signs of a moderate realism. Supply the particulars, allow the significations to emerge of themselves. A procedure pioneered by Daniel Defoe. Robinson Crusoe, cast up on the beach, looks around for his ship-mates. But there are none. "I never saw them afterwards, or any sign of them," says he, "except three of their hats, one cap, and two shoes that were not fellows." Two shoes, not fellows: by not being fellows, the shoes have ceased to be footwear and become proofs of death, torn by the foaming seas off the feet of drowning men and tossed ashore. No large words, no grief and despair, just hats and caps and shoes.

For as far back as he can remember, his mother has secluded herself in the mornings to do her writing. No intrusions under any circumstances. He used to think of himself as a misfortunate child, lonely and unloved. When they felt particularly sorry for themselves, he and his sister used to slump outside the locked door, making tiny whining sounds. In time the whining would change to humming or singing, and they would feel better, forgetting their forsakenness.

Now the scene has changed. He has grown up. He is no longer outside the door but inside, observing her as she sits, back to the window, confronting, day after day, year after year, while her hair slowly goes from black to gray, the blank page. What doggedness! She deserves the medal, he thinks, this one and many more. For valor beyond the call of duty.

The change came when he was thirty-three. Until then he had not read a word she had written. That was his reply to her, his revenge on her for locking him out. She denied him, therefore he denied her. Or perhaps he refused to read her in order to protect himself. Perhaps that was the deeper motive: to ward off the lightning stroke. Then one day, without a word to anyone, without even a word to himself, he took one of her books out of the library. After that he read everything, reading openly, an the train, at the lunch table. "What are you reading?" "Onc of my mother's books."

He is in her books, or some of them. Other people, too, he recognizes; and there must be many more he does not recognize. About sex, about passion and jealousy and envy, she writes with an insight that shakes him. It is positively indecent.

She shakes him; that is what she presumably does to other readers too. That is presumably why, in the larger picture, she exists. What a strange reward for a lifetime of shaking people: to be conveyed to this town in Massachusetts and feted and given money! For she is by no means a comforting writer. She is even cruel, in a way that women can be but men seldom have the heart for. What sort of creature is she? Not a seal, certainly: not amiable enough for that. But not a shark either. A cat, perhaps. One of those large cats that pause as they eviscerate their victim and, across the torn-open belly, give you a cold yellow stare.

There is a scene in the restaurant, mainly dialogue, which I will skip. I pick up events back at the hotel, where Elizabeth Costello asks her son to run through the list again of the people they have just met. He obeys, giving each a name and function, as in life. Their host, William Brautegam, is dean of arts at Appleton. The convener of the jury, Gordon Wheatley, is a Canadian, a professor at McGill, who has written on Canadian literature and on Wilson Harris. The one they call Toni, who spoke to her about Henry Handel Richardson, is from Appleton College. She is a specialist on Australia and has taught there. Paula Sachs she knows. The bald man, Kerrigan, is a novelist, originally Irish, now living in New York. The fifth juror, the one who sat next to him, is named

Moebius. She teaches in California and edits a journal. She has also published stories.

"You and she had quite a tête-à-tête," says his mother. "Attractive, isn't she?"

"I suppose so."

She reflects. "But, as a group, don't they strike you as rather . . ."

"Rather lightweight?"

She nods.

"Well, they are. The heavyweights aren't interested in this kind of show. The heavyweights are wrestling with heavyweight problems."

"I'm not heavyweight enough for them?"

"No, you're heavyweight all right. Your failing is that you're not a problem. What you write hasn't been shown to be a problem. Once you present a problem, you might be shifted over into their court. But for the present you're not a problem, just an example."

"An example of what?"

"An example of writing. An example of how someone of your station and your generation and your origins writes. An instance."

"An instance. Am I allowed to protest? After all the effort I put into not writing like anyone else?"

"Mother, there's no point in picking on me to argue with. But you must surely concede that at a certain level we write like everyone else. Otherwise we would be writing private languages. It's not absurd — is it? — to be interested in what people have in common rather than in what sets them apart."

There is another literary debate the next morning. John goes down to the hotel gymnasium and there bumps into Gordon Wheatley, chairman of the jury. Side by side on exercise bicycles they have a shouted conversation. His mother will be disappointed, he tells Wheatley, not entirely seriously, if she hears she has won the Appleton Award because 1995 is the year of Australasia.

"What does she want to hear?" shouts Wheatley back.

"That she is the best," he replies. "In your jury's honest opinion. Not the best X or Y, just the best."

"Without infinity you can't do mathematics," shouts Wheatley. "But that doesn't mean that infinity exists. It's just a construct, a human construct. Of course we say that Elizabeth Costello is the best. We just have to be clear what a statement like that means, in the context of our times."

The analogy with infinity makes no sense to him, but he does not pursue the argument. He hopes that Wheatley does not write as badly as he thinks.

Realism has never been comfortable with ideas. It could not be otherwise: realism is premised on the idea that ideas have no separate existence, can exist only in things. So when it needs to debate ideas, as here, it is driven to invent situations — walks in the countryside, conversations — in which characters give voice to contending ideas and thereby in a certain sense embody them. The notion of embodying is cardinal. In these debates, ideas do not and indeed cannot float free: they are tied to the speakers by whom they are enounced, are generated from the matrix of individual interests out of which their speakers act in the world. Thus, for instance, the son's concern that his mother not be treated like a Mickey Mouse Third World writer, or Wheatley's concern not to seem an old-fashioned absolutist.

At eleven he taps on the door of his mother's room. They have a heavy schedule before them: an interview, a trip to the college radio station for a recording session, then, in the evening, the presentation ceremony and the speech that goes with it.

At the radio station the two of them are separated. He is shown into the control booth. The interviewer, he is surprised to see, is the elegant Moebius woman he had sat beside at dinner. "This is Susan Moebius, the program is *Writers at Work,* and we are speaking today to Elizabeth Costello," she says. She proceeds to give a crisp introduction. "Your most recent novel," she continues, "called *Fire and Ice,* is set in the Australia of the 1930s and is the story of a young man struggling to make his way as a painter, against the opposition of family and society. Did you have anyone in particular in mind when you wrote it? Does it draw upon your own early life?"

"No, I was still a child in the 1930s. Of course we draw upon our own lives all the time — they are all we have. But no, *Fire and Ice* isn't autobiography. It's a work of fiction. I made it up."

"It's a powerful book, I must tell our listeners. But do you find it easy, writing from the position of a man?"

It is a routine question, opening the door to one of her routine paragraphs. To his surprise, she does not take the opening.

"Easy? No. If it were easy it wouldn't be worth doing. It's the otherness that is the challenge. Making up someone other than yourself. Making up a world for him to move in. Making up an Australia."

"Is that what you are doing in your books, would you say — making up Australia?"

"Yes, I suppose so. But it's not so easy nowadays. There's more resistance, a weight of other Australias made up by other people, that you have to push against. That's what we mean by tradition, the beginnings of a tradition."

"I'd like to get on to *The House on Eccles Street*, which is the book you are best known for in this country, a path-breaking book, and the figure of Molly Bloom. Critics have concentrated on the way you have claimed or reclaimed Molly from Joyce, made her your own. I wonder if you would comment on your intentions in this book, particularly in challenging Joyce, one of the great father figures of modern literature, on his own territory."

Another clear opening, and this time she takes it.

"Yes, she is an engaging person, isn't she, Molly Bloom — Joyce's Molly, I mean. She leaves her trace across the pages of *Ulysses* as a bitch in heat leaves her smell. Seductive you can't call it; it's cruder than that. Men pick up the scent and sniff and stare and circle around and snarl at each other, even when Molly isn't on the scene.

"No, I don't see myself as challenging Joyce. But with certain books there is such prodigal inventiveness that there's material left over when the action is finished. Material that almost invites you to take it up and build something of your own."

"But you've taken Molly out of the house — if I can pick up on your metaphor — taken her out of the house on Eccles Street where her husband and her lover and in a certain sense her author have confined her, where they have turned her into a kind of queen bee, unable to fly, and turned her loose on the streets of Dublin. Wouldn't you see that as a challenge on your part, a response?"

"Queen bee, bitch . . . Let's revise the figure and call her a lioness, rather, stalking the streets, smelling the smells, seeing the sights. Looking for prey, even. Yes, I wanted to liberate her from that house, and particularly from that bedroom, with its creaking bedsprings, and turn her loose — as you say — on Dublin."

"If you see Molly — Joyce's Molly — as a prisoner in the house on Eccles Street, do you see women in general as prisoners of marriage and domesticity?"

"You can't mean women today. But yes, to an extent Molly is a prisoner of marriage, of the kind of marriage that was available in Ireland in 1904. Her husband, Leopold, is a prisoner too. If she is shut into the conjugal home, he is shut out. So we have Odysseus trying to get in and Penelope trying to get out. That's the comedy, the comic myth, which Joyce and I in our different ways paid our respects to."

Because both women are wearing earphones, addressing the microphone rather than each other, it is hard for him to see how they are getting on. But he is impressed, as ever, by the persona his mother manages to project: of genial common sense, lack of malice, yet of sharp-wittedness too.

"I want to tell you," the interviewer continues (a cool voice, he thinks: a cool woman, capable, not a lightweight at all), "what an impact *The House on Eccles Street* made on me when I first read it. I was a student, I had studied Joyce's book, I had absorbed the famous Molly Bloom episode and the critical orthodoxy that came with it, namely that here Joyce had released the authentic voice of the feminine, the sensual reality of woman, and so forth. And then I read your book and realized that Molly didn't have to be limited in the way Joyce had shown her, that she could equally well be an intelligent woman with an interest in music and a circle of friends of her own and a daughter with whom she shared confidences — it was a revelation, as I say. And I began to wonder about other women whom we think of as having been given a voice by male writers in the name of their liberation, yet in the end only to speak and serve a male philosophy. I am thinking of D. H. Lawrence's women in particular, but if you go further back they might include Tess of the D'Urbervilles and Anna Karenina, to name just two. It's a huge question, but I wonder if you have anything to say about it — not just about the lives of Marion Bloom but about the project of reclaiming women's lives in general."

"No, I don't think there's anything I would want to say, I think you've said it all very fully. Of course, fair's fair, men will have to set about reclaiming the Heathcliffs and Rochesters from romantic stereotyping too, to say nothing of poor old dusty Casaubon. It will be a grand spectacle. But seriously, we can't go on parasitizing the classics forever. I'm not excluding myself from the charge. We've got to do some inventing of our own."

We skip to the evening, to the main event, the presentation of the award. Elizabeth Costello's son John finds himself in the first row of the audience, among the special guests. The woman to his left introduces herself. "Our daughter is at Appleton," she says. "She is writing her honors dissertation on your mother. She's a great fan. She has made us read everything." She pats the wrist of the man beside her: her husband. They have the look of money, old money. Benefactors, no doubt. "Your mother is much admired in this country," she says. "Particularly by young people. You should tell her that."

All across America, young women writing dissertations on his mother. Adherents, disciples. Would it really please her to be told?

The presentation scene itself I will skip. Generally speaking, it is not a good idea to interrupt the narrative too often, since story-telling works by lulling the reader or listener into a dream state in which real-world time and space fade away, superseded by the time and space of the fiction. Breaking into the dream draws attention to the constructedness of the story and plays havoc with the realist illusion. However, unless I skip certain scenes we will be here all day. The skips are not part of the text, they are part of the performance.

The award is made. Then his mother is left alone at the rostrum to give her acceptance speech, which in the program is entitled, "What Is Realism?" The time has arrived for her to perform, to show her mettle.

She puts on her glasses. "Ladies and gentlemen," she says, and begins to read.

"I published my first book in 1955, forty years ago. I was living in London, at that time the cultural metropolis for Australians. I remember clearly the day when a package arrived in the mail, a copy of the book, an advance copy. I was of course thrilled to have it in my hands at last, the real thing. But there was still one thing that nagged me. I got on the telephone to my publishers. 'Have

the deposit copies gone out?' I asked. And I would not rest until
I had their assurance that the deposit copies would be mailed the
same afternoon, to the Bodleian and the other places, but above
all to the British Museum. That was my great ambition: to have
a place on the shelves of the British Museum, rubbing shoulders
with the great C's: Carlyle and Chaucer and Coleridge and Conrad. (The joke is that my closest literary neighbor turned out to be
Marie Corelli.)

"One smiles now at such ingenuousness. Yet behind my anxiety
there was something serious, and behind that seriousness in turn
something pathetic that is less easy to acknowledge.

"Let me explain. Besides all the copies of the book you have
written that are going to perish — that are going to be pulped
because there is no sale for them, that are going to be opened and
read for a page or two and then yawned at and put aside forever,
that are going to be left behind at seaside hotels or in trains —
besides all these lost ones we must be able to feel there is at least
one copy that will not only be read but be taken care of, given a
home, given a place on the shelf that will be its own in perpetuity.
What lay behind my anxiety about deposit copies was the wish that,
even if I should be knocked over by a bus the next day, this first-
born of mine would have a home where it could snooze for the
next hundred years, and no one would come poking with a stick
to see if it was still alive.

"That was one side of my telephone call: if I, this mortal shell,
was going to die, let me at least live on through my creations."

Elizabeth Costello proceeds to reflect on the transience of fame,
the transience even of deposit libraries. I skip, and resume.

"Let me now turn to my subject, 'What Is Realism?'

"There is a story by Franz Kafka in which an ape, dressed up for
the occasion, makes a speech to a learned society. It is a speech,
but a test too, an examination, a *viva voce*. He has to show not only
that he can speak his audience's language but that he has mastered
their manners and conventions, is fit to enter their society.

"Why am I reminding you of Kafka's story? Am I going to
pretend I am the ape, torn away from my natural surroundings,
forced to perform in front of a gathering of critical strangers? I
hope not. I am one of you, I am not of a different species.

"Those of you who know the story will remember that it is cast in the form of a monologue, a monologue by the ape. There is thus no means, within the world of the story, for either speaker or audience to be scrutinized with an outsider's eye. For all we know, the speaker may not 'really' be an ape, may be simply a human being like ourselves deluded into thinking himself an ape, or a human being presenting himself, with heavy irony, for rhetorical purposes, as an ape. For all we know, too, the audience may consist not, as we imagine, of bewhiskered, red-faced gents who have put aside their bush jackets and topis for evening dress, but of fellow apes, trained, if not to the level of our speaker, who can mouth complicated sentences in German, then at least to sit and listen; or, if not trained to that pitch, then chained to their seats and trained not to jabber and pick fleas and relieve themselves openly.

"We don't know. We don't know and will never know, with certainty, what is really going on in this story: whether it is a man speaking to men or an ape speaking to apes or an ape speaking to men or a man speaking to apes (though the last is, I think, unlikely) or even just a parrot speaking to parrots.

"There used to be a time when we knew. We used to believe that when the text said, 'On the table stood a glass of water,' there was indeed a glass of water, and a table, and we had only to look in the word-mirror of the text to see them both.

"But all that has ended. The word-mirror is broken, irreparably, it seems. About what is really going on in the lecture hall your guess is as good as mine: men and men, men and apes, apes and men, apes and apes, whatever. The lecture hall itself may be nothing but a zoo. The words on the page will no longer stand up and be counted, each saying, 'I mean what I mean!' The dictionary that used to stand beside the Bible and the works of Shakespeare above the fireplace, in the place occupied by the household gods in pious Roman homes, has become just one code book among many.

"This is the situation in which I appear before you. I am not using the privilege of this platform to make idle, nihilistic jokes about what I am, ape or woman, and what you are, my auditors. That is not the point of the story, say I, who am nevertheless in no position to dictate what the point of the story is. There used to be a time, we believe, when we could say who we were. Now we are just performers, speaking our parts. The bottom has dropped

out. We could think of this as a tragic turn of events, were it not
that it is hard to have respect for whatever the bottom was that
dropped out — it looks to us like an illusion now, one of those
illusions sustained only by the concentrated gaze of everyone in
the room. As soon as you look away, the mirror falls to the floor
and shatters.

"There is every reason, then, for me to feel less than certain
about myself as I stand before you. Despite this splendid award,
for which I am deeply grateful, despite the promise it makes that,
gathered into the illustrious company of those who have won it
before me, I am beyond the reach of time's envious grasp, we all
know, if we are being realistic, that it is only a matter of time before
the books which you honor, and with whose genesis I have had
something to do, will cease to be read and eventually cease to be
remembered. And properly so. There is a limit to the burden of
remembering we can impose on our children and grandchildren.
They will have a world of their own, of which we will be less and
less part. Thank you."

The applause starts hesitantly, but then swells. His mother takes
off her glasses, smiles. It is an engaging smile: she seems to be
relishing the moment. Actors bathe in applause like this all the
time, ill deserved or well deserved: actors, singers, violinists. Why
should she not have her moment of glory too?

The applause dies down. Dean Brautegam leans into the microphone. "There will be refreshments — "

"Excuse me!" A clear, confident young voice cuts through the
dean's.

There is a flurry in the audience. Heads are turning.

"There will be refreshments in the foyer, and an exhibition
of Elizabeth Costello's books. Please join us there. It remains for
me — "

"Excuse me!"

"Yes!"

"I have a question."

The speaker is standing up: a young woman in a white T-shirt.
Brautegam is clearly nonplused. As for his mother, she has lost her
smile. He knows her look. She has had enough now, she wants to
be away.

"I am not sure," says Brautegam, frowning, looking around for support. "Our format tonight does not allow for questions. I would like to thank — "

"Excuse me! I have a question for the speaker. May I address the speaker?"

There is a hush. All eyes are on Elizabeth Costello. Frostily she gazes into the distance.

Brautegam pulls himself together. "I would like to thank Ms. Costello, whom we have gathered tonight to honor. Please join us in the foyer. Thank you." And he switches off the microphone.

There is a buzz of talk as they leave the auditorium. An incident, no less. He can see the girl in the white T-shirt ahead of him in the throng. She walks stiff and erect and seemingly angry. What was the question going to be? Would it not have been better to have it aired?

He fears that the scene will repeat itself in the foyer. But there is no scene. The girl has left, gone out into the night, perhaps stormed out. Nevertheless, the incident leaves a bad taste; say what one might, the evening has been spoiled.

What was she going to ask? People huddle together, whispering. They seem to have a shrewd idea. He has a shrewd idea too. Something to do with what Elizabeth Costello the famous writer might have been expected to say on an occasion like this, and did not say.

He can see Dean Brautegam and others fussing around his mother now, trying to smooth things over. After all they have invested, they want her to go home thinking well of them and of Appleton College. Nevertheless, they must already be glancing ahead to 1997, hoping that the 1997 jury will come up with a more winning winner.

I skip the rest of the foyer scene, move back to the hotel.

Elizabeth Costello retires for the night. Her son, who is in many ways the main actor henceforth, watches television in his room, then grows restless and goes down to the lounge. There, for the second time that day, he sees the woman who interviewed his mother for radio, Susan Moebius. She waves him over. She is with a companion, but the companion soon departs, leaving the two of them alone.

He finds her attractive. She dresses well, better than the conventions of the academy permit. She has long, golden blond hair; she sits upright in her chair, squaring her shoulders; when she tosses her hair, the movement is quite queenly.

They skirt the events of the evening. They speak about the revival of radio as a cultural medium. "An interesting session you had with my mother," he says. "I know you've written a book about her, which I haven't read — I'm sorry. Do you have good things to say about her?"

"I hope I do. She is a key writer for our times. The book isn't about her alone, but she figures strongly in it."

"But is she a key writer for all of us, or just for women? I got the feeling during the interview that you see her as a woman writer or a woman's writer. Would you still consider her a key writer if she were a man?"

"If she were a man?"

"All right: if you were a man?"

"If I were a man? I don't know. I've never been a man. I'll let you know when I've tried it."

They smile. There is definitely something in the air.

"But my mother has been a man," he persists. "She has also been a dog. She can think her way into other people, into other existences. I've read her; I know. It's within her powers. Isn't that what's most important about fiction, that it takes us out of ourselves, into other lives?"

"Perhaps. But your mother remains a woman all the same. Whatever she does, she does as a woman. She inhabits her characters as a woman does, not a man."

"I don't see that. I find her men perfectly believable."

"You don't see because you wouldn't see. Only a woman would see. It's something between women. If her men are believable, good, I'm glad to hear so, but finally it's just mimicry. Women are good at mimicry, better than men. At parody, even. We have a lighter touch."

She is smiling again. See how light my touch can be, her lips seem to say. Soft lips.

"If there's parody in her," he says, "it's too subtle for me to pick up." There is a long silence. "So is that what you think," he says at last, "that we live parallel lives, men and women, that we never really meet?"

The drift of the conversation has changed. They are no longer speaking about writing, if they ever were.

"What do you think?" she says. "What does your experience tell you? And is difference such a bad thing? If there were no difference, what would happen to desire?"

They are alone in the elevator. Not the elevator he is used to: a different shaft. Which is north, which south, in this hexagon of a hotel, this beehive? He presses the woman against the wall, kisses her, tasting smoke on her breath. Research: will that be her name for it afterward? Using a secondary source? He kisses her again, she kisses him back, kissing flesh of the flesh.

They exit on the thirteenth floor. He follows her down a corridor, turning right and left. He loses track. Where is it, the core of the hive? His mother's room is 1254. His is 1220. Hers is 1307. He did not know there was a thirteenth floor. He thought that floors went from twelve to fourteen, that that was the rule in the hotel world. Where is 1307 in relation to 1254: north, south, west, east?

I skip again, a skip this time in the text rather than in the performance.

When he thinks back over those hours, one moment comes back with sudden force, the moment when her knee slips under his arm and folds into his armpit. A shapely thigh, he thinks, appraising, approving. Curious that the night should be dominated by a single recollection, not obviously significant, yet so strong that he can almost feel the ghostly knee against his skin. Does the mind by nature prefer sensations to ideas, the tangible to the abstract? Or is her knee just a mnemonic, from which will unfold the rest of the night?

They are lying in the dark, flank to flank, in the text of memory, talking.

"So, has it been a successful visit?" she asks.

"From whose point of view?"

"Yours."

"My point of view doesn't matter. I came for Elizabeth Costello's sake. Hers is the point of view that matters. Yes, successful. Successful enough."

"Do I detect a touch of bitterness?"

"None. I'm here to help — that's all."

"It's very good of you. Do you feel you owe her something?"

"Yes. Filial duty. It's perfectly natural among humankind."

She ruffles his hair. "Don't be cross," she says.

"I'm not."

She slides down beside him, strokes him. "Successful enough —
what does that mean?" she murmurs. She is not giving up. A price
has yet to be paid for this time in her bed, for this conquest.

"The speech didn't come off. She was disappointed. She put a
lot of work into it."

"There was nothing wrong with the speech in itself. But the title
was mystifying. And she shouldn't have used Kafka. There are
better texts."

"Are there?"

"Yes, better, more suitable. This is America, the 1990s. People
don't want to hear the Kafka thing yet again."

"What do they want to hear then?"

She shrugs. "Something more personal. Not necessarily more
intimate. But audiences don't react well to heavy historical self-
ironization anymore. They might at a pinch accept it from a man,
but not from a woman. A woman doesn't need all that armor."

"And a man does?"

"You tell me. If it's a problem, it's a male problem. We didn't
give the award to a man."

"Have you considered the possibility that my mother has got
beyond the male-female opposition? That she has explored it as
far as it will go, and is now after larger game?"

"Such as?"

The hand that has been stroking him has paused. The moment
is important, he knows. She is waiting for his answer, for the
privileged access it promises. He can feel the thrill of the moment,
electric, reckless.

"Such as measuring herself against the illustrious dead. Such as
paying tribute to the powers that animate her. For instance."

"Is that what she says?"

"You don't think that is what she has been doing throughout
her life — measuring herself against the masters? Has no one in
the profession recognized that?"

He should not be saying this. He should be keeping out of his
mother's business. He is in a stranger's bed not for his bonny blue
eyes but because he is his mother's son. Yet here he is spilling the
beans like a nincompoop! He sees now how spy-women work.
Nothing subtle to it. The man is seduced not because his will to

resist is overcome but because being seduced is a pleasure in itself. He falls in order to fall, for the pleasure of falling.

He wakes once during the night, in a state of deep sadness, such sadness that he wants to cry. He touches the naked shoulder of the woman beside him, but she does not respond. Lightly he runs a hand down her body, breast, flank, hip, thigh, knee. Handsome in every detail, in a blank kind of way.

He has a vision of his mother in her big double bed, crouched in sleep, her knees drawn up, her back bared. Out of her back, out of the waxy, old person's flesh, protrude three needles: not the tiny needles of the acupuncturist or the voodoo doctor, but thick, gray needles, steel or plastic: knitting needles. The needles have not killed her, there is no need to worry about that, she breathes regularly. Nevertheless, she lies impaled.

Who has done it? Who would have done it?

Such loneliness, he thinks, hovering over the old woman in the bare room. His heart is breaking; the sadness pours down like a gray waterfall behind his eyes.

He should never have come here, to room thirteen whatever it is. A wrong move. He ought to get up at once, steal out. But he does not. Why? Because he does not want to be alone. And because he wants to sleep. Sleep, he thinks, that knits up the raveled sleeve of care. What an extraordinary way of phrasing it! Not all the monkeys in the world, picking away at typewriters all their lives, would come up with those words. Out of the dark emerging, out of nowhere: first not there, then there, like a newborn child, heart working, brain working, all the processes of that intricate electrochemical labyrinth working. A miracle. He closes his eyes.

She is already at breakfast when he comes down. She is wearing white, she looks rested and content. He joins her.

From her purges she takes something and lays it on the table: his watch. "It's eight hours off," she says.

"Not eight," he says. "Sixteen. Canberra time. So that I won't forget who I really am."

Her eyes rest on his, or his on hers. Green-flecked. He feels a tug. A continent still unexplored, and he about to leave! A pang, a tiny pang of loss, shoots through him. Pain not without pleasure, like certain grades of toothache. He can conceive of something quite serious with this woman, whom he will not see again.

"I know what you are thinking," she says. "You are thinking we won't see each other again. You are thinking, What a wasted investment."

"What else do you see?"

"You think I have been using you. You think I have been trying to reach your mother through you."

She is smiling. No fool. A capable player.

"Yes," he says. "No." He draws a deep breath. "I'll tell you what I really think. I think you are drawn, even if you won't acknowledge it, by the mystery of the divine in the human. You know there is something special in my mother, yet when you meet her, she turns out to be just an ordinary old woman. You can't square the two. You want an explanation. You want a clue, a sign, if not from her, then from me. That's what you think. It's all right, I don't mind."

Strange words to be speaking over breakfast, over coffee and toast. He did not know he had them in him.

"You really are her son, aren't you. Do you write too?"

"You mean, am I touched by the god? No. But yes, I am her son. Not a foundling, not an adoptee. Out of her very body I came, caterwauling."

"Will I have a chance to say goodbye to your mother?"

"You can catch her before the television interview. It's at ten, in the ballroom."

The television people have chosen the ballroom because of the red velvet drapes. In front of the drapes they have set up a rather ornate chair for her, and a smaller chair for the woman who will ask the questions. Susan, when she comes, has to cross the whole length of the room. She is ready to travel; she has a calf-leather satchel over her shoulder; her stride is easy, confident. Again the pang comes, but light as a feather.

"It's been a great honor to get to know you, Mrs. Costello," she says, taking his mother's hand.

"Elizabeth," says his mother. "Excuse the throne."

"Elizabeth."

"I want to give you this," says Susan Moebius, and from her satchel produces a book. The cover shows a woman wearing an antique Grecian costume, holding a scroll. *Reclaiming a History: Women and Memory,* says the title. Susan Kaye Moebius.

"Thank you, I look forward to reading it," says his mother.

At the end of the interview Susan Moebius's book is almost left behind. He is the one who picks it up from under her chair.

"I wish people wouldn't give one books," she murmurs. "Where am I going to find space for it?"

"I have space."

"Then you take it. Keep it. You're the one she is really after, not me."

He reads the inscription: To Elizabeth Costello, with gratitude and admiration. "Me?" he says. "I don't think so. I am just" — his voice barely falters — "a pawn in the game. You are the one she loves and hates."

He barely falters; but the word that came to mind was not "pawn," it was "clipping." A toenail clipping, that one steals and winds up in a tissue and takes away.

His mother does not reply. But she does give him a smile, a quick, sudden smile of joy and — he cannot see it in any other way — triumph.

Their duties are over. The television crew are packing up. In half an hour a taxi will take them to the airport. She has won, more or less. On foreign turf too. An away win. She can go home bearing her true self, leaving behind an image, false, like all images.

What is the truth of his mother? He does not know, does not want to know. He is here simply to protect her, to bar the way against the relic seekers and the sentimental pilgrims. Yet there is also an impulse in him to speak out before he goes, to whoever will hear. This woman, he wants to say, whose words you hang on as if she were the sibyl, is the same woman who, forty years ago, would lie in bed in her bed-sitter in Hampstead all day, crying soundlessly to herself, crawling out in the evenings into the foggy streets to buy the fish and chips on which she lived, then falling asleep in her clothes. She is the same woman who stormed around the house in Melbourne, hair flying in all directions, screaming at her children, "You are killing me! You are tearing the flesh from my body!" (He lay in the dark with his sister afterward, comforting her while she sobbed: he was seven; it was his first experience of fatherhood.) This is the secret world of the oracle. How can you understand her before you know who she really is; and how, knowing who she is, can you understand her?

He does not hate his mother. (As he thinks these words, other words echo at the back of his mind: the words of one of William Faulkner's people insisting with mad repetitiveness that he does not hate the South. Who is it?) He does not hate her. Quite the contrary. If he had hated her, he would long ago have put the greatest possible distance between the two of them. He does not hate her. He serves at her shrine, cleaning up after the excitement of the holy day, sweeping up the petals, collecting the offerings, putting the widows' mites together, ready to bank. He may not share in the frenzy, but he worships too.

A mouthpiece for the divine. But "oracle" is not the right word. Not in the Greek mold. More like Tibet or India: a god reincarnated in a child, who is then wheeled from village to village, applauded, venerated.

Then they are in the taxi, driving through streets that already have the air of streets about to be forgotten.

"So," says his mother. "A clean getaway."

"I do believe so. Have you got the check?"

"The check, the medal, everything."

A gap. They are in Boston, at the airport, at the gate, waiting for the flight to be called that will take them on the next stage of their journey home. Faintly, over their heads, with a crude, driving hunt, a version of *Eine Kleine Nachtmusik* is playing. Opposite them sits a woman eating popcorn out of a paper bucket, so fat that her feet barely touch the floor.

"Can I ask you one thing?" he says. "Why realism? No one here wanted to hear about it. Why such a grim subject?"

Fiddling in her purse, she says nothing.

"When I think of realism," he goes on, "I think of peasants frozen in blocks of ice. I think of Norwegians in smelly underwear. Why are you interested in that kind of thing? And where does Kafka fit in? What has Kafka to do with it?"

"With what? With smelly underwear?"

"Yes. With smelly underwear. With people picking their noses. You don't write about it. Kafka didn't write about it."

"No, Kafka didn't write about people picking their noses. But Kafka had time to wonder where and how his poor educated ape was going to find a mate. And what it was going to be like for him in the dark with the bewildered, half-tamed female that his keepers eventually produced for his use. Kafka's ape is embedded in life.

It is the embeddedness that is important, not the life. His ape is embedded as we are embedded, you in me, I in you. The ape is followed through to the end, to the bitter, unsayable end, whether or not traces are left on the page. Kafka stays awake during the gaps when we are sleeping. That is where he fits in."

The fat woman is observing them frankly, her little eyes flickering from the one to the other: the old woman in the raincoat and the balding man who could be her son, having a fight in their funny accents.

"Well," he says, "if what you say is true, it's repulsive. It's zookeeping, not writing."

"What would you prefer? A zoo without keepers, where the animals fall into a trance when you stop looking at them? A zoo of ideas? A gorilla cage with the idea of a gorilla in it, an elephant cage with the idea of elephants in it? Do you know how many kilograms of solid waste an elephant drops in twenty-four hours? If you want a real elephant cage with real elephants, then you need a zookeeper to clean up after them."

"You're off the point, Mother. And don't get so excited." He turns to the fat woman. "We're discussing literature, the claims of realism versus the claims of idealism."

Without ceasing to chew, the fat woman removes her eyes from them. He thinks of the cud of mashed corn and saliva in her mouth, and shudders. Where does it all end?

"There's a difference between cleaning up after animals and watching them while they do their business," he starts again. "We're talking about the latter, not the former. Don't animals deserve a private life as much as we do?"

"Not if they're in a zoo," she says. "Not if they're on show. Once you're on show, you have no private life. Anyway, do you ask permission from the stars before you peer at them through your telescope? What about the private lives of the stars?"

"Mother, the stars are lumps of rock."

"Are they? I thought they were traces of light millions of years old."

"Boarding will now commence for Flight 323, nonstop to Los Angeles," says a voice above their heads. "Passengers requiring assistance, as well as families with young children, may step forward."

On the flight she barely touches her food. She orders two

brandies, one after the other, then falls asleep. When, hours later, they begin the descent to Los Angeles, she is still asleep. The stewardess taps her on the shoulder. "Ma'am, your seat belt." She does not stir. They exchange looks, he and the stewardess. He leans across and clips the belt across her lap.

She lies slumped deep in her seat. Her head is sideways, her mouth open. She is snoring faintly. Light flashes from the windows as they bank, the sun setting brilliantly over southern California. He can see up her nostrils, into her mouth, down the back of her throat. And what he cannot see he can imagine: the gullet, pink and ugly, contracting as it swallows, like a python, drawing things down to the pear-shaped belly sac. He draws away, fastens his own belt, sits up, facing forward. No, he tells himself, that is not where I come from, that is not it.

BRIAN DOYLE

Altar Boy

FROM THE AMERICAN SCHOLAR

I will go up to the altar of God
The giver of youth and happiness.
— Psalm 43

Introit

I MISSED one Mass as an altar boy — the Tuesday dawn patrol,
6:00 A.M., Father Dennis Whelan presiding. He was a good-natured
fellow, a cigar smoker, although he was a little young for it, that
kind of guy, but he was furious when I trudged back to the sacristy after sitting through the second half of Mass in the very last
pew.
 Where were you?
 I was late, Father.
 You miss another and you're out of the corps.
 I'm very sorry, Father.
 It's no joke to be all alone out there.
 Yes, Father.
 I knew why he was peeved: I was the key to his famous twenty-
two-minute Mass. He pulled off this miracle week after week, without ever looking at his watch. His Mass drew the faithful by the
dozens, especially businessmen trying to catch the weekday 6:30
train into New York City. One time Whelan had the 6:00 on St.
Patrick's Day, and we had nearly fifty people in the church — still
a record for our parish, I bet.

Working with Whelan was a pleasure; he was a real artist, someone who would have made his mark in any field. He had all the
tools — good hands, nimble feet, a sense of drama, a healthy ego,
the unnerving itch to be loved that all great performers have. He
did not rush his movements, mumble, or edit his work. He was
efficient, yes — he'd send his right hand out for the chalice as his
left was carving a blessing in the air, that sort of thing — but every
motion was cleanly executed and held in the air for the proper
instant, and he had astounding footwork for such a slab of meat.
He was one or two inches over six feet tall, 250 pounds maybe, big
belly sliding around in his shirt, but he was deft on the altar and
could turn on a dime in the thick red carpet. He cut a memorable
double pivot around the corners of the altar table on his way to
his spot, and he cut that sucker as cleanly as a professional skater
before a Russian judge.

My job was simple: I was the wizard's boy, and the whole essence of being a great altar boy was to be where you needed to be
without seeming to get there. Great altar boys flowed to their
spots, osmosed from place to place. They just appeared suddenly
at the priest's elbow and then slid away like Cheshire cats. There
were other arts — quick work with the hands, proper bell ringing,
a firm hand with matches and candles, the ability to project a sort
of blue-collar holiness on the stage, that sort of thing — but
the flowing around like a five-foot-tall column of water was the
main thing, and it was damned hard to learn. Rookies spent their
whole first year, and often two, lurching around the altar like zom-
bies, a tick behind Father's moves, which led to, horror of horrors,
an irritated Father gesturing distractedly for what he needed.
Extra gestures from the wizard were the greatest sins, and we re-
coiled in horror when we saw them when we were at Mass with
our families and out of uniform. At such moments, when the clod
on the altar forgot to ring the bells, or brought the wrong cruet,
or knelt there like a stone when he should have been liquiding
around the altar in a flutter of surplice sleeves, I closed my eyes
in shame and in memory, for my rookie year was a litany of er-
rors too long to list, and my graduation from rookie to veteran was
a source of great pride to me.

Gloria

Whelan was all business out there from the moment he strode purposefully through the little doorway from the sacristy. He had to duck a bit to get under the lintel easily, but even this dip was done smoothly and powerfully, as if he had trained for it. This quick duck-and-rise move made it appear that he was leaping onto the stage, and he always startled the rail birds getting in a last ask before the lights went up; by the time Whelan was front and center, the old birds were back in their pews doing the rosary ramble.

Whelan ran his Mass like clockwork, and God help the boy who was still sleepy, because the man knew our marks like they were chalked on the floor, and he expected us to be quick with the equipment of the Mass — glassware, towels, smoke. Cruets were to be filled to the neck, incense respectfully removed from the boat and properly lit in the thurible, hand towel clean and folded over the left arm, Mass book open to the right page, bells rung sharply at exactly the instant he paused for the sharp ringing of the bells. He also liked his wine cut with water in advance, half and half. Most priests liked to mix it themselves during Mass. Some drank mostly water, with only a touch of wine for color and legitimacy; some drank the wine straight, with barely a drop of water. Few priests drank a full load of wine; even the heavy hitters found cheap burgundy distasteful at dawn. We did, too, although there were more than a few boys who drank wine in the musty stockroom, and every altar boy at some point gobbled a handful of Communion wafers to see how they tasted fresh from the box. They tasted like typing paper. After I discovered that the hosts came wholesale from a convent in New Jersey, the consecrated Host never tasted quite as savory again.

Oremus

I joined the altar boys because my older brother was in the corps and because my parents expected it. Also, you could get out of class for funerals. Funerals didn't pay anything but weddings did, usually a buck, although there were rumors of five-dollar weddings, and it was said of one boy that he had once received a twenty-dollar bill from a bride's father who was drunk. Baptisms didn't pay — a quarter, maybe, if you were doing twins. The way to make money was to do funerals and to work the banks of candles on either side of the altar. The big ones were on the left and the little ones were on the right — "big ones for the horses and little ones for the dogs," as Mr. Torrens, the altar master, said with an enigmatic smile. He was a horseplayer, I think.

People would come up to the candles before and after Mass, and if you were there in uniform, they'd hand you the money, even though the steel box was right in front of them. Large candles were a dollar and small ones were a quarter.

Light a big one for my grandmother, they'd say, crumpling a bill into your hand.

Here's a quarter for my boy at sea.

Here's a quarter for a marriage.

A quarter for the pope's health.

Two smalls, for my intentions.

A dollar for the dead.

The code among us was that coins placed in your hand were yours; bills went into the box. The theory was that we were just standing there and the women (they were mostly women) were handing us money out of the goodness of their hearts. This was the first tickle of sin for some of us, and while the practice enriched some boys, it was by no means universal, partly because our cassocks had no pockets and partly because Mr. Torrens learned about it from a first-year boy and after that kept a sharp eye on us from the sacristy door. A boy named Frank Rizzo (not the Philadelphia mayor) was asked to leave the corps because of this, and it caused great embarrassment to his family. He became a bully in adolescence and probably still is.

The Poem of the Twenty-two Rites and Thirteen Masses

When I was an altar boy, there were twenty-two rites for the Mass, and we were expected to know them even though we were to be witnesses and assistants at only one, the Roman rite, by far the world and Olympic champion in Western civilization. There were actually two other Western rites and a startling total of nineteen Eastern Catholic rites. All twenty-two rites remain in my mind not unlike a poem, and so I chant the Poem of the Twenty-two Rites, which I dedicate to Father Dennis Whelan, wherever he may be: Abyssinian, Albanian, Ambrosian, Armenian, Bulgarian, Chaldean, Coptic, Georgian, Greek, Hungarian, Italo-Albanian, Malabar, Malankar, Maronite, Melkite, Mozarabic, Roman, Romanian, Russian, Ruthenian, Serbian, and Syrian. I even remember that the Ambrosian rite was used only in Milan, and the Mozarabic rite only in Toledo and Salamanca in Spain. And then there are the thirteen Masses within the Roman rite: the Missa Cantata, or Sung Mass (or "High Mass"), sung by a priest and a choir, the Gregorian Masses (a series celebrated for thirty consecutive days, for the release of a soul in purgatory), the Low (the "usual Mass," like the ones I assisted Father Whelan with), the Pontifical (said by a bishop), the Solemn (sung by a priest with acolytes, choir, deacon, and subdeacon), the Votive (priest's choice of intentions), Missa Pro Populo (said by pastors by Church law eighty-eight times a year), Mass of a Saint, Mass of Exposition, Mass of Reposition, Mass of the Catechumens (the first half of Mass, before the big moment), Mass of the Faithful (second half), and Mass of the Presanctified (part of the Good Friday Mass during the Passion of Christ).

To remember all this, is that prayer or foolishness?

Mass of the Faithful

After Father Whelan was on his mark, facing the congregation from behind the altar, Mass was under way. The pieces of it snicked into place like oiled parts of an engine. Opening prayers, prayer for the intention of the day, Gospel, Eucharist, serving of Eucharist along the rail, left to right and back again, cleanup and closing prayers, back to the front of the altar for the brisk procession back into the sacristy. Or, in the order of the Latin prayers we learned and then unlearned, *aufer a nobis, oramus te, Kyrie* (Greek, left over from the first and second centuries A.D., before the Mass went Latin), *Gloria, Alleluia, Credo, Dominus Vobiscum, Oremus, Sanctus, Te igitur, Communicantes, Hanc igitur, Quam oblationem, unde et memores, Supra quae, Supplices, per quem, per ipsum, Pater Noster, Libera nos,*

Agnus Dei, Domine, Ite missa es, placeat, and then a rush for the door, or, in the case of the priest and the altar boy, a dignified retreat to the sacristy.

As Whelan ducked back under the sacristy lintel, he was a different man, and even before he was across the room you could see the steel go out of his body. At the counter, he took off his alb and hung up his rope belt on the inside of his closet door. Then he peeled his surplice off over his head like a boy yanking off a sweater, and then he sat down on his stool and lit a cigar. By then my surplice and cassock were hanging in my locker and I was sitting in one of the two chairs by the door. It was considered bad form to leave the sacristy before Father left. Some boys waited impatiently by the door, but I rather liked Whelan and enjoyed the postmortem:

Good job out there, son.

Thank you, Father.

Could do the bells a little sharper.

Yes, Father.

Then still them with your off hand.

Yes, Father.

Are we on next week?

Monday for me, Father.

Ah, that'll be Father Driscoll.

Driscoll was another brisk guy, although not quite so smooth as Whelan. He was a good deal younger, and he lingered over the prayers a bit. It was said that he had a hair shirt and the stigmata, and we watched his hands closely when he carved the prayers during Mass. You couldn't really tell about the stigmata; there were marks there, but he could have cut himself working in the priests' garden, which was the domain of a short Italian Jesuit who made pickles and such. Driscoll's small hands were always moist, and he had the unusual habit of shaking hands with his altar boys after a Mass; he did this as part of his disrobing ritual, and he would actually come into our little locker room to shake hands if we'd forgotten about it. He always seemed out of place there, and he didn't stay any longer than the handshake.

Once a visiting Franciscan who didn't know the custom wandered into our locker room after a Sunday Mass and sat down companionably. There were four of us boys there at the time, two just finished and two suiting up, and I remember the uncomfortable silences after the priest's friendly questions; we weren't used to a priest in our room, and he was an oddity anyway, with his hooded brown robe and bare feet in enormous sandals. He had gnarled feet like the roots of oak trees. The veins on his feet looked like cables and his toenails were as big as quarters. He finally realized the score and left, after shaking our hands. His hands were a lot bigger and drier than Father Driscoll's. He didn't have the stigmata.

Years later I realized with a start that Christ probably looked a good deal like the Franciscan, with his dusty feet and pocked face, and I had ignored the guy, wished him gone no less than shaky Peter had wished Jesus gone from his past before the cock crowed; Peter standing there in the icy darkness, the fire at his feet sparking up into the dangerous night, sharp voices coming at him like needles, and he shifts uneasily from foot to foot and damns his friend as easily, as thoughtlessly, as you might crush a beetle; then a shooting pain of light in the sky, dawn crawls over the hills, and right in his ear, as loud and shrill as a scream, comes the shriek of a rooster and the horrible knowledge that he has betrayed the man he loves . . .

Consecration

Actual belief in the miracle was mixed among the boys, although all of us watched the priests' hands with awe at the instant the Host was changed into the living, breathing Body of Christ. We did not expect actually to see change steal over the Host itself, as we had been told ad infinitum by the nuns that the miracle was beyond human ken, but we did half expect to see a priest's hands burst spontaneously into flame as he handled the distilled essence of the Mind that invented the universe. There was some discussion about what we should do if a hand fire broke out. There were two general camps: the first insisted that the water cruet should be flung at the fire, and the second advised a sprint away from the awful miracle and toward the janitor, who spoke only shards of English but who knew how to deal with shards of glass, fire, locked doors, broken bicycle chains, vomit, heart attacks, dog bites, broken teeth, broken noses, blood, and sobbing first graders who wet their pants because they were too shy to raise their hands and ask Sister if they could go to the bathroom.

I could never turn my eyes away from that key moment, though. It was and is the single most mysterious and bizarre belief of my faith, and it was in many ways the thing that set us apart from all other Christian denominations. In later years I would sit in Congregationalist and Episcopalian and Lutheran services and observe the Communions of those faiths, the passing of torn bread among the faithful and the circulating cups of wine, and while these acts seemed friendlier to me, more communal than the shivering magic of the Transubstantiation, they seemed insubstantial, too, muted, more like a casual brunch than a heartbreaking Last Supper. I always wanted to like the Communions of other faiths, but they seemed pale to me. I suppose being dipped in miracles every day inoculates you against the mundane; or at least it shoots your sense of perspective all to hell. I still expect miracles, and I have seen some: my wife, my daughter coming out of my wife, my twin sons coming out of my wife one after another like a circus act, the bolt of light that shot around the room when my uncle died.

Requiem

Recently I went to Mass in the Cathedral of the Madeleine in Salt Lake City. This edifice, a monument to the staying power of Catholicism in the heart of Mormon country, is the church where my late father-in-law was an altar boy in the 1920s. He was also a student there, as the cathedral once housed a grade school in its nether regions (four Congregation of the Holy Cross nuns taught eight grades). But it was the altar itself that I was interested in. During Mass I deliberately detoured past the immense stone altar and proscenium, thinking of the man who once knelt there, garbed in acolyte's robes, draped in youth, not yet the affable patriarch who would sire six children and build a business and hammer a home out of the Oregon woods and die there suddenly among his pastures and gardens, his breath sliding to a halt as his lungs filled with fluid, his wife holding him in her arms as he slumped helplessly to one side of the bed, the look on his face more confusion than pain, his death a great surprise to him on a lovely April morning, the scents of horses and blackberry trickling in the window.

I don't know what I expected to see there, amid the pomp and circumstance of Mass in this garish old castle. I suppose I was looking for the marks of his knees, or the hovering nugget of his soul. He died before I met him, before I could thank him for his daughter and show him my daughter and sons. I have looked for him in the woods and in the wood of the house he made. I have been closest to him near a small pond that he labored to clear from the woods, but the forest in Oregon is a tenacious thing, and it took the pond back after the man died.

Adolesensuous

Certainly, being an altar boy was training for the priesthood, in the way that baseball's Little Leagues are training grounds for the big leagues. We were encouraged to go on outings with the younger priests, who took us to carnivals and baseball games (always the Mets, never the Yankees) and bowling alleys. The eighth graders made a pilgrimage to the seminary at Garrison, New York, every year; the year I went, the school had just opened a vast and gleaming sports center, and a quiver of athletic lust went through me like winter wind when the doors to this Xanadu swung open and revealed an oceanic swimming pool and a glittering gymnasium with polished hardwood floors and *glass backboards*. We nearly fainted with desire. The young priest showing off this gem had the wit to remain silent as we gaped at Neverland, and my friends and I spent the rest of the day envisioning ourselves sprinting and spinning and scoring thousands of points on that perfect floor, the stands throbbing with local girls tantalized not only by our patent skill but by the thought that we were tadpole priests — how much more enticing to lure a prospective saint down into the willow trees by the river, and there slip a tongue in his mouth and get his hand on your breast and see if the Catholic Church in the vaguely sanctified person of this gangly zit of a boy was indeed convinced that asceticism was a road to holiness.

Combine this athletic Xanadu with the sweeping view of the Hudson valley below, and the lush playing fields terracing off into

the distance, and the sense that a boy living at a high school fully
two hours from home was an independent and mature creature,
and you had a potent draw for boys on the lip of puberty; but then
we were served mystery meat for lunch, in a dank military-style
cafeteria, and shown through the cold moist barracks, where narrow metal cots stretched away for miles, where a thousand boys
had pulled the pud in a thousand slate-gray stalls, and they lost us.
All the way home Father Driscoll chirped the virtues of the seminary, but we were silent, each boy afraid to be the first to burst the
poor man's bubble. He might, after all, bear the stigmata; plus we
felt sorry for him. He had once been sentenced to a narrow cot
and horse burgers and dismal mornings in a dank gray stall where
cockroaches did the fandango through scummy puddles.

We went home to our bright houses with joy.

Catechumens

On mornings when I had the 6:00 Mass, I would awake in the
woolly dark and leave my brothers snoring like bears and pedal
through the empty streets with my fists clenched in my jacket
pockets and my collar turned up against the whip of dawn. The
church was silent and dark. The only light in it was the tabernacle
lamp, and the only sign of human life the stray Styrofoam coffee
cups filled with cigarette butts in the back of the church, the spoor
of the Nocturnal Adoration Society, which met once a month to
conduct a vigil with the Blessed Sacrament, which reposed inside
a monstrance on the altar; teams of men would arrive every hour
and replace the team in the church, each team yawning as it passed
the other, each exchanging muted greetings, a handshake here
and there in the dark air, the men checking their watches and
settling down on their knees like old horses waiting for dawn.

There were seven lay societies: the Altar Society (for women),
the Blessed Virgin Sodality (for young women), the Holy Name
Society (for men), the Legion of Mary, the Mothers' Club, the Nocturnal Adoration Society, and the Rosary Society (for women).
While my ambition was someday to join my father in the Nocturnal
Adoration Society, my admiration was highest for the Altar Society,
whose members worked like bees to keep the church and its
accoutrements sparkling. "It was they who undertook the launder-

ing of altar linens, communion cloths and surplices, the polishing
of the brass candelabra and altar vases, as well as the disposal of
withered flowers, ferns, and pot plants," the Irish writer Mary Lavin
recounts in her story "A Voice from the Dead." They were an
efficient lot, friendly but brisk, and the good Lord himself could
not help a boy who got in their way when they were stripping the
altar linens; more than once I was shouldered against the cold wall
of the sacristy by a brisk Altar Society woman with an armful of
God's laundry, on her way purposefully, moving through the waters
of the day like a battleship, toward her dank basement laundry
room and the magic Maytag thundering away down there like the
monstrous engine in a tramp steamer.

Incense

Almost always I was at the church before Father Whelan. I would
hear his steps in the courtyard and smell his cigar. He smoked
villainous cigars, execrable things that smelled like peat moss and
burned fitfully if at all. He was always at them, lighting, relighting,
puffing determinedly, moaning with despair at the shoddy plug
that hung like a zeppelin between his lips. He got them from the
tobacconist in the village, a seedy man with a harelip who gave the
priests a break, 20 percent off, probably in exchange for future
considerations. I knew the price because I once bought a box for
Whelan after Mass; he'd been caught short, and after thrashing
his pockets like a man with bees in his pants, he sat me down in
the sacristy.

I need a favor, son.
Yes, Father.
It's unorthodox.
Yes, Father.
I need cigars.
Cigars?
Cigars. A box of them.
Yes, Father.
You'll have to go up to the village. You have a bike.
Yes, Father.
Get a box of panatelas. Here's a fiver.
Yes, Father.

Don't smoke any.
No, Father.
Keep the change.
Yes, Father.
None of these coronas, now.
Yes, Father.
What?
I mean no, Father.

Memento

I remember the dark scent of the church at dawn, the dense purple light, the smells of incense and cigars and dust. I remember the dry shuffling of shoes as communicants shambled toward the Host. I remember the twisted faces of saints in the windows, Veronica's pale hand outstretched with a cloth for the face of Christ, the bulging Popeye forearm of Simon as he supported the collapsing Savior. I remember the groaning organ and the reverberating yowl of an infant being baptized in the nave. I remember the stiff black cloth under which you hid all desire and personality as you prepared to assist at a miracle that you did not and could never understand but which you watched for ravenously, like a hawk after meat. For a time we were expected to wear ties under our cassocks, but eventually this stricture was lifted and we were allowed to wear shirts. No jeans, no sneakers, no sandals — this last despite the gnarled treelike feet of the Franciscans on the altar once a month. You buttoned your cassock from the bottom up, to be sure of symmetry, and then you slipped on the starched white surplice. A simple uniform, black and white, unornamented, memorable.

Credo

I have come, in my middle years, to a passionate belief in a Coherence — a pervasive divineness that I only dimly comprehend and cannot at all articulate. It is a feeling, a sense. I feel it most near my elfin daughter, my newborn sons. Last night I stood over the huddled body of my daughter, asleep in her crib, her hair flowing around her like dark water. She had fallen asleep only

minutes before, sobbing herself to sleep after soiling herself and
her bedding and her bear. She is very sick and cannot control her
bowels, and she is humiliated and frightened by this; she fell asleep
in my wife's arms, her sobs muffled in the folds of my wife's deep,
soft flannel shirt. I stand above her now in the dark. She is curled
like a question mark in the corner of her crib. My body curls itself
into an ancient gesture of prayer and humility and I place my
hands together and begin to weep — for love of this child, in fear
of illness, in despair at my helplessness. I make a prayer in the
dark. I believe so strongly, so viscerally, in a wisdom and vast joy
under the tangled weave of the world, under the tattered blanket
of our evil and tragedy and illness and brokenness and sadness
and loss, that I cannot speak it, cannot articulate it, but can only
hold on to ritual and religion like a drowning man to a sturdy ship.

Benedicamus Domino

"And so the Mass comes to an end, in a whirl of purifications and
postscripts that do not seek to impress themselves deeply on the
mind; one has not enough capacity left for receiving impressions,"
wrote Ronald Knox. "'And every man went to his own house,' as
it says frequently in the Old Testament and once in the New, and
that is what we do; we must be alone."

Many a time I was alone when it was all over, when the rail birds
had gone from the rail, when the businessmen were walking briskly
to their trains. When the audience was gone, the janitor would
whip through the church slamming the kneelers back up and
slipping missals and songbooks back into their racks behind each
pew. Then he would bow before the altar and slip out a side door
toward the school. I would wait for the click of the side door closing and then wander out of the sacristy and sit down in a pew
and think and listen and wait for something to happen. The building groaned and creaked, the candles fluttered and sizzled, bees
and flies bounced off the windows. In the windows were the saints,
red and blue and green and pink, their faces and bodies and
fluttering hands outlined in lead. After a few minutes I would walk
down the aisle, past the empty pews and kneelers and missals and
Stations of the Cross, and push through the massive oak door and
into the broad fat light of the new day, dazzled.

ANDRE DUBUS

Witness

FROM THE NEW YORKER

THURSDAY during the school year is a wheelchair day; they are all wheelchair days, but some more than others. On Thursdays I drive thirty minutes to Andover, the town where my daughters live. They are Cadence and Madeleine, fourteen and nine. I go to their school and park on the road that goes through the grounds and wait for their classes to end at three-twenty. My right leg hurts when I drive; it hurts when it is not at a ninety-degree angle, and most nights it hurts anyway. While driving I have to place my foot to the left of the brake pedal, and that angle makes my leg hurt sooner, and more. Often my back hurts. Years ago I learned that pain and wheelchair fatigue — *sitting*, and worrying about what can go wrong because I can't stand or walk — take most of my energy; I cannot live as normals do, and I must try to do only what is essential each day. So on Thursdays I neither write nor exercise. I make snacks for my daughters, wrap two ice packs around my leg, drive and wait, then take them to my house for dinner, then back to their house, and then I return to host a writers' workshop at my home. I like Thursdays.

I could leave my house at two-thirty or so, and my leg would not start hurting till after three, my back not till after four, or even later, or not at all. But I try to leave by one-thirty. I bring lunch and a book, and drive to the school. I park and eat a sandwich, drink water, and read. There is no telephone. I have a car phone, which I would not have as a biped. It is harmless. It can ring only when the ignition is on, and no one knows its number; I don't know its number. In the car, I read. The pain starts. At home the phone rings and rings, and when I am writing I don't answer; but when I am reading I feel that I should answer it. But even with the pain, there is peace in the car. The moral torque is that by the time the girls come out of school the pain is tiring me. I have to be wary of impatience and irritation. A few days ago I read that a samurai philosophy is to refrain until you can respond instead of reacting. I must work on that.

This fall, in 1996, there is another difficulty: the girls have a dog. And on Thursdays the dog is alone in the house and by late afternoon it needs to be walked, to relieve itself, be a leashed animal outdoors. So from school we drive to the house where the girls live with their mother, and they go inside. The house has front steps, so I have never been in it. I would need a man to get me inside, probably three — depending on the men — to go upstairs to the rooms where my daughters sleep. While I wait in the car, I cannot imagine what the girls are doing in the house whose walls and ceilings and furniture and rooms do not exist as images in my mind. Inside the girls are invisible and soundless; they do not come out with the dog. I admire what I call their anarchy. I cannot make them hurry, not even to a movie or a play, which I tell them will start whether or not we are there; they remain insouciant. I am flesh enclosing tension: we have never been late for a movie or a play. In the car, my leg and back do not admire the girls' anarchy. Patience is leaving, irritation arriving. I read. Then, to my right, I glimpse motion; I look and see the girls finally coming out of the house, the brown short-haired dog ahead of them. Cadence holds the taut leash. The dog is of medium size, younger, eager, wagging her tail, sniffing the air. They cross the street behind me, I watch them in the mirror, then they go through a tree line — again they are invisible — and into a large field. When they disappear I'm briefly frightened; someone could do something to them. I read, I smoke, sometimes I grunt or moan.

I want the girls to have a dog, and I want them to be happily walking the dog in the field. But I also want my leg to stop hurting. I want to be home with my leg on the wheelchair's leg rest. I want to be there eating dinner with my daughters.

A woman who was my Eucharistic minister, bringing me Communion when I could not go to Mass for more than a year after I got hit, once said to me, "Don't think about what you want; think about what you need." What do I need, sitting in this car? Courage? Patience? I can think only that I need the pain to leave me. My energy is flowing into it. And it is not bad pain. For bad pain there are good drugs. By now the ice packs are thawed. What I need, waiting for my girls, is for this part of the day to end. It does. After twenty-five minutes or so, they come through the tree line and cross the street and return the dog to their house. Time passes. Then they come out and get into the car and I drive to my home where a woman I pay is cooking dinner. It is five o'clock. The girls go to Cadence's room and shut the door and play classical music for the potted plants. They study, I answer phone messages, throw away mail, keep what I have to answer or pay. At five-thirty we eat.

On a Thursday in late October, I drove with my girls from the school to their house. The sky was blue, the air warm, and there were yellow and red autumn leaves; and at the girls' house, to relieve the pain in my leg, I got out of the car. I do this by lowering my wheelchair from a carrier that holds it on the roof. With Joan Didion's *The Last Thing He Wanted,* I got in my chair and went to the front of my car, using it as a shield against the very few moving cars on this street with houses and trees. My leg rested in front of me. Soon it would stop hurting. Two young boys wearing helmets were on skateboards in the road. My daughters have new neighbors across the street. Out of that house came a brown-haired woman in her thirties, carrying a very young boy. She looked at me, then called to the skateboarding boys, told them they could not play in the street. They stalled, pleaded, then skated to the sidewalk. She looked at me again. The boy in her arms wore glasses, and was squirming. The woman came to me, looking down now at my face. She said, "I've been wanting to talk to you for some time. I saw your accident."

"You did?"

"I was with my friend at the call box."

Ten years, three months, and one day before this lovely October afternoon, between midnight and one in the morning, on I-93 north of Boston, I saw a car stopped on the highway. It was a four-lane highway, and the car was in the third lane. There was another car in the breakdown lane, and two women were standing at an emergency call box. Now one of those two women was here, and I felt as I might if she had told me that long ago we were classmates. We introduced ourselves, shook hands. She said she had just moved to this street and had been talking to neighbors and had realized that I was the man she saw that night. She saw two men hit; the other one died within hours.

She said, "You're an author?"

"Yes."

The boy, not yet three, twisted in her arms, grunted, reached for my wheelchair. His thick glasses made his eyes seem large.

"You were hit by a silver — " She named a car I know nothing about, but not the right one.

I said, "It was a Honda Prelude."

"And it paralyzed you?"

"No. Only my leg's useless. I'm very lucky. I had three broken vertebrae in my back. But my spine was okay. My brain." I felt that I was reciting; as I spoke I was seeing her at the call box while I drove up to the driver's side of the car that had stopped, the last one I ever walked to. "Where were you coming from?" I asked.

"Joe's American Bar and Grill. My friend and I ate there, and had some drinks."

"The one at the mall?"

After we see a play, my girls and I eat at a seafood restaurant near Joe's at a mall; I was imagining us doing that, connecting places with this woman standing beside me.

"No. In Boston."

"Where were you going?"

"Andover. I haven't driven the same since that night."

"Neither have I."

The boy was strong and kept turning, lunging, reaching. She said, "I have to get his stroller."

She carried him across the street and into her house, and I sat among fallen leaves near the curb and looked up at yellow leaves and branches and the sky, and saw the woman and her friend at the restaurant, then at the call box. The two skateboarding boys were not ten years old; since that night she had borne three sons; and my daughter Madeleine had been born. The woman came out with her son strapped into a stroller and crossed the street. The boy reached for the leg rest of my chair. She said, "He goes to a special school. He sees a lot of kids in wheelchairs."

"What's wrong with him?"

"Probably autism. He's too young for the tests."

He was looking at a book with pictures. Then he started tearing it, its cover, too; he tore it in half, then into quarters. He was concentrating, grunting. I said, "He's very strong."

She smiled, and said, "They aren't supposed to be able to tear them."

"He's got a life in there."

"Oh, he does. It's me who's frustrated. Because I can't talk to him. And I know he's frustrated because he can't talk."

The girls came out with their dog and looked at me and the woman, and I said, "Have you met your neighbor?" They came to the sidewalk, and I said, "She was there the night I got hit."

Madeleine looked intently at her; Cadence's mouth opened, and in her cheeks color rose, and she said, "You *were?*"

I saw in her face something that was in my soul, though I did not know it yet; I felt only the curiosity you might feel on hearing an unusual sound in the dark outside your window; Cadence looked as though she had just heard something painful, but it had not yet fully struck her. I introduced the woman and her son to my girls, then they went off with their dog. I looked up at the woman, seeing her beside the highway watching me fly over the car, land on its trunk. My blood wanted to know; it rushed. She said, "The woman in the broken-down car was running around in the highway."

"She was standing in the speed lane. I was trying to get her off the road." The man who died was her brother.

For a moment I was there: a clear July night, no cars coming, everything I had to do seeming easy. I said, "I'm glad you had already called the state troopers. They saved my life. I might have bled to death."

"Someone else would have called."

"Maybe. But *after* I was hit."

The boy was trying to get out of his stroller; he reached for my leg rest, for a wheel of the chair, lunged and twisted in the straps.

"I have to take him in," she said.

I wanted to ask her what she saw, but I could not; it was like waiting to confess something, waiting for that moment, for the words to come. When I got hit, I did not lose consciousness, but have never remembered being hit, only flagging down a car for help, then lying on its trunk.

I watched her cross the street with her son and, at her stairs, lift him from the stroller and carry him inside. I began reading again. Soon a car turned the corner behind me and stopped at the woman's house; I watched a man go inside; he was not big, but his shoulders and chest were broad, and he walked with an energy that sometimes saddens me. When my daughters and their dog returned from the field, I moved to my car door, put the leg and arm rest into the back seat, and got in. Before I raised the wheelchair to its carrier, the man came out of the house, carrying his son, and walked to me. He reached over the wheelchair and we shook hands and exchanged names. His face did not have that serious look of some men, as though all play were gone from their lives, and there was only work, money, the future they may not be alive for. He was a man who could be joyful. I can now see his face more clearly than I see his wife's; when I try to remember her, I see her standing at the call box, a body whose face I could not see in the night.

"My wife said she talked to you."

"It's incredible. I've never met anyone who saw me get hit."

"She called me that night. What's it like for you, after ten years?"

"It's better. I'm used to some things. I still can't drive alone to Boston, at night on 93."

"Oh, that's a protective device."

"Really? You mean I don't have to think of myself as a wimp?"

"No, no. I believe everything we have is a gift."

We talked about his work, and his son, who was moving in his arms, and he said he'd like to have a beer with me sometime; he would get me up his steps. I told him I would like that. In his face were the sorrow and tenderness of love as he strongly held his writhing son, looking at the small face that seemed feral in its isolation. We shook hands and he went inside.

I started the car, picked up the switch that's attached to a wire on the floor, and pressed it, and the carrier on the roof lowered, two chains with an elongated hook, which I inserted into a slot under the chair's seat. I flicked the switch again, this time in the other direction, and the chains pulled the chair up. But when it reached the frame of the carrier, it stopped. The motor was silent. I released the switch, tried it again. It clicked. The chair did not move. I kept pushing the switch. Its click was disproportionately loud, a sound without promise; yet I kept doing it. The chair was too high for me to reach it and try to take it off the hook, and a thirty-inch metal frame was jutting out from my car.

This is why I have a car phone: for circumstances that require legs. My son-in-law, Tom, is a mechanic. I called him, thirty minutes away in southern New Hampshire. He said he would come. I was calm. I have never been calm when the wheelchair carrier fails, and usually I am not calm for hours after Tom has fixed it. But that day I was calm, maybe because I had started the day by going to Mass — this always helps — or maybe because my spirit was on the highway on the twenty-third of July in 1986.

I would not have the time to be rescued, then drive my daughters to my house for dinner at five-thirty. My daughters were still inside. When they came out, I told them, and we kissed goodbye, and they went back inside. I phoned the woman at my house, and said we would not need dinner. I read Didion. Tom came in his truck, looked under the hood, worked there for a while, then said it was fixed, for now, but he would have to get a part. My knowledge of things mechanical is very small: pens, manual typewriters, guns. I drove home, feeling that I was on the circumference of a broken circle whose separated ends were moving toward each other. Soon they would meet. Next time I saw her, I would ask everything.

Around seven-twenty, writers began arriving for the workshop, and some of us waited on the sundeck for those still on the road. I told them about the woman and said that next time I would ask her if she saw me get hit; when I heard myself say that, I was suddenly afraid of images I have been spared, and I said no, I would not ask her. We went to the living room, and I told the story again, to the people who had not been on the deck; this time, as I talked, curiosity and wonder left me, as though pushed out of my mouth by the dread rising from my stomach. I looked at the faces of the women and men sitting on the couch, the love seat, the window seat; we formed a rectangle. I was alone at one end. I felt faint, as if I had lost blood. I said, "I think I'll go into a little shock tonight, or tomorrow."

But I was calm that night, and Friday, and Saturday. On Sunday we had a family dinner with three of my grown children, their spouses, the older son's two small children, and Cadence and Madeleine. That morning the sky was blue, and I was on my bed, doing leg lifts. When I swung my leg and stump up for the fiftieth time, I began quietly to cry. Then I stopped. I made the bed, dressed, ate yogurt and strawberries, showered, dressed on my bed. The tears were gone and would not come back, but my soul was gray and cool, and pieces of it were tossed as by a breeze that had become a strong wind and could become a storm. I drove to the girls' house. They live on the corner of the street, and when I turned onto it I saw the woman in her yard. She was doing some kind of work, her back was to me, and I looked away from her, at the girls' house, and I phoned them to say I'm here.

At my house we cooked on the grill, and I sat on the deck, my face warmed by the sun, and talked with my children and enjoyed the afternoon. I looked up at my two sons and told them of suddenly crying while doing leg lifts, of being fragile now, and as I talked to them I made a decision I never make, a decision about writing, because my decisions usually gestate for months, often more than a year, before I try to write anything: I told them I would start writing this on Monday, because meeting the woman, shaking her hand, hearing her voice, seeing her sons, especially the youngest one, and shaking her husband's hand, hearing his witness — *She called me that night* — had so possessed me that I may as well plunge into it, write it, not to rid myself of it, because writing does not rid me of anything, but just to go there, to wherever the woman had taken me, to go there and find the music for it, and see if in that place there was any light.

Next day I woke to a wind that brought sorrow and fear and rain, while beyond the glass doors in front of my desk the sky was blue, and leaves were red and yellow, and I wrote. For ten days I woke and lived with this storm, and with the rain were demons that always come on a bad wind: loneliness, mortality, legs. Then it was gone, as any storm. They stop. The healing tincture of time, a surgeon told me in the hospital. On the eleventh day, I woke with a calm soul, and said a prayer of thanks. While I wrote this, the red and yellow leaves fell, then the brown ones, and the nights became colder, and some days, too, most of them now in late November, and I did not find the music. Everything I have written here seems flat: the horns dissonant, the drums lagging, the piano choppy. Today the light came: *I'm here.*

JOSEPH EPSTEIN

Will You Still Feed Me?

FROM THE AMERICAN SCHOLAR

I KNOW IT'S no great achievement — I realize people are doing it every day — but I am rather smugly pleased to have reached the stately age of sixty. I am pleased because, while the actuarial tables suggest I ought to have made it, nonetheless I have "the imagination for disaster," in the phrase of Henry James, who claimed to have "seen life indeed as ferocious and sinister." I am always not so secretly delighted when the worst doesn't happen. James also called death, at his final illness, "the Distinguished Thing." The Distinguished Thing has not come knocking at my door, at least not yet, though it regularly pays check-out calls on people my age and much younger: Harold Ross at fifty-nine, Whittaker Chambers at sixty, and François Truffaut at fifty-two were required to pack their bags.

The few friends to whom I have mentioned that I am sixty seem mildly impressed. I am a little impressed by it myself. My birthdays have until now not much moved me. I have always felt my age, and I have tried to act my age, too, which, in a society that vaunts youthfulness, hasn't always been easy. I used to see my official retirement date — 2002, when I shall be sixty-five — on documents and viewed the number as more properly belonging to the realm of science fiction. I read the other day that Chicago, the city in which I live, hopes to have the Olympics in 2008, and I wonder if I shall be around to attend them.

As I clicked off the decades in my own life, I made note of what they were supposed to represent: thirty — the end of young manhood; forty — the onset of true earnestness; fifty — midlife, the halfway point (though, chronologically, not really), the age that evokes all sorts of empty symbolism. But sixty, sixty I think is fairly serious. There is nothing ambiguous about being sixty, the way there is about being in one's fifties. If one takes to chasing young women in one's sixties, for example, one is, officially, a dirty old man. At sixty it is even too late to undergo that greatest of all masculine psychological clichés, a midlife crisis. If one does so, one is not in a crisis but is merely being a damn fool.

In a Mavis Gallant story called "An Unmarried Man's Summer," the hero is told by his father, "If your life isn't exactly the way you want it to be by the time you are forty-five, not much point in continuing." He adds, "You might as well hang yourself." I suspect that the advice — apart from the hanging — is sound if the age, in accord with the longer-gevity of our own day, were set at sixty. At sixty, one probably does well not to expect wild changes, at least not for the better. Probably best not even to expect a lot in the way of self-improvement. Not a good idea, I think, at this point to attempt to build the body beautiful. Be happy — immensely happy, in fact — with the body still functional.

At sixty I am now too old to die young, which is, somehow, pleasing. I am too old to expect a dramatic shift, apart from illness, in my life: too old to turn gay, or go motorcycle or Hasidic. The cards have been dealt, I have taken my draw, and I must play out the game. I happen to think I drew a pretty good hand. (A joker or two, I realize, are still to come.) Had I my first six decades to live over, there are lots of things I might have done differently. Yet I realize that had I done them differently, I might not have been able to do most of the things that I am now glad to have done. If you are satisfied with your life and its few accomplishments — and I, for the most part, am — even serious mistakes made early in life come to seem not only sensible but necessary. If you are not pleased with your life, of course, the reverse applies, and everything seems both a mistake and unnecessary.

Can you bear much more of this smugness? I'm not sure that I can. One of the nice things about *Hamlet,* it has been said, is that at least Polonius, who may himself have been around sixty, gets stabbed. To become Polonius-like, to start dispensing vast quantities of advice, is one of the temptations of growing older. When with young people, I find I already have to guard against playing the kindly old gentleman. I have sworn off all sentences that begin, "You may not remember this, but . . ." or "When I was a kid . . ." or "During World War II, I remember . . ." or "In my day . . ." At sixty, one begins to feel one is entitled to such sentences — and one is, of course, wrong. Better, I think, to save them until age ninety-six or ninety-seven.

Sixty can have this strange effect on people, rather as if one is suddenly driving in a different gear. The most radical case of a sudden shift at sixty I know about belonged to W. H. Auden, an odd enough man in his own way before sixty but very odd indeed after sixty. It was as if at sixty precisely Auden was able to live as the old man he had earlier longed to be. He had carried carpet slippers around with him before, but now he began wearing them full time and in all sorts of weather. He rarely changed his clothes. He would tell the same anecdotes over and over, often to the same people and within a brief span of time. "At my age," he averred, "I'm allowed to seem a little dotty."

After sixty, Auden emphasized all the little crankinesses that had earlier added to his charm but now chiefly irritated his friends. He became tyrannical about other people being punctual. He insisted on early bedtimes, and would leave other people's dinner parties at nine, or chase people from his own apartment at the same time. He liked to say that he had given up sex. (He hadn't.) He allowed himself mildly right-wing views, which he repeated to the point where they became set pieces. He became a monologist. He ceased to exercise. ("A *walk?* What on earth *for?*") Friends said that he had lost all spontaneity and that he longed for death. By sixty-two he seemed, in the words of one of these friends, Margaret Gardiner, "a very old man." Sixty, for W. H. Auden, was clearly a serious mistake.

If turning oneself into a mangy old coot at sixty is a grievous error, what are the other possibilities? Philip Larkin, on his sixtieth birthday, wrote that he looked "forward to the decent obscurity of autumn." With his excellent deadpan, he wrote to a friend that he thought it "a bit hard to call someone sixty just because they've been fifty-nine for a year." Yet he felt "being sixty is rather grim," adding, with just the right measure of Larkinesque rue, "I can't say I *feel* unduly old; I'm bald and deaf and with a Falstaffian paunch, but these have been with me for several, if not many, years.

A chap in the *Guardian* said that the best thing about being sixty is that it isn't being seventy, and while this is true it's something that time will cure, as Pitt said when accused of being too young."

Auden said seventy was a good age to die, though he thought he would live to eighty-three; in fact, he pegged out, in 1973, at age sixty-six. Larkin, who was always conscious of passing time and of the time left to him, departed the planet at sixty-three. "Who am I now?" Auden wrote, in a poem called "Prologue at Sixty": "An American? No, a New Yorker,/who opens his *Times* at the obit page . . ." I am myself a Chicagoan who also opens his *Times* at the obit page. No news more interesting than that having to do with those who have left the court. It seems, at this point, as if someone I know, or someone connected to someone I know, dies nearly every other day. I consider a fine morning one on which the *New York Times* prints obituaries about five people — four who died in their early nineties and one who died at eighty-nine. A bad morning is one on which three of the deceased are younger than I and two are just a few years older. This means that the machine gunner is out and firing indiscriminately. It would be a great help if one knew the exact date of one's own death — one's own true, so to say, deadline — though I am sure that, even with years of warning, one would still manage to be unprepared. I have always regarded the phrase "untimely death" as the poorest possible usage; hard to imagine, for oneself, a timely one.

Meanwhile, small warnings keep cropping up. I note what look like a few mottles, or age spots, on the top of my left hand. Graying of hair, rotting of teeth, loosening of flesh — all seem nicely on schedule. ("What is life," said Carlyle, "but a continual dying!") My handwriting, never very good, begins to approach the indecipherable. An eleven-year-old girl, with the utter candor of kids, one night at dinner said to me, "You don't have an upper lip." When I checked in the mirror, this turned out to be quite correct. I am getting a mortgage banker's mouth: two thin lines with teeth in between. Standing before the mirror, I practice the sentences "You should have thought of that earlier. I'm sorry, but we are going to have to foreclose on the farm."

In the press, I see photographs of people — chunky men with ringed pates of white hair, women in what appears to me an advanced state of decrepitude — and, *sacrebleu!*, they turn out to be four years younger than I. People even much younger hold jobs I assumed would always be held by people much older than I. Our poet laureate was the student of a contemporary of mine; the current secretary of state once worked for my wife.

I see photographs in the press of people a year or two older than I, and I tell myself that surely I don't look anywhere near as old as that. Yet when I last went to the movies, I gave the young woman selling tickets a twenty, and, as I counted my change, I noted that she had charged me the senior-citizen rate. I put down a book on the counter at my Korean dry cleaner's, and the owner asked me if the photograph on the back is of me. It is, in fact, a photograph of Isaiah Berlin, who was a mere eighty-eight when he died in November 1997.

I am thought to have a good memory. What I have, in fact, is a writer's memory. For mysterious (and extraordinarily lucky) reasons, I seem to be able to call up all sorts of odd facts and memories required by things I happen to be writing. But when not writing prose, I have become quite as forgetful as other people my age. Names drop away, titles of books and movies frequently aren't there when I need them, odd bits of information get lost: the other day, for example, I could not recall the word "spleen"; a few days earlier, I mislocated the name "Borsolino," the Italian hatter. I seem especially bad at keeping past time straight. Events that I recall as being five or six years past turn out to be eight or as many as ten years past. I remember scarcely anything of trivial movies that I have seen as recently as three or four years ago. It is rather charming, really, allowing me to come to these ephemeral entertainments as if afresh.

Please do not get me wrong. The ongoing struggle, as the Communists used to say, keeps on going. A significant decision about growing older, it seems to me, has to do with whether or not one wishes to keep roughly abreast of new technologies, computers chief among them. I think that, had I been ten years older, I might have taken a pass on the computer age, contenting myself with using the computer only for its word processing. But I decided to hang in there. I haven't my own Web page, but I am, in a limited way, a World Wide Webster, partial, like nearly everyone else who uses it, to e-mail and unable to read anything of any length on the Internet. I am even a disappointed and now lapsed subscriber to

Wired, a magazine that suggests the promise of computer technology bringing about a new sensibility. After reading *Wired* for more than a year, I have decided to stay with my old one.

Hanging in there, I continue to read young novelists and short story writers: Cathleen Schine, Nicholson Baker, Mark Leyner, Julie Hecht, David Foster Wallace. I read these writers partly because much of my education has been through fiction, partly because I still love the novel and short story above all other literary forms, and partly because I hope they will tell me things I do not know about the way we live now. I find I do learn some of these things, though I am not sure I am getting a healthy return on my investment. But, then, I may have reached the age when nothing seems quite new and everything begins to remind me of everything else. I may be coming to a time when only amusing children and acts of inexplicable goodness are capable of blowing me away.

A certain distaste for change has begun to set in, even — perhaps especially — in minor matters. I find I do not wish to contemplate the notion that there is now a football team called the St. Louis Rams. The Rams have been in Los Angeles for as long as I can remember, and they ought to have had the decency to stay there — at least for my lifetime. When a house or building is razed along one of my habitual routes of travel, I feel a touch of loss, as I would after losing a back tooth that I hadn't hitherto been conscious of. A good deal of what passes for elegant food in modish restaurants seems to me overly ambitious, and I long for plain good food. Not all my positions and emotions are rearguard. I find, with the help of Pierre Boulez, that I am coming to enjoy modern musical composition, though only when I am in the room where it is being played. But I am most content when in familiar surroundings and among old friends.

I pick up a literary quarterly to discover that there is an interview with Alice Fulton by Alec Marsh. I don't know who Alec Marsh is. I don't know who Alice Fulton is either, or why she is worthy of being interviewed. Turns out she's a poet, has written a book with the amusing title *Sensual Math,* and seems to be interested in the issue of "the poet's relationship to our electronically mediated world." By me, as the poker players say, as they toss in their cards. I used to know the names of all the poets. Also those of all published short story writers, novelists, critics, reviewers, key publishing editors. I knew the mastheads of all the magazines, including those in exceedingly small print in *Time* and *Newsweek*. Now — by me.

My interests seem more limited generally. Am I, subconsciously, delimiting them? The list of things I no longer know about — and, perhaps more significant, no longer care to know about — grows. I know the names of fewer and fewer movie stars, United States senators, major league pitchers. I am not interested in politics — either its nuts and bolts or its larger structures. I can on occasion be shocked, but I am less and less surprised. I recently read an entire book on prostate cancer.

Just as my interests seem more limited, so have my fantasies become more sparse and attenuated. I am no longer able to dream my way into complex sexual intrigues with beautiful women with lush foreign accents. Staring at striking young women is an activity I now consider to be at a scale of seriousness three levels below that of window-shopping. I have no power fantasies whatsoever: I don't wish to be CEO of General Motors, editor of *The New Yorker*, president of Yale, secretary of HUD. My fantasies now include picturing myself enjoying long stretches in peaceful settings, amid the people I love, with an utter absence of aggravations, small and large.

Age consciousness has begun to set in. With the exception of classical music concerts, the places I frequently find myself in — restaurants, movies, plays — are places where I am often the oldest guy in the joint. "I think I have been more than most men conscious of my age," wrote Somerset Maugham. "My youth slipped past me unnoticed, and I was always burdened with the sense that I was growing old." Maugham reports, in *A Writer's Notebook*, that he always seemed older than his contemporaries, and adds that "it is not a very pleasant thing to recognize that to the young you are no longer an equal. You belong to a different generation. For them your race is run. They can look up to you; they can admire you; but you are apart from them; and in the long run will always find the companionship of persons of their own age more grateful than yours."

I have many younger friends. I used to have many friends much older than I. But by now, I believe the balance between younger and older has shifted. I do not myself feel a great gap between us, though perhaps my younger friends feel our age difference more than I. Can it be that they want from me what I wanted, in my turn, from my older friends: regard, respect, finally admiration to set the seal on my own less-than-sure estimate of my quality? It may seem odd to require the approval of one's elders when in one's fifties, but I felt this and still feel intense pleasure when I learn that someone I admired as a young man now has a good opinion of me.

Maugham goes on to report that one of the pleasures of growing older "is that on the whole you feel no need to do what you do not like." He adds that you are less likely to care what people think of you, whereas when young one is "bound hand and foot with the shackles of public opinion." Henry James, in a letter written in his sixtieth year to his friend Grace Norton, corroborates this, affirming that he has "reached a state of final beatitude in which one cares not a fraction of a straw what any one in the world *thinks* of one." I tend to agree. I might go a bit further and say that I am rather pleased to have some of the enemies I do; their dislike, I feel, honors me. When one gets to sixty, one is reconciled with oneself; one is what one is. Injustice of opinion matters less and less. Only true justice hurts; and, lucky fellow, I have come this far without having to undergo it.

What makes sixty feel rather different from, say, fifty-seven, is that finitude sets in in a big way — finitude combined, even now, with hope. If I can make it, I say, I'd like to teach ten more years. God willing, I say, five years from now I hope to have cleared the decks to work on an extended book I have long planned. With a little luck, I say, I can write another eight books before the lights go out. Knock wood, I say, if I can only make it to eighty, my grandchild will be twenty-seven and I will have helped see her into relatively safe harbor.

This notion of finitude, of no longer playing with a fully loaded shot clock, has been with me for some time. I note an entry in my journal for October 10, 1992: "Autumn setting in in earnest. Sweater weather. Leaves near peak of color change. How many more autumns will I see? God knows — and nobody else — and it is not clear how much He cares."

With the reign of finitude well in place, one's resignation becomes greater. No sooner does one begin to recognize how quickly

time is moving — it's not the minutes, it's those damn decades —
than one recognizes as well all that one won't accomplish, at least
in this life. "In the next life, *perhaps*," I find myself more and
more saying, trying to get the italics into my voice, whether I am
referring to not being able to acquire a new foreign language, or
read a multivolume work, or play the piano, or go into retailing.
I now know for certain that there are many things I shall never do:
own a mansion, cook elegant dishes, read musical scores. I can, as
they say, live with this; in fact, I am hoping to live for a good while
with it.

One is resigned, too, to the world's comedy: idiots rising to the
top, fanatics dressed up as idealists, boobs confidently in control.
Henry James, in a formulation on which I cannot improve, noted:

> Life *is* a battle. On this point optimists and pessimists agree. Evil is
> insolent and strong; beauty enchanting but rare; goodness very apt to
> be weak; folly very apt to be defiant; wickedness to carry the day; im-
> beciles to be in very great places, people of sense in small, and man-
> kind generally, unhappy . . . In this there is mingled pain and delight,
> but over the mysterious mixture there hovers a visible rule, that bids us
> learn to will and seek to understand.

I wish that by now, at sixty, I could say that my own understanding of life is deep. It ain't. I remember, at twenty, taking a
Shakespeare course in the University of Chicago's adult education
program and being struck by how in the dark about life so many
of my fellow students, many of them then in their forties and fifties,
seemed. I don't know that I myself am currently all that much
more enlightened. I like to think I am a little less connable than
I was twenty or thirty years ago. I like to think I now at least
understand how things *don't* happen, which is not at all the same
as understanding how they *do* happen. I have never fallen for
either of the two big stories of our century — Marxism and Freudi-
anism — but that doesn't mean that I have come up with any big
story of my own. In the Hegelian triad, I am all antithesis. I am
left, really, with a few self-invented folk sayings: "In for a penny, in
for a pounding" is one; "You live and you yearn" is another.

One of the things I yearn for, of course, is greater understanding. I don't at all like the idea of leaving the theater without
understanding the play. Shall I be able to build up enough small

insights to allow the parts to begin to approximate a whole? I continue to hope to get better at my work. For some years now, I have been telling myself that, as a writer, I have not yet begun to get worse, though I could use a good quality-control guy. Will I know about it when it happens? Short of dying or simply ceasing to write (as I type out this introductory phrase, the two seem to me almost the same), is there any way that getting worse can be avoided? Short of early death, probably not.

Being sixty changes a sentient person's notion of the future. Curt Gowdy, the old sports announcer, used to say of young athletes that they had their whole future ahead of them. Where else, I wondered, would anyone's future be? But, growing older, I begin to sense that much of my future is behind me. Certainly, I think differently of the future. It is no longer all open doors and wide horizons, enticing prospects and endless possibilities. If one has children and grandchildren, one's sense of futurity is bound up with them. I myself listen to the plans of the young — and the young tend to be full of plans — and try not to smile, remembering the old joke: "Know how to make God laugh? Tell him your plans."

If sixty changes one's sense of the future, it absolutely knocks the hell out of one's sense of progress. What, at this point, is one progressing toward? And yet life, without a sense of progress, can seem an arid thing. My dear friend Edward Shils, then in his late seventies, told me that he had to have a sense of intellectual progress if he were to continue as a teacher and a scholar. Without this sense, teaching becomes empty, scholarship barren. Edward, practicing what he preached, broadened and deepened his own knowledge of China when in his early eighties, and he began to teach courses in Sinological subjects.

When younger, one tends, brimming with hope, to assume progress: that next year will be better than this; that one will continue to grow smarter; that fortune will smile on one. At sixty, it is no longer quite so easy to believe such things. Candide, after all, was a young man. Had Voltaire made him sixty, he would have been not merely a fool but an utterly hopeless idiot.

"It is *difficult* to know something," says Wittgenstein, "and to act as if you did not know it." What one knows at sixty is that time is beginning to run out. So one lessens one's expectations, limits one's possibilities, resigns oneself to the hard facts of life — and yet plays on through. Life may be a mug's game — a game, that is, one cannot finally win — but it still seems well worth playing. In an unexpected way, these limitations can make things seem even richer: one loses passion and gains detachment, gives up ambition and hopes for perspective. The comic element of life seems, in some ways, greater than ever.

Perspective is the trick of life, and I have not come anywhere near mastering it. Such perspective as I do have applies almost exclusively to other people, not to myself. Another of the pleasing things about attaining a certain age is that one begins to make out the arc of other people's careers. One sees patterns in their lives — the intellectual of poor character who has no real work to his credit as he nears fifty; the woman, stimulated by worthlessness in men, left alone in her sixties; the academic of profoundly bad taste who has wasted more than a decade of his adult life promoting a dreadfully dopey idea. These and other lives are amusing to contemplate.

I am, I fear, a sucker for the notion, first formulated by Novalis, that character is destiny. I feel reassured when people of strong character win out and people of poor character go down the drink. Evidence of a clean cause-and-effect relation clears the intellectual sinuses. Unfortunately, too often people of good character also go down the drink — for want of energy or because of bad breaks and crucially mistaken decisions — while the shoddy, the dreary, and the miscreant flourish, as the Greeks said, like the green bay tree. Naturally, I ascribe my own little successes in life to good character, though such character as I have is owing to my wish to avoid guilt and shame and to the loss, fairly early in life, of my taste for serious delinquency.

Writing to his friend Lady Georgiana Morpeth, who was going through a patch of depression, Sydney Smith recommended, among twenty different points, that she "be as busy as you can," "live as well as you dare," and have "short views of human life — no further than dinner or tea." Sound advice, especially the part about short views. At sixty, a long view may not, after all, be that long. Living with short views, enforced short views, may be one of the most interesting things about being sixty. Like hanging, it concentrates the mind — or at any rate ought to.

Does it concentrate it, however, too much on depression? Mild depression seems to me a natural and even sensible state to be in when entering late middle age. More than half the game is over, and one's equipment is in less than dazzling condition. A reader of a short story I not long ago published wrote me a letter in which he remarked on my *Weltmüdigkeit,* or world-weariness. He went on to say: "I hope I'm not being flip or jumping to a conclusion here — I'd guess that you, like many guys in their fifties and sixties, who have to preoccupy themselves with their own mortality (I am now in my middle seventies!), are also depressed." I prefer to think I'm not. I don't think of myself as being able to sustain depression beyond a few hours. But, maybe, it comes with the territory.

At sixty, one begins to spend a fair amount of time, at least mentally, with the dead. Oddly, I think less about my own death and more about dead friends and family. I miss them and find myself often talking to them. I cannot bear to remove from my Rolodex the names of such dead friends as Erich Heller, John Wain, and Samuel Lipman. The other day at the Paulina Market butcher shop I felt the presence of the now dead friend who first took me there; my wife's uncle came strongly to mind as I passed Schulien's, a neighborhood German restaurant where he and I sometimes met before Cub games; my mother pops up everywhere, so often, in fact, that I may spend more time thinking about her now than I did when she was alive.

If one is lucky — that is to say, long-lived — at some point one's dead friends figure to outnumber one's living friends. Slowly, but increasingly, conversation about health with contemporaries begins to dominate; it already has begun with me. The other day's mail brought a catalogue from a necktie manufacturer in Vermont. Two of his ties seemed to me rather pleasing, but then I thought of all the neckties I now own — perhaps sixty of them — and decided that I already have enough, in the English phrase, "to see me out." Edward Shils would not agree. In his early eighties, he sometimes stopped to buy some piece of kitchen equipment; he claimed that doing so gave him a feel for the future; even on his deathbed, he still seemed pleased to acquire a new book.

But his was a remarkable generation. Someone recently said to me that he thought of the generation now in its late seventies and eighties as "the strong generation." Something to it. They lived through the Depression, fought in World War II, came into man- and womanhood early, and lived their lives as, if you will pardon the expression, grownups. This gave so many of them not merely substance but gravity of a kind I do not find in my own or sub- sequent generations. Is it natural to think of one's own generation as a bit thin? Did such people as Joseph Conrad, Willa Cather, or William Faulkner think of their own generations as "thin"? Seems doubtful.

The feeling has begun to set in with me that I shall never again meet people as extraordinary as people I have met who are now departing the scene. As I view this scene, I find few celebrated people whom it would thrill me to meet: no one in scholarship, no one in sports, scarcely anyone in the arts. I cannot summon the awe. A few years ago, I was invited to a lunch at the White House for the presentation of medals to artists. When I was told I could not bring along a "spouse" — one of the ugliest words in the language — I declined, saying that I would instead content myself with a sandwich at home. I felt absolutely no regrets. Is this what is meant by being jaded?

I begin to take a keener interest in old age. I now cringe at stories about people who have sent up the yellow flag of senility. I note carefully the way younger people shun the very old, as if they were lepers, which has caused the phrase "the leprosy of old age" to pop into my mind, never, I fear, to be dislodged. I have begun to be a connoisseur of death, thinking a fair amount about the various diseases and modes of departure. I think, too, of styles of dying. A friend recently told me about his former lawyer, who loved opera. Knowing that his death from a debilitating disease was imminent, he arranged to travel to London and, seated in a wheelchair, he watched and listened to opera at Covent Garden on the last thirty evenings of his life. I read in Primo Levi's *Periodic Table* a description of Levi's Uncle Bararicô: in his old age, "he ate almost nothing, and in a general way he had no needs; he died at over ninety, with discretion and dignity." To die with discretion and dignity — that seems a fine thing.

Yet better, I realize, to live with discretion and dignity. What turning sixty, that fatidic age, has done is make me want to live more carefully in the years left to me. Observe I say "carefully," not "cautiously," though caution may enter into it too. I wish to mini- mize my stupidity, maximize my intelligence. "For those who are not angry at things they should be angry at are fools," wrote Aristotle, and yet, I sense, to be angry is, somehow, to be wrong. I want to limit to amused contempt my response to life's irritations. I realize that I cannot stand in the way of regress. I wish to live with a respect for the complexity of life without unduly complicating my own life. (*"Complexe mais pas compliqué"* was one of Ravel's mottoes for his art.) Which is another way of saying that I long for the perspective that is supposed to accompany my age.

I dearly want to learn at last to live in the moment. From early adulthood, I have spent much of my time living, mentally, in the future. Ah, when I'm older, when I've achieved this or that, when things have at last fallen into place, then life will begin in great glorious earnest. The current temptation, now that the future has arrived, is to begin living in the past: to remember the good old days when I thought so much about the future. Enough already. I have to lose my yen for then, suture the future, and at long last put the pow! in now — to make each day, that is, as delight-filled as possible.

In his poem "Lullaby," W. H. Auden writes, "Let your last thinks be thanks." A good deal to that. Especially in my case, since, as has become apparent to me, I have been one of the world's lucky people: paid for doing what I like most to do, rich in friends, in good health, lucid, still laughing. I have had a very good roll of the dice.

Not that I am in any way ready to pass these dice along. Ten years ago, in Florence, in a shop outside the Church of San Lorenzo, I purchased an ascot — brilliant blue, niftily splashed with red, and flecked with gold. I have yet to wear it, thinking it too pretentious even for me, who normally doesn't at all mind a touch or two of pretention. How much longer do you suppose I have to wait to get away with wearing this ascot? My neck, already aflap with loose skin, is certainly ready. But am I? Not quite there yet, I feel. Perhaps in another decade.

Yes, at seventy, if I get there — I have just touched wood — I shall be ascotted and ready to roll. You will see me coming. You won't be able to miss me. I shall be this old dandy, Italian silk at his throat, looking a bit distracted, because he is still thinking of the future while living in the past — and wondering where all the time has gone.

IAN FRAZIER

Someplace in Queens

FROM DOUBLETAKE

OFF AND ON, I get a thing for walking in Queens. One morning, I strayed into that borough from my more usual routes in Brooklyn, and I just kept rambling. I think what drew me on was the phrase "someplace in Queens." This phrase is often used by people who live in Manhattan to describe a Queens location. They don't say the location is simply "in Queens"; they say it is "someplace in Queens," or "in Queens someplace": "All the records are stored in a warehouse someplace in Queens," "His ex-wife lives in Queens someplace." The swooning, overwhelmed quality that the word "someplace" gives to such descriptions is no doubt a result of the fact that people who don't live in Queens see it mostly from the windows of airplanes landing there, at La Guardia or Kennedy airports. They look out at the mile after mile of apparently identical row houses coming up at them and swoon back in their seats at the unknowability of it all. When I find myself among those houses, with their weightlifting trophies or floral displays in the front windows, with their green lawns and nasturtium borders and rose bushes and sidewalks stained blotchy purple by crushed berries from the overhanging mulberry trees, and a scent of curry is in the air, and a plane roars above so close I think I could almost recognize someone at a window, I am happy to be someplace in Queens.

Queens is shaped sort of like a brain. The top, or northern border, is furrowed with bays and coves and salt marshes and creeks extending inland from the East River and Long Island Sound. To the west, its frontal lobe adjoins the roughly diagonal

line running southeast that separates it from Brooklyn. At its stem
is the large, solid mass of Kennedy Airport, at its east the mostly
flat back part that borders Nassau County, Long Island. To the
south stretches the long narrow peninsula of Rockaway Beach,
which does not really fit my analogy. Queens is the largest New
York City borough. It has the longest and widest avenues, the most
freeways, and the most crowded subway stations. It has more ethnic
groups and nationalities than any other borough; observers say
that it has more ethnic diversity than any other place its size
on earth. Some of its schools are the city's most overcrowded. In
one Queens school district, a dozen or more new pupils enroll
every week during the school year, many speaking little English.
Classes meet in bathrooms and on stairways; kids use stairs as desks
when they practice their spelling and teachers go home hoarse
every night from trying to make themselves heard. Immigrants
open stores along the avenues beneath the elevated-train tracks in
Queens, the way they used to under the old Second Avenue El on
the Lower East Side. Queens has more miles of elevated tracks than
any borough, and the streets below them teem.

I like to walk under the elevated tracks early on summer mornings, before people are up. At six-thirty, a steeply pitched shaft of
sunlight falls between each pair of dark iron pillars. On down the
avenue you see the shafts of light, each tinted with haze, receding after each other into the distance. Sun here is secondary, like
sun in a forest or on a reef. Some of the shadows of the El on the
empty pavement are solid blocks, some are sun-and-shadow plaid.
Traffic lights overhang the intersections from the El's beams and
run through their cycles at this hour for no one. Security gates
on all the stores are down. There's a sharp tapping as an Asian
man turns a corner hitting the top of a fresh pack of cigarettes
against his palm. He tears off the cellophane, throws it on the
ground, opens the pack, hurries up the steps to the station. Each
metallic footstep is distinct. When the noise of the train comes,
it's a ringing, clattering pounding that fills this space like a rioting
throng. The sound pulses as if the train were bouncing on its
rails, and, in fact, if you stand in the station the floor does seem
to trampoline slightly beneath your feet. Then there's the hiss of
the air brakes, a moment of quiet, the two notes of the signal
for the closing doors, and the racket begins again. In the world

under the El, speech-drowning noise comes and goes every few minutes.

Queens specializes in neighborhoods that nonresidents have heard of but could never place on a map. Long Island City, for example, is not someplace out on Long Island but on Queens's East River side, across from midtown Manhattan. High-society families had estates there when that side of the river was New York's Gold Coast. Today, it is Con Ed property, warehouses, and movie-equipment supply places. You can buy a used police car there for a third off the book price. Astoria is near La Guardia Airport, just across the river from Rikers Island, which is in the Bronx. Sunnyside is southeast of Long Island City, and below Sunnyside is Maspeth, and below Maspeth is Ridgewood, one of the most solidly blue-collar neighborhoods in the city. Springfield Gardens, in southeast Queens, has many wood-frame houses, and that general area has the city's highest fire-fatality rate. Queens used to be the city's vegetable garden and orchard, and in certain places the old farmland still bulges through the borough's concrete lacings. In Fresh Meadows, in the east middle of the borough, a cherry tree survives that was planted in about 1790. It stands on a small triangular relic of field now strewn with Chinese-restaurant flyers and abutted by the back of a beverage store, a row of small businesses, and some row houses. This year, the tree bore a crop of cherries, just as it did when it was out in the country and Lincoln was a boy.

In Forest Hills, in the middle of the borough, flight attendants in blue uniforms with red scarves wheel suitcase caddies up its sloping sidewalks. Woodside, on the northwest border, is the city's most integrated neighborhood. St. Albans and Cambria Heights, on the east of the borough, are almost all black and middle class. In Queens, the median black household income is higher than the median white household income — $34,300 a year compared to $34,000 a year. Howard Beach is just west of Kennedy Airport. It became famous some years ago when a white mob killed a black man there. Ozone Park, just north of it, has houses in rows so snug you can hardly see the seams between them, and each house has a lawn the size of a living room rug: some of the lawns are bordered by brick fences with statuettes of elephants raising their trunks, some are thick with flowers, some with ornamental shrubs in rows.

People water in the mornings there, and get down on all fours to pick pieces of detritus from the grass. In front of 107-44 110th Street, a house with gray siding and black trim and a picture window, several men came up to the owner, Joseph Scopo, as he got out of a car one night in 1993, and they shot him a number of times. He made it across the street and died near the stone-front house at 107-35. The front yard of Mr. Scopo's former house is all cement; for many years, he was the vice president of Local 6A of the Cement and Concrete Workers of New York City.

On Kissena Boulevard, in Flushing, I passed a two-story brick row house with a dentist's office on the first floor and the sign "D. D. Dong, D.M.D." By now, my feet were hurting and my legs were chafed and I was walking oddly. At the end of a sunlit alley, a pink turban leaned under the hood of a yellow cab. A yellow-and-black butterfly flew over a muffler-repair shop. A red rose grew through coils of razor wire and chain-link fence. At a juicing machine on the street, I bought an almost-cool Styrofoam cup of sugarcane juice, grassy-tasting and sweet. Then I was among the Cold War ruins of Flushing Meadow Park, site of the 1964–65 World's Fair, which is now a mostly empty expanse coexisting with about half a dozen freeways at the borough's heart. No place I know of in America looks more like Moscow than Flushing Meadow Park: the heroic, forgotten statuary, all flexed muscle and straining toes; the littered grounds buffed by feet to smooth dirt; the vast broken fountains, with their twisted pipes and puddles of olive-colored water. I leaned on the railing of a large, unexplained concrete pool thick with floating trash and watched a sparrow on a soda can do a quick logrolling number to stay on top. No matter what, I could not get out of my mind "D. D. Dong, D.M.D."

Legally, you can buy wigs made of human hair in Queens, and two-hundred-volt appliances designed to work in the outlets in foreign countries, and T-shirts that say "If you can't get enough, get a Guyanese," and extra-extra-large bulletproof vests with side panels, and pink bikini underwear with the New York Police Department shield and "New York's Hottest" printed on the front, and pepper-spray personal-defense canisters with ultraviolet identifying dye added, and twenty-ounce bottles of Laser Malt Liquor, whose slogan is "Beam me up," and a cut-rate ten-minute phone call to just about any place on earth, and a viewing of the Indian movie *Sabse Bade Khiladi,* featuring "the hottest song of 1995, 'Muqubla Muqubla.'" Illegally, if you know how, you can buy drugs in bulk, especially cocaine. Drug enforcement officers say that Queens is one of the main entry points for cocaine in the United States, and that much of the trade is engineered by Colombians in the neighborhoods of Elmhurst and Jackson Heights, a district called Little Colombia. On the Elmhurst–Jackson Heights border, at Eighty-third Street just below the Roosevelt Avenue El, is a pocket-sized park of trees and benches called Manuel de Dios Unanue Triangle. It is named for a journalist killed in Queens in 1992 by agents of a Colombian drug cartel.

Manuel de Dios Unanue was born in Cuba, graduated from the University of Puerto Rico, and worked as a newspaper reporter in New York. In 1984, he became the editor of *El Diario–La Prensa,* the city's largest Spanish-language newspaper. At *El Diario,* he was, according to various accounts, obsessive, crusading, blindly self-righteous, possessed of a brilliant news sense, delusional, uncompromising, vain. He chain-smoked. He believed that the United States should open political discussions with Castro, a view that angered anti-Communist terrorist groups, and he printed many articles about the drug trade. He received death threats with a regularity that became a joke between him and his colleagues. Once, someone painted black zebra stripes on his white car and left a note saying he would "get it."

In the eighties and the early nineties, drug money flowed into Queens. Police said that check-cashing places and travel agencies and other businesses in Elmhurst and Jackson Heights were laundering it. Steamer trunks full of submachine guns traced to a realty company on Queens Boulevard led to the discovery of apartments with stashes of drugs and money elsewhere in the city. Colombians died by violence in Queens all the time. One year, 44 of the borough's 357 homicide victims were Colombians. Pedro Méndez, a political figure who had raised money for the 1990 campaign of Colombia's new antidrug president, was shot to death near his home in Jackson Heights the night before that president's inauguration. At a pay telephone by a florist's shop on Northern Boulevard, police arrested a man named Dandeny Muñoz-Mosquera, who they said was an assassin wanted for crimes that included the murders of at least forty police officers in Colombia. Although the authorities believed he had come to Queens to kill somebody, at his arrest they could hold him only for giving a false name to a federal officer. In prison, he requested that Manuel de Dios do an interview with him.

Manuel de Dios had left *El Diario* by then, fired in 1989 for reckless reporting, according to some accounts. On his own, he wrote (and published) a book called *The Secrets of the Medellín Cartel*, an antidrug exposé. He began to publish two magazines, *Cambio XXI* and *Crimen*, in which he identified alleged drug traffickers and dealers and the local places where they did business, with big photographs. In Colombia, some people — according to federal agents, José Santacruz Londono and Gilberto Rodríguez-Orejula, of the Cali drug cartel, among others — decided to have him killed. Someone hired someone and his wife, who hired someone, who hired Wilson Alejandro Mejía Vélez, a sixteen-year-old employee of a chair factory in Staten Island. One afternoon the boy put on a hood, walked into the Mesón Asturias restaurant in Queens, and shot Manuel de Dios twice in the back of the head as he finished a beer at the bar.

The *Times, The New Yorker,* Salman Rushdie, and others decried the murder. Police said they would solve it soon, and sixteen months after the killing, on a tip from an informant, they caught the killer and some of the conspirators, not including the higher-ups in Colombia. The killer and four others stood trial, were convicted, and went to jail. The triggerboy got life without parole. Manuel de Dios's magazines ceased publication after his death. His book cannot be found in the Spanish-language bookstores in Elmhurst, or *Books in Print.* People in Elmhurst know the name of the book, and they say the name of its author in a familiar rush, but they cannot tell you where you might find a copy. Recently, the number of local drug-related murders has gone down; people say this is because the victory of one big drug cartel over another has brought stability to the trade.

The Mesón Asturias restaurant is just across Eighty-third Street from the Manuel de Dios Unanue Triangle. On a hot July afternoon, I went into the restaurant, sat down at the bar, and had a beer. The bartender, a short, trim man with dark hair, put a bowl of peanuts by me and cut some slices of chorizo sausage. We watched Spanish TV on cable and commented on a piece about the running of the bulls at Pamplona. The bartender said that an American had been killed and that you had to know how to be with the bulls. I paid for the beer and got up to leave. I asked, "Is this where the journalist was killed?"

"Oh, yes," the bartender said.

"Were you here?"

"No, I was outside."

"Did you know him?"

"Yes, he was a regular."

"He must have been a brave man," I said.

The bartender stood not facing me and not facing away. He pushed the dollar I had left for a tip across the bar, and I pushed it back at him. For a while the bartender looked off toward the dim, gated window. "Well," he said, "you never know your luck."

The oldest house in Queens — perhaps in the city — is a frame farmhouse built in 1661 by a man who later suffered banishment for letting Quakers meet there. His neighbors in the town of Flushing sent the Dutch governor a Remonstrance stating their belief in religious freedom not only for Quakers and other Christians but also for "Jews, Turks, and Egyptians." Today, the house, called the Bowne House, sits on a small patch of lawn between a four-story apartment building and a city playground. The theoretical Jews, Turks, and Egyptians are now real and living nearby, but nearest are the Koreans. Almost all the signs you see in downtown Flushing are in Korean, and the neighborhood has a Quaker meetinghouse, Korean Buddhist temples, and Korean Catholic and Protestant churches. At the end of the No. 7 Flushing subway line, pamphleteers for a city council person hand you fliers saying that the line is going to hell, while other people hand you fundamentalist Christian tracts saying that you are. Pentecostal churches in storefronts all over Queens have signs in the window advising, for example, "Do nothing you would not like to be doing when Jesus comes," in Spanish and English. A multimillion-dollar Hindu temple, the largest in the city, recently went up in Flushing. Many Hindus, Buddhists, and Sikhs have recently added small celebrations of Christmas to their traditional worship calendars. Groups of Gnostics meet in Queens, and Romanian Baptists, and followers of the guru Sri Chinmoy, who sometimes express their faith by doing enough somersaults to get into the *Guinness Book of World Records*. When summer comes, big striped tents rise on outlying vacant lots with billboards advertising tent meeting revivals led by Pastor John H. Boyd.

In Douglaston, a far Queens neighborhood that still has the feel of a town, I sat on the lawn of an Episcopal church at the crest of a hill. The ancient gravestones in the churchyard leaned, the daylilies along the driveway bloomed, and the white wooden church panted discreetly in the heat through its high open windows. In Astoria, I visited St. Irene's of Chrysovalantou Greek Orthodox Church, home of the icon of Saint Irene, which witnesses say wept on the eve of the Persian Gulf War. A short woman all in black said, "Why not? Why not?" when I asked if I could see the icon, and she led me slowly up the aisle in fragrant, dusky church light. The icon, a six-by-eight-inch painting, is in a large frame made of gold bracelets, jeweled wristwatches, and rows of wedding rings donated by parishioners. On a wooden rail below it are inhalers left by asthma sufferers whose breath Saint Irene has restored. In Richmond Hill, I stopped in at Familiar Pharmacy, managed and co-owned by Mohammad Tayyab, who knows the Koran by heart. He is thirty-nine, has a neatly trimmed beard, and wears his baseball cap backward. He told me that, growing up in Multan, Pakistan, he memorized verses from the Koran almost every day, morning to night, from when he was six until he was twelve. The Koran is about the length of the New Testament. A person who knows the Koran by heart is called a *haviz*. Mohammad Tayyab recites the whole Koran once a year in a mosque during the fast of Ramadan, and reviews three chapters every night, to keep fresh. The stored-up energy of his knowledge causes him to radiate, like a person who has just been to a spa.

In Montefiore Cemetery, in another far part of Queens, the Grand Rebbe of the Lubavitcher Hasidim, Menachem Schneerson, lies in a coffin made of boards from his lectern. By the time of Rebbe Schneerson's death, in 1994, at the age of ninety-three, some of his followers had come to believe he was the Messiah. Tens of thousands of Lubavitchers from around the world have visited his grave, sometimes annoying the black families who own homes nearby. Neighbors complained that the Lubavitchers were singing loudly, drinking beer, trespassing, and asking to use their bathrooms. The sect has since bought a house near the grave for the convenience of visitors. I went to see the grave myself, on an anniversary of the Rebbe's death. Cars with out-of-state plates lined the boulevard by the cemetery gate; some cars had their doors open to the curb, and shoeless Lubavitchers lay asleep on the seats. Along the paths to the gravesite ran that orange-webbed plastic security fence in which we now routinely wrap important public events. Some of the Lubavitchers were pink-cheeked teens with blond sidecurls. Cops not much older leaned against the cemetery gate and smoked, thumbs hooked in their belts, cigarettes between their first two fingers.

Black-clad Lubavitchers in black hats were coming and going. In the patio behind the nearby Lubavitcher house, many were reciting prayers. Occasionally, an impassioned voice would rise like a firework, bursting higher than the others. A man about my age who pointed the way to the grave suggested that I remove my shoes before approaching it: "Remember, this is a holy place," he said. My running shoes looked as bright as a television ad on top of the pile of functional black brogans of many sizes already there. I ducked through a low door to an anteroom filled with candles. It led into an enclosure of walls maybe twelve feet high, and open to the sky. At the center of the enclosure was a knee-high wall around the grave itself. Men were standing at the graveside wall and praying, chanting, flipping expertly through small prayer books in their palms, rocking from side to side with the words. Heaped on top of the grave like raked-up leaves, spilling onto the smooth pebbles next to it, drifting into the anteroom, were hundreds or thousands of small square pieces of paper on which people had written prayers for special intercessions. There are so many hopes in the world. Just out of the line of sight past the higher wall, 747s descended slowly to Kennedy Airport like local elevators stopping at every floor. Across the street just out of earshot, long-legged girls jumped double-Dutch jump rope, superfast.

WILLIAM H. GASS

The Test of Time

FROM THE ALASKA QUARTERLY REVIEW

1

WHAT MUST a work of art do to prepare to pass the Test of Time? Is it a written test, this test? And does it appear at a certain period in a work's life the way final exams do, or tenure reviews, or professional boards?

In perhaps an odd way, the answer to these questions is yes.

Is it related to "the survival of the fittest" and the idea that the last one standing is the winner?

Sure, somewhat.

Is the test graded, and if so, by whom?

There can be no doubt that some works are felt to have stood the Test of Time better than others. The Test of Time is not simply pass/fail. One of the severest examiners is Time itself.

Is it therefore possible to receive a C-minus on the Test of Time?

Well, the equivalent.

Or is the test more like an ordeal which cars and trucks and airplanes are put through, to see if they are safe and well made?

Certainly, for a work must sustain a lot of hard knocks, neglect, and rejection before it can say it has passed.

Is the Test of Time an exam which must be periodically repeated, like those for a driver's license?

More than that. The test is continuous.

Is there a theological component like damnation, redemption, and salvation?

Alas, yes.

What happens to works which fail to pass the Test of Time?

Nobody cares.

Is the Test of Time something the State administers, or a professional board, or a training school, or is it a private kind of thing like a questionnaire in a magazine which will tell you, say, if you are sufficiently outgoing?

The State and its cultural agents administer part of it, but professions contribute, and schools share. It is also very much a private, nearly internal test, which works employ in the process of their creation.

So works which pass the Test of Time are never again ignored, misunderstood, or neglected?

No. Works which fail find oblivion. Those which pass stay around to be ignored, misunderstood, exploited, and neglected.

But they bring their authors honor, their creators praise?

Those responsible are all dead.

So what is the personal gain from making immortal works, if the maker isn't immediately rewarded?

None whatever.

Is the Test of Time a rescuing argument?

Frequently.

When is it most commonly employed? In a rescue?

Yes.

Is the Test of Time, then, a good test, with a reasonable record of success?

The Test of Time is not a test at all. It is an announcement of temporary victory: "I am still alive." The dead do not report. As such, it is only old news.

So what happens, finally, to works which have withstood the Test of Time?

They become timeless.

2

We also frequently say: "Time will tell," when actually it is we who read the expression on the clock, because Time's voice is simple and singular like the rattle of an alarm or the rouse of a rooster. And generally it means that we intend to postpone judgment; that we shall have to wait to find out if a marriage will be happy or a business successful, or whether some evaluation or prediction will be verified. Will the wine improve? Time will tell.

My last example was somewhat misleading. In time, Time may collect its toll, but taste will tell.

There is no more popular appeal, when considering the merit of works of art, than the one to Time, and when I say "popular" I mean across the board and up and down the scale. It is assumed that there is no better reason for granting greatness to an artist than the fact that his or her works, after several centuries, are still being seen and admired, heard or performed, or read and written of. The quality of being constantly contemporary — or of stubbornly surviving the vicissitudes of history, taste, and the whimsicalities of fashion — is the single quality most commonly found among major works of art, when all their other characteristics — medium, subject, attitude, length, complexity, profundity, range of feeling — differ considerably.

Conversely, there is no sign of future failure that's more reliable than the popularity of the moment, and by "popularity" I mean across the board in the noisy markets of popular culture, as well as up and down the scale from the cribs of country music and the pillows of sentimental romance through midcult's porncorn bloodletting or foreign film idolatry to the most recent academic trend and intellectual fawning, with its high-fashion fields of influence and its pompous lockjaw jargons.

The Test of Time is a stretch of Time conceived as a gauntlet to be run. And any long stretch will do, as if Time battered its principals equally through every section. We don't say: the period from 1750 to 1912 was particularly benign, and almost everything written then survived until they hit the bit between 1913 and 1938, which we now regard as a quarter century of catastrophe, a typhoon of a time when most works of art were lost without remainder.

Another way of envisioning the test is spacial. Our creative acts fill the creative sky like stars. There are dim ones and bright ones. The constellation Rhetoric which contains Cicero and Quintilian is more distant from our system than the brilliant nova of the Greeks. Vico shines but not as brightly as Plotinus.

We must remember, too (so we can discount them), that there are works which so adorn their era, and wrinkle their age, you can't study the period without studying their role in it.

Since we live in a society concerned mainly with money and amusement, it might be appropriate to examine an early use of the Test of Time: when it was employed to defend Utilitarianism from the charge that the Principle of Utility was an instrument of the Philistine — one of those rare cases in which the defendant defends himself, since Utilitarianism and Philistinism are identical twins. Jeremy Bentham had asserted that pushpin was as good as poetry as far as the hedonistic calculus was concerned, if pushpin did indeed give as much pleasure to as many people as poetry did. We might replace pushpin with some mechanical amusements like arcade or video games. How would we determine the differing amounts, since a subjective inventory is impractical? Just as the level of pain for a person might be measured by the degree to which the entire organism is affected by it and mobilizes to respond, so we might estimate the expected pleasure of a particular activity indirectly by assessing the amounts of time, energy, interest, and money that are spent to achieve it — like packing a picnic lunch and driving six kids and two dogs to the beach — as well as considering the actual pleasure received through the frequency of the activity's repetition. Six kids and two dogs? That thin stony beach? Never again.

On this basis, video games would appear to be far more important than poetry if we consider society as a whole. Mass culture is what it is because the masses prefer it. And they prefer it because it is easy to obtain (it does not require training or an advanced education or even an IQ). It amuses; it consoles; it allows people to vent their feelings in a relatively innocuous manner; it permits easy identification and promotes illusions of control; it establishes communities of common experience and provides the middle class and middle-class intellectuals with something they can talk about as if they had taste, brains, and breeding. Although the middle class would like to disavow any membership in the masses, the middle class is now far too large to be anything else. Besides, its taste is in no way more refined than that of the lower, only better packaged and more hypocritical. A taste for Bach partitas is not middle class. Academics, who one might expect would be willing to support at least some examples of cultural quality, keep a hamper of towels handy to throw in the ring if any blows are actually struck. As Harold Bloom remarks in *The Western Canon:* "The morality of scholarship, as currently practiced, is to encourage everyone to replace difficult pleasures by pleasures universally accessible precisely because they are easier." And why not? Why play wild bird in a world full of feeders? Whereupon, the tough-minded Benthamite might rest his case.

And shrug when accused of cultural leveling.

John Stuart Mill had a softer head (and poorer logic). Shakespeare might lose out to Mighty Morph in the short run (he, in effect, said), but if we consider the long haul, well, these lowlife entertainments disappear like morning mist, other amusements replace them, whereas great poetry, theater, fiction, and art endure, and in so doing pile up pleasure points. In the long run, Proust will outplease pushpin, pinball, pachinko, and indoor soccer. To the Greatest Happiness for the Greatest Number (to which Mill had to tack on the stipulation that each person was to count as one and no one for more than one) must be added the phrase "In the Long Run," with the long run no twenty-six-mile marathon, but rather a race millennial in length. How long? The suspicion is: for as long as it takes to restore the canon to its eminence.

To the quantitative sum of pleasure and pain we could insist upon including a judgment of quality as well, which might require the employment of competent observers: those able to experience the pleasures of video games and Bach chorales equally, and be in a position, then, to judge the qualitative superiority of one pleasure over another. So modified, the principle of utility is: the Greatest Happiness of the Highest Kind for the Greatest Number capable of experiencing the Highest Kind, otherwise watch football, drink beer, and eat ice cream, you happy slobs.

Although there may be a few persons capable of enjoying honkytonk and High Mass, pot pies and puff pastry, celli concerti and retch rock, and therefore be in a position to pronounce upon the quality of each of these endeavors as well as the cultural level of other pleasures, it should be clear that a life of idiocy and a life of civility are rarely joined, and that we have probably stretched our standard beyond its useful limit; for how do we know when the pleasures of the Bobbsey Twins have been thoroughly felt, so that if they appear to be losing out on the qualitative side to Samuel Beckett's tramps, it may be because only the most devoted fans of each have enjoyed their favors fully, and that no one can manage to be equally crazy about both.

There are at least two other problems. It may be true that *Hamlet*

will outlast *Hill Street Blues,* and therefore amass more pleasure
credits, but this will require *Hamlet* to survive on its merits in order,
eventually, to please so many more; it won't be its pleasure-giving
qualities at any moment which keep it alive, but its aliveness which
makes its pleasure-giving possible; moreover, the proper contest is
not between the latest bad play about AIDS and a distant boom
from the canon, since the Nonce is meant to be consumed and
discarded in order to make way for more Nonce of the same
ninnified kind. Why recite Rilke or stage Racine one more time
when Rap will release one's venom better than most snakes, and
when the visual jokes and verbal snickers which make up sleazy
sitcoms will restore deserved dignity to big boobs and deep cleav-
age where Matisse and his odalisques flatly fail. Any popular pas-
time is soon replaced by another of the same sort, so that the
competition we are contemplating should be between similar kinds
of empty amusement or consoling kitsch in one corner, and the
pot of paint lately flung in the public's face in the other — between
crap as a class and the classy as a class — and this contest is no
contest; it is a mismatch of monumental proportions: the balance
continues to favor whatever is compliant, cheap, and easy.

Occasionally those who confuse an egalitarianism which is politically desirable with a cultural equality which is cowardly, dam-
aging, and reprehensible remind us of the good old days when the
masses (how many?) flocked to the pit of the Globe and laughed
their lungs out (at what?) at the bad puns and tomfoolery of
Shakespeare's clowns, or of the crowds who filled the Athenian
theater to be cautioned by Sophocles, or of the thousands who
read Dickens devotedly and wept at the death of little Nell, or of
the many comrades who filled Communist arenas to hear their
Russian poets rant, and brought flowers to heap at their feet as if
they were prima donnas. In short, some poetry has beaten pushpin
in the past, and we ought to take a peek at why, instead of whining
about popular taste. They hope the upshot of such an examination
will support their view that "higher" culture no longer appeals to
the people because it has forgotten the people (who are its roots,
its audience, its aim), becoming elitist, hopelessly avant-garde, and
out of touch with real life and real life's real problems.

However, the evidence is that whenever people have a choice
(under communism citizens had none) they will select schlock with

a greed and certainty of conviction which leaves no doubt where their preferences lie; that furthermore they have always done so: in churches they kneel in hundreds at the gaudiest shrines; they troop in thousands to the loudest and least talented rock spectacles; they take pasteboard passions and paper mysteries onto planes; they purchase period furniture and prechewed food; they flock to movies which glorify stupidity; their idols are personalities, their dreams are sentimental, their realities dubious gossip.

And why not? What has hoity-toity culture ever done for them? If they go to the cinema to watch Abel Gance's *Napoléon* instead of flocking to the flicks to snicker at Steve Martin, they will still be robbed on the way home; their hearts will remain in the same chest; their eyes will stay fixed on the main chance; it will take aspirin to hide their aches and pains; and not a single simple-minded belief will be changed. Levelers can find some comfort in the fact that the cultivated (society dames, academics, intellectuals, professional people), although they may not murder their spouses or rob banks as regularly as the poor and ignorant, manage to envy, conspire, cheat, abuse positions of power, begrudge or resent the success of others, lie and otherwise control events, embezzle, defraud, betray, with an eagerness equal to any, and in numbers sufficient to suggest no major moral differences between the classes exist.

The Russian novel, English poetry, German music, Italian and Spanish painting, French food, American movies, Italian opera, the English stage, Flemish tapestries, French wine, Viennese operettas, Czech toys, Chicago architecture, Parisian style, Dutch diligence, have enabled these nations and their cities to act with piety, circumspection, and respect for others, to be sensitive to needs and fears far from their own, to avoid aggression, aggrandizement, and exploitation, in order to act always to produce the greatest happiness for the greatest number — everyone counting, but no one counting for more than one. Thank heaven for these higher cultures who have brought peace and security, certainly prosperity and comfort, to the world.

A derisive noise is appropriate here. As the moral educators of mankind, masterpieces have been one big floppola.

That is why the Test of Time has to be invoked, because the Test of Time puts people at some distance from their selfish selves, allows them to correct more immediate mistakes, permits missing manuscripts to be found, contexts of interest to be enlarged, local prejudices to be overcome. The visionary and the vulgar, the discriminating and the sentimental, the precise and the vague, are so frequently, and against all rational expectation, found together in the same bed, that the finer qualities present are compromised and besmirched in the eyes of those otherwise fit to see them. The crude laugh out loud or easily weep at the scandalous scene set before them, the way Dickens's readers giggled and gasped at the doings portrayed in his lively but sentimental cartoons. However, Dickens's language, his rhetoric, which rises sometimes to Shakespeare's level (as well as so much else which rises with it), is ignored by those bent on melodrama, while it is discounted by the snobbishly fastidious who see it servicing only soap opera and special pleading. The Test of Time sieves inhuman failings like silt through a prospector's pan, leaving a residue which is clearly either gold or gravel.

So conceived and supported, the Test of Time is nevertheless made ineffective by the intractable naiveté of its assumptions. For isn't it naive to suppose that history will allow only the best to survive? Is it that considerate? Does history spare cultural icons when it does not hesitate to defeat virtue, or when it permits the truth to be trampled under the feet of four-year-olds? Does it cry out Halt! when a fine building is about to be destroyed? Does it reroute bombs? Does it encourage care and stewardship for the Fine while forgetting the False? Haven't we been told that the human race made progress when it replaced the great Greek gods with a bewhiskered tyrannical granddad whose mean spirit is as big as his beard?

In what world do we live if we think only the good guys win and virtue is always rewarded? In a free market, the vulgar, we have learned, will grab all the meat and potatoes, and elbow the refined, empty-handed, out the door. People are wicked because wickedness gives them an advantage. When the Romans overran Greece they took bare-assed marble boys and busty girlies home to decorate their villas, and melted bronzes down to make pitiless the points of their spears. Pagans, Christians, Moslems took turns burning the books of Alexandria's library. Invaders loot, sack, pillage, rape, and burn. Whoever they are. Whatever it is. They steal to sell. They steal to display, to vaunt, to collect. Indian mounds are leveled like harvested fields, and gold and slaves are sent back to the capital. Those who rise up against criminal divinities stupidly burn down the temples of the superstitious (which may be glorious and beautiful) instead of the superstitions of the superstitious (which are ignorant, ugly, and obscene).

Of course, we should not blame "history." History is not an agent who goes about trampling traditions into dust, ending lives, stifling others, despoiling the land and poisoning the sea. History is humanity on its rampage. Considering the frequency of natural calamities, our treatment of warfare as a seasonal sport, and the insatiable squirrelyness of human greed, it should be an occasion for surprise that anything excellent survives.

3

How indeed do they? In the same way that Elvis Presley does. They have fans. The devoted gather, often slowly at first, each fan feeling alone with her enthusiasm and despised for it; odd-eyed because El Greco or Modigliani or Picasso pleases; odd-eared because Schönberg or Ives or Bartók is thrilling; conceptually queer because Celan makes instant sense, or Hopkins thrives, or Musil musiks the mind. Or because WOW man.

When the work which is worshiped has been roundly reviled, it becomes even more precious. It shows society up. It verifies the fan's feeling of being isolated and unappreciated, in a foreign land, surrounded by indifference or hostility. The "new" architecture is attacked because it is felt to be opposed to present preferences; the "new" music undermines an entire tradition; the "new" painting accuses reality of appearance; the "new" writing is incomprehensible, obscene, blasphemous, politically incorrect; thus each art finds its "new" adherents among those similarly disaffected.

"Fan" is a shortened form of "fanatic," and it is true that the fan's love is often half-sighted if not entirely blind, often fueled as much by the dislike its object provokes in others as by the love its object inspires in him; so that the fan often falls for a message which isn't there, is moved by emotions which aren't expressed, by strategies which haven't been employed.

Fans form clubs or find other ways in which to share their enthusiasms. The fan's love does not resemble romantic passion in every way, because it is rarely possessive; it is more like chauvinism in the sense that the fan's feelings make him the member of a defining cult or tribe. He's prepared to love anybody Irish, anyone French. A fan is prepared to devote far more time to the pursuit and glorification of his idol than most people are, even those who find the composer's music or the author's works intriguing or uncommonly fine. Eventually, fans will found a holy shrine. These shrines, in their turn, will employ professional "keepers of the flame"; they'll put out bulletins and publish magazines; they'll manufacture relics, peddle icons, sponsor gatherings; and before you can say "Mickey Mouse" or "Bobbie Burns" there'll be a group in place whose livelihood, not just their enthusiasm or donated time, will depend upon the continued idolization of the idol — and by the enlistment of greater and greater numbers. Economic interests are generally more reliable and enduring than love. Social status hangs upon money like a fob from a watch, and power from both. The keepers of the flame, like the clergy, will have many more reasons than adoration to carry out their duties. Any adoration which isn't drama, spectacle, and public relations — which is simply rich understanding and deep appreciation — can come last.

In short, the work of art, the performer, the beneficial idea have become "the treasures of" an institution — the Mona Lisa in the Louvre. It is the institution and its interests which carry their symbol before them like a flag, a chalice, a trophy, across the treacherous bournes of Time. If you think it is hard to find true virtue hidden somewhere in this story, you are right. The institutions, in their turn, become tools for large ones: if a young nation, a new movement, needs heroes and poets, some Longfellow will be chosen and brought to the schools like a captive in chains, or some hero like Nathan Hale will be installed in the national story like a bishop in the church; this painted pop-up history to be taught to helpless kiddies to confirm the prejudices of their parents so that the myth of a magically united and superior society can be passed on to its prospective citizens that they may each equally enjoy the pleasures of chauvinistic self-satisfaction, and in order to conserve their oh-so-common cultural values, preserve the legitimacy of the status quo, and guarantee, consequently, the continued power of the State and its teams of pickpockets.

If there is someone sane you wish to drive mad, merely institutionalize him; if there is some Good you wish to besmirch, some Truth you wish to undermine, organize it; if there is some noble and glorious career you wish to destroy, parade its accomplishments past a committee.

The canon — Shakespeare, Dante, Chaucer, Cervantes, and so on — blessed by Harold Bloom — are alas not there because greatness is both steed and shield to carry them on through the indifference of history, past its nervous overseers and their obedient serfs. Leaders — political, religious, economic — care nothing for merit; they value only use. And they succeed because the led are no differently inclined. The poor may not be poor because they are poor of mind and heart (as some suggest), but their minds and hearts are certainly not a bit better for it. Their sort of simple life is simple-minded; a life close to the soil is lived near the grave; the workman's pride in the work of his hands was long ago mechanized; the rhythms of Have and Want and Get never change. Those who are "out" are not better for being there, otherwise why would they seek a change?

But they — those who fancy they are not making out very well like other folks are supposed to be making out in the wonderful world of those other folks — will be quick to see in what direction the canon fires, and will have the rhetoric I have just rehearsed as handy as spit in their mouths. They will memorize the ways they have been cheated; they will have care-baskets of truth on their side; they can point to a campaign of discrimination, injury, neglect; they can quite rightly complain of unfairness and bigotry and misuse. They will advance their own art, their own neglected texts, their own critical methods, their own mythologies in opposition to the cultural icons in place. Nothing could be more natural, nothing more righteous than their indignation. It will seem that they alone love literature; let it act importantly; help it to shape their communities; and to a degree — lacking money, power, and other forms of glue — they will be right; but make no mistake, like the Puritans, they'll love liberty only when facing their enemies who don't want them to have it. It will turn out, moreover, that the struggle against their common adversary will not permit internal divisions. For a time, freedom of thought and action will have to be sacrificed to the goals of the group, and so on — how often have we heard it? Not bold new behavior, not innovative notions, but conformity and compaction are the consequences.

Since minorities have no armies and few fields to fight on, their members bicker like faculties over the most minor matters, bitterly opposing this or ardently espousing that, as if a schedule change would alter the course of the Gulf Stream, an appointment in the history of igloo design revolutionize the building code. But these quibbles screen the truth from outsider eyes. Disciplines have been derailed, departments destroyed, careers ruined, so that "right thinking" might prevail. Tweedledum and Tweedledee are fighting with nothing over nothing because they haven't guns yet. Then it will be life-and-death.

Groups squabble about literature because they have other than literary uses for the literary. The schools, which are busy finding ways to get the answers to the Test of Time smuggled to their chosen favorites, like coaches' answers to their players, so they may pass the latest examination, will now and then speak of Art and claim a disinterested purity. And there are an unorganized few (the unhappy few whom I should like to represent, "the immense minority," as Juan Ramón Jiménez so significantly puts it) who sincerely love the arts. There are those for whom reading, for example, can be an act of love, and lead to a revelation, not of truth, moral or otherwise, but of lucidity, order, rightness of relation, the experience of a world fully felt and furnished and worked out in the head, the head where the heart is also to be found, and all the other vital organs.

I have the good luck not to live in an English department, so I have not had to observe directly or suffer intimately the sophistical poses of pluralism and the opportunistic fads of fashion which the courtiers of our culture have paraded on its runways, but my feeling is "it has been ever thus." Philosophy departments, where my presence has been more frequent, have, during my brief sojourn in their narrow halls, practiced the prejudices of Idealism, Pragmatism, Positivism, Existentialism, Phenomenology, and served the interests of special groups (a practice they once despised) by offering biomedical or business ethics, game theory, philosophical psychology, and feminist studies.

Inside the Academy, at the Symphony, within Museum walls, each warring faction will boast that god is on their side, and claim transcendence for their values and opinions. This is done by trying to ensure that only their ideas, and works correctly expressing them, get put before the public in the future, and by reanalyzing the past for as far back as the catalogue has cards (a deliberately out-of-date metaphor) in order to show, as I previously characterized their internecine struggles, that "it has been ever thus," whatever it is they say it is now.

Outside, in the vendors' streets, there are nothing but temporary tents. The lasting, the universal, are despised (except by those who are still peddling the classics to old fogies). But who really wants reruns of already winded warhorses? Well, only those arrogant and rapacious revivalists who set *Rigoletto* in the Bronx and who want Dido and Aeneas to sing about their love while costumed as colonials.

The ideal cultural product comes powerfully packaged, creates a mighty stir, can be devoured with both delight and a sense of life-shaking revelation, provides an easy topic for talk, is guaranteed to be without real salt or any actual fat — contain no substance of any substantial kind — so that after you have eaten it, for days you will only shit air.

So are all these works, which appear to have persisted the way postmen once did through dark nights and bad weather (the past's periodic eclipses of reason, and other ages of ice), here now only through evil machination or by odd accident? The poet may duck, escape his time, as Quevedo writes:

> Retired to the peace of this desert,
> with a collection of books that are few but wise,
> I live in conversation with the departed
> and listen to the dead with my eyes.
> [Quoted by Octavio Paz in *The Other Voice,* New York:
> Harcourt Brace, 1991, p. 111.]

but the work cannot choose its companions or by itself steer a favorable course. Yet, oddly, something like that happens. Minds find minds. The intelligent heart beats in more than one head, and a wise book contains a consciousness which has at last made something wonderful of the world.

For when I follow Thoreau's prose, I am in no ordinary footsteps. *Walden* has been read, and reread; it is hallowed; it is an
American classic; it sells because generations of students at all sorts
of grade levels are asked to answer questions about it; and it is still
seen to support this group, that cause, have relevance. How full of
these tourists the woods are, how trampled the paths, how bored
or nervous or put upon the picnickers feel, forced to spread their
blankets over these placid pages.

Have they felt a sentence start like a rabbit from beneath their
eye? Or watched a meadow made small by the sky, or studied a
simple street, or felt the wind flutter a row of wash like flags hung
from a window? And been taught by such a sentence what it is to
be alive?

> Are we, perhaps, *here* just to utter: house,
> bridge, fountain, gate, jug, fruit tree, window —
> at most: column, tower . . . but to *utter* them, remember,
> to speak in a way which the named never dreamed
> they could *be*.

Gertrude Stein wondered more than once what went into a
masterpiece: what set some works aside to be treasured while
others were abandoned without a thought, as we leave seats after
a performance; what there was about a text we'd read which
provoked us to repeat its pages; what made us want to remain by
its side, rereading and remembering, even line by line; what led
us to defend its integrity, as though our honor were at stake; and
to lead it safely through the perils that lie in wait for excellence in
a world where only mediocrity seems prized. She concluded that
masterpieces were addressed not to the self whose accomplishments might appear on some dossier, the self whose passport is
examined at the border, the self whose concerns are those of
the Self (I and My and Me and Mine), but to the human mind,
a faculty which is everywhere the same and whose business is with
universals. Masterpieces teach that human differences are superfi-
cial: that intelligence, not approved conclusions, counts; that richly
received and precisely appreciated sensations matter, not titillation
or dolled-up data; that foreplay, not payoff, is to be preferred; that
imagination and conceptual solutions, not ad hoc problem solving, are what such esteemed works have in common. And we, who

read and write and bear witness and wail with grief, who make
music and massacres, who paint in oils and swim in blood — we
are one: everywhere as awful, and as possibly noble, as our natures
push us or permit us to be.

Say a sort of "amen" to that. But the trouble with transcendence
is that the transcendent must rise, and in order to do that it must
lighten its load, dump detail as worse than unwanted, toss aside
everything that thickens life and leads us to lick it like gravy.
Overboard go all gross things, as if the crude and hollow and im-
permanent weren't recurrent. Transcendence is not what master-
works teach me: they teach me immersion. They teach me that
the trivial is as important as the important when looked at importantly. They tell me that evil is lasting and complex and significant
and profoundly alluring, and that it requires our appreciative and
steadfast gaze more than grace and goodness do, who receive it
like starlets — only too often ready to giggle in reply.

And we, who must be transcendent, too, if Universals are to take
any notice of us, lose ourselves in the course of this diet: our little
habits, simple pleasures, traits which set us aside as a certain someone — perhaps a lovely leg we shave and sand and wax as if it
held up period furniture, or a voice we exercise as we would a
show horse, or the way we cheat at parchesi or treat the sweet tooth
we suffer and adore with weekend sundaes, or try to defeat the
line which a strategic elastic has left on our body by undressing in
the dark, and relying on the skin's resilience to erase its statement
by morning.

Even ideas (and certainly their abstractness recommends them),
when they are thought, are drenched in the particularities of time
and place and mood and purpose, because minds, it turns out, are
as particular as toenails, and are always like a working part of a
tired foot too, companion to the other toes; so that your belief in
God and my belief in the divinity of the dance aren't just notions
we've put mustaches on to differentiate them, but are as peculiar
to us as our visage is, our fingerprint, our taste in clothes, our
loyalty, our laugh.

As Ernst Cassirer said of the aim of Kant's critical philosophy:
"To step into the infinite it suffices to penetrate the finite in all its
aspects."

We are in cahoots with art. We want everything to survive, even flies. And there they are, on that slope of Rilke's lines: the gate, the house, the fruit tree, the window — waiting for our look to be realized, not as house or tree or window but as a smeared gray pane, a pane as gray as the walk is where it proceeds through that skimpy sick grass there past a leafless tree up to the weathered front door, ajar as if to welcome our entry, but actually left open by the whole of Yesterday when that Time went, with its features and its friends, never to return. If we took note of the weathered top of the kitchen table, when we entered, and how a dim gray light puddled in some of its scars and leaked the length of its cracks; if we saw, when we entered, how the blue pitcher stood amid crumbs of bread like a bird that's just been fed, and how a dish towel hung for an hour over the ladderback of a kitchen chair, drying its sweat-shaped patches of damp before being taken up to be dampened again; had we found the paint or prose or pipe for them; had we rhymed a skillet's sear with a knife's scratch, then we'd have them still, still as Walden's water was, when Thoreau skiffed at night across it and cast a line:

> Sometimes, after staying in a village parlor till the family had all retired, I have returned to the woods, and, partly with a view to the next day's dinner, spent the hours of midnight fishing from a boat by moonlight, serenaded by owl and foxes, and hearing, from time to time, the creaking note of some unknown bird close at hand. These experiences were very memorable and valuable to me, — anchored in forty feet of water, and twenty or thirty rods from the shore, surrounded sometimes by thousands of small perch and shiners, dimpling the surface with their tails in the moonlight, and communicating by a long flaxen line with mysterious nocturnal fishes which had their dwelling forty feet below, or sometimes dragging sixty feet of line about the pond as I drifted in the gentle night breeze, now and then feeling a slight vibration along it, indicative of some life prowling about its extremities, of dull uncertain blundering purpose there, and slow to make up its mind. [*Walden*, IX, "The Ponds."]

We cannot say with certainty what will live, and survival, by itself, is no guarantee of quality; but I think we can say something about what is deserving. Thoreau's two unsimple sentences put me out on that pond, in prose as clear as its water is. Now I can mourn its present turbid state, and fashion a fine romance from my memory of a time when kids could stay out late to fish, and feel the distant friendship of the stars like the lights of Atlantis in the water. But the magical stillness in the prose, its easy motion, depends upon its calm and measured breathing, its quiet but ever-present music, its unhurried and appreciative perceptions, like a slow swallow of wine.

All those numbers would paralyze most paragraphs. However, here, as I move my mind along the line, holding its hush in my ear, of course I do not see the dimpling surface of the lake — the lake is miles from me, the time is out of reach, the categories of existence clash; but my consciousness *conceives* the seeing, *conceives* the thirty rods of distance to the shore, *conceives* the twitch a nibble makes, how the rod's handle tickles the angler's palm, and consequently understands the decision slowly forming down there from the nudge of the fish's nose.

There's no moment too trivial, too sad, too vulgar, too rinky-dink to be unworthy of such recollection, for even a wasted bit of life is priceless when composed properly or hymned aright — even that poor plate of peaches slowly spoiling while its portrait is being painted — not, however, the peaches themselves, which must rot to realize their nature, and not a sore tooth's twinge, and not a battle's loss, or love's loss, or the cutest darling dimple, or a bite of pie the peaches could have been better put to use in; no, rather their rendering — that's priceless: the Cézanne which gives to the mountain more than it merits, the juice that runs from alongside that aching tooth when the topmost peach is bitten, but only when a sentence performs the biting, and the juice is wiped off by the word "sleeve," and the smile of satisfaction can be read as it spreads across the face of the page.

When Hopkins wondered "how to keep," whether there was "any any," "none such, nowhere known some, bow or brooch or braid or brace, lace, latch or catch or key to keep back beauty, keep it, beauty, beauty, beauty, . . . from vanishing away," he knew, of course, the answer; which was yes, "there is one," there is a place where "the thing we freely forfeit is kept with fonder a care, fonder a care kept than we could have kept it, kept far with fonder a care"; but he said it was "yonder," in effect, up in the air, as "high as that," when all the while he knew where it was: it was there under his forming fingers; it was in his writing, where the real god, the god he could not avow — dared not worship — worked, wrote, writing his rhetorical regrets, putting his question so perfectly the proof was in the putting.

Hopkins, in one mood, writes, "Nothing is so beautiful as spring — when weeds, in wheels, shoot long and lovely and lush," while in a wintertime time, when his faith nears icy cinder, he complains, "no worst, there is none. Pitched past pitch of grief, more pangs will, schooled at forepangs, wilder wring"; but there's no contradiction here; it's not that one of them is right; that he should buck up and be brave or leave off sentimentalizing about one more season; and the fact that for a moment, in his heart, his faith is renewed or shaken, while in mine, his reader, belief being absent, faith has no place to stand or snow in which to shiver — that difference makes no difference; it is irrelevant as yesterday's air, because opinions, principles, philosophies, systems of belief, are also a part of the passing world, beauties themselves, some of them, rich in invention, as full of our longing as legs in long pants; and our longings are real, if what they long for isn't; they also need their celebration, since each of them is like a baited line sunk into a Deep beyond our seeing — searching — waiting for the nose of something there to twitch it, waiting for a nibble.

Celebrate sorrow — why not? Celebrate pain, invent an Iago, bring on the awfuls, Bosch's brush awaits to do its best by the worsts. Christ hangs from the cross like ill-hung clothes, yet the meaning of his suffering is our redemption. My heresy is: redemption is on the canvas, in the image and its pigments.

4

How best to pass the Test of Time in a world where everything good happens later than you'd have liked, and everything bad breaks out before you expected it? Good times do pass and bad ones, dear heart, for all your poetizing, are bad; the good is quick as a bird, the bad is slow as ooze, and, dearie, for all your whistling Dixie, evils are not nice. If Hopkins is down in the dumps, he is miserable down there, and no fine lines will redeem the dumps, or save him from his doubts, or relieve him of the truth: God's not going to pluck him out of the earth where he will surely lie and surely rot, not as if he were a root crop pulled clear and shaken clean: say maybe a carrot suits the clergy, turnip perhaps, onion,

leek, parsnip for a poet. Anyway, rinsed of the grave, he'd only be
headed for the soup.

Thoreau went boating as a boy, and dropped his line, and never
did it happen in prose of any kind, including his own: the line's
great curve behind him as he trolled was drawn in cold pond water,
crystalline. Now Walden is threatened by developers every year,
and the water has been soiled by decades of rancid runoff. What
has been saved then, what has been preserved, what has withstood
time . . . and the sawyer's saws? The Binsey poplars were suddenly
felled, as if in front of Hopkins's saddened eye, blunt stumps lining
the bank where he passed as faithfully as the river, their short life
shortened by someone who could cut, and could cancel his care
before it came up into consciousness . . . who could ax one and
watch it fall and then another. "My aspens dear, whose air cages
quelled, quelled or quenched in leaves the leaping sun, all felled,
felled, are all felled."

"Wake and feel the fell of dark not day." This is how; this is why.
The paragraphs of Walden form in words what never happened. I
agree: events encouraged those words, events surprised them even
into existence; but Thoreau made his memory, created water that
never was . . . oh yes, they tossed the brands they burned to lure
the fish up out of nighttime as if the sun had risen, they tossed
the brands like firework and listened to them return to enter the
water with a kiss; but they did so by swinging their arms then, and
not in so many, not in any, words: ". . . and when we had done, far
in the night, threw the burning brands high into the air like
sky-rockets, which, coming down into the pond, were quenched
with a loud hissing, and we were suddenly groping in total darkness." Thoreau was not Thoreau, then, just a boy, playing a flute
to charm the perch, catching pouts with threaded worms, and not
a word, I'm sure, disturbed the serenity of that life.

So had it not happened — and where is that Walden now? — it
would have happened anyway, but not in Time who allows the ax
to swing like a second hand, but in the prose or in the poem where,
down in the dumps, a pun appears to point out to us that life, that
misery, does not pun and does not rhyme and has no rhythm,
sprung or otherwise, so inadequate is it; and why not let life pass
then, get along; life, thank god, happens only once and its pains
are merely painful, hurtfully plain; while, in the poem, pain is

wrung from the poet as if he were wet wash, but, since he's been pitched past pitch of grief, the ringing has a pealing sound: the pangs of pain, the procession of those *p*'s.

Didn't the poplars cage — quell — the sunlight themselves, so how can they complain? And weren't those burning brands quenched as well? One light went while rising, the other fell. Time holds occasions open like opportunities, but the poet's poem never was "in time" like the trees or his grief or Walden's water was midnight. They, those things, the terrible sonnets, every one, were composed, brought by Hopkins into being, not when he was down in the dumps, not while he was Hopkins, but when he was a Poet, truly on top of the world, the muse his mother; and the poems supplant their cause, are sturdier than trees, and will strip the teeth of any saw that tries to down them.

Because when the poplars went they went without the poet's passion for them as present as their leaves. And we, as readers, are not brought to Walden Pond in some poetic time machine. We experience Walden as it passed through Thoreau's head, his whole heart there for us to pass through too, his wide bright eyes the better to see with, the patient putting together of his prose to appreciate. Of the pond, the trees, the pain, the poet may retain — through the indelibilities of his medium — moments which, in reality, went as swift as a whistle away; but he will also give them what was never there in the first place: much afterthought, correction, suggestion, verbal movement, emotion, meaning, music. The result is the combination of occasion, consciousness, and artful composition which we now — oh so fortunately — have. Thus the night was not as it was described, neither the fishing, nor the pain; events, actions, objects didn't repeat; and the feelings were never felt, the wringing and the quelling, they were as baked as biscuits; and the thoughts were never thought that way — what thoughts there were are as long gone as the row of trees — they were composed; in sum, the pond we know, the trees, the pain, the poet's passion for each actual thing, the philosopher's concerns, mourning the fallen trees, they never were anywhere but in these words: "when we hew or delve: after-comers cannot guess the beauty been. Ten or twelve, only ten or twelve strokes of havoc unselve the sweet especial scene, rural scene, a rural scene, sweet especial rural scene."

That is half our answer. It was lovely to be on Walden Pond at midnight, fluting the fish, but lovelier and more lasting in the verbal than in the fishing lines. It is painful to lose faith even for a moment or see a row of crudely hewn trunks where your favorite rustic scene once was, but mutilation's sorrow is inspiring in the reading, although we realize the poem does not soften the blows felt by the trees.

Here is the other half. Don't take the test. Poetry makes nothing happen, because it refuses to be a happenstance. Poems are not events. They are realities remarkably invested with value. They are a woman, a man, a mind made of words, and have no body, and hence no needs.

So be advised. For works of art, the rule reads: Never enter Time, and you will never be required to Exit.

ELIZABETH GRAVER

Two Baths

FROM SHENANDOAH

Sometimes first impressions gather up some of the residue of centuries.
— John Berger

1

I WAS, at this first bath, twenty, spending the year studying in
France, but traveling for a week with an American friend in Germany. Why Germany? Because it was cheap, because my eye landed
on it as I sat in Chartres in the Bibliothèque André-Malraux and
stared at an enormous atlas; because I liked the name Baden-
Baden — the way it repeated on the tongue and meant Bath-Bath.

For a few days we had been walking in the outer fringes of the
Black Forest, a landscape that reminded me of the New England
mountains where I grew up — the same gentle shapes and deep
pine colors, only here you could eat rich, dark cake in cafés, pour
tea from iron kettles with acorns on their lids, climb wooden
lookouts on the trails and sleep in clean youth hostels where
Canadians planted flags on their night tables, lest someone mistake them for Americans.

We were Americans though we bore no flags, privileged young
women traveling on our parents' money. We were dark and funny,
a comedy team, eager to talk to strangers, quick to hitch a ride
from a man in a black turtleneck, black jeans, and black Mercedes.
A count, I remember imagining as I sat in the back seat. He might
take us home to his castle. He might wine and dine us. Or rape
us. The thoughts slid calmly across my mind and disappeared.

We were also Jewish, a fact that kept lighting my head in flashes I tried to ignore — in the train, for instance, as we rode so precisely from one town to the next; in the way something in me curdled when I heard the German language, my ears unable to find music there, though I knew all words held music if you listened right. I hadn't come to Germany for history, but it kept prodding me. I found that in this country I, always a bit outside myself, was even more outside, looking, looking at myself — my black hair, fair skin, long nose, long face: can they tell, is it obvious? And how weak and skinny I felt there, next to the strapping couple who ran the café we sat in for hours — a man and a woman as tall, blond, and leggy as giraffes.

We went to the baths to relax after days of walking in the Black Forest. Like two girls in a tale, we climbed the marble steps, clutching money whose worth we didn't know how to tally, walking into a palace where we didn't quite belong. Our clothes were sweaty and dirty from days of traveling. My hair was pulled back with a purple shoelace; my friend's hair was cropped close to her head like a boy's. I felt far from home and wanted a bath the way a child does — for its cradling water, the lathering of my skin, the tipping of my head into capable hands. I wanted heat, too, for it was late November and we'd been cold in the mountains. We paid our marks and went inside.

Where I saw, at first, nothing but beauty: tiles covered with green peacocks, beaded with water; damp white floors and high windows; rooms leading, maze-like, one into another, each room with its own clean purpose — salty or steamy, hot, cold, or in-between. There were signs on the walls but we couldn't read them; we moved by our senses, from here to there. In the first room, stripping off our clothes, I remember stretching and feeling small and puny, and (somehow, at the same time) firm and lucky. Next to me, my friend unhooked her bra, stepped out of her underpants, taller than I was, a bit rounder, and on her hip (unseen, as of yet, by her parents) the blurry tattoo of a blue rose.

Looking back, I know I must have had the body of a girl — the flat stomach and smooth thighs of a twenty-year-old who'd had an easy life and never given birth. All around us old European women bent over their long breasts, soaped at their wrinkled skin, sat on benches and rubbed pumice stones along the tired soles of their feet. So much skin, I remember thinking, so much loose flesh, and I wanted and did not want to look, feeling my own flesh as so firm, so new, and yet knowing at the same time that I might be witnessing a vision of my future. Time, in this bath, came to me as a folded, pleated thing, and I recognized that, before I knew it, I'd be thirty looking back (as indeed, now, I am), and then forty looking back, and then it came to me (standing there so far from home, my pores yawning open) that even if I were lucky enough to live a long life, one day I would die.

It came to me, perhaps, because the steam blurred things so that the edges of bodies almost disappeared and matter came apart along its seams. There I was, surrounded by strangers, each one naked, touching her own skin. I wanted a towel or a skirt, but the women around me seemed utterly unselfconscious, even as they were covered with the nicks and marks of age. Everywhere I looked I saw bareness — the sharp angle of an elbow, the dip of a breast, the dark line between buttocks — women with bodies, concentrating on themselves. Naked the way animals are, I thought, and I watched a squat woman bend over and scrub between her legs like a monkey cleaning itself.

And then a flash again, a vision on the outer fringes of my mind: here we were, my friend and I, in a bath where we couldn't read the signs. And at any moment the gas would come in, invisible as air, and we would crumble, draw our last breaths, and who was to say what the woman in the white dress like a nurse's costume wanted with us? Who could decipher the language, rough and throaty as a dog's bark, that sprang from her throat as we passed by?

Cover yourself, I thought. And yet here I was, a tourist, having willingly paid my money, shed my clothes. Don't be paranoid, I told myself. Don't make these people pay for their ancestors' crimes. But for an airless moment I couldn't look at the clean white ceiling, the hard white walls, without seeing the texture of bleached bone.

Then we were in the next room, lying, each of us, face down on benches built into the edges of a large stone structure like a pyramid with steps. And before I could protest or question, another woman in a nurse's uniform was leaning over me with a loofah sponge.

I want to leave, I thought. Please let me go.

The sponge was hurting me, and I hadn't signed up for this, but here she was touching me, leaning over me like a surgeon, taking off my skin. I lay on my stomach, my teeth gritted, my muscles clenched, feeling the stone hard beneath my hipbones, breasts, and cheek. When she was done, she tapped me on my back and showed me the loofah mitt and my own arm — both covered with limp, gray threads of skin.

"*Ja?*" she said, and I nodded, smiled weakly, and looked for my friend, who was under the mitt of another woman, only she was laughing, calling out *Nein nein,* and the mitt woman was laughing too and roughly batting at my friend.

I'm not sure how long we spent in the bath in Baden-Baden; time grew heavy as a towel soaked in water. I know we stayed longer than we should have, determined to get our money's worth. We lingered long enough so that we suddenly found ourselves walking, dazed, into a room filled with both men and women, the men looking up at us, perhaps forty pairs of eyes, twenty penises, most of them old and shriveled in the water. Laughter struck me, then; something like mirth or discomfort or both cramped my stomach. Only later did someone tell us that at four o'clock the bath became mixed. Mixed, I remember thinking: men and women, Jews and Christians, Germans and foreigners, our skin and theirs, everyone only half pretending not to look.

"Are you twins?" an old woman asked us in English as we sank into the water.

We giggled and shook our heads. Twins? Why would we be twins? My friend was a good four inches taller than I was, my eyes hazel, hers brown, our bodies not at all the same shape.

What she means, I thought, is: Are you Jews? Then I kicked myself for my assumptions. You're paranoid, I told myself again, and I remembered how the mother of a childhood friend posted a picture of children in a concentration camp on her family's gleaming fridge, to remind her daughters of how lucky they were and how unlucky their history was — a strange mixed message that left her family reeling. Her girls could not eat, starved them- selves, binged and purged inside the mansion where they lived with a mother who read books about the Holocaust each night before bed.

"It's all right," my grandmother said to my mother when, as a girl, she shattered an eggshell-blue teacup made in Japan. "There goes another Jap!"

At the end of our hours in the bath, a woman with strong arms came up and cocooned us in white sheets until, hemmed in, we couldn't move our arms and could walk only by taking baby steps along the polished floor. She gestured, then, at a huge circular room with cots arranged around its edge, and we minced along until we reached two metal cots. To lie down we had to flop ourselves backward all in one motion, and then there we were, blanketed and snug as infants, trapped and held as prisoners, flat on our backs in an elegant white room where the light slanted down through a high dome and steam wafted through the door and all around us strangers slept. There we were, limbs tied, hungry now and dizzy and slipping toward something like mirth.

When the laughter came, it was sharp and hard and brought us close to gagging, for we couldn't sit up, quite, or get out from our wrappings. Inside our laughter lived too many things to describe: our own lightheadedness, certainly (the heat, the water, hours without food), but also a thick, teary sense of how hard it was to fix on anything in this place so far from home — a place where women who cleaned us like mothers reminded us of gas chambers; where we stepped outside ourselves and saw our bodies in their youth and in their death; where we were not quite sure if we were being coddled or choked.

"Shhh," I said to my friend, which only made her laugh harder. From other cots, people turned their heads and glared at us. And then a nurse-woman stomped in, frowned, unwrapped us, and sent us out to where our clothes lay waiting.

Later that afternoon, we met an old woman on a bus and she took us home for tea and showed us pictures of her family — men in SS uniforms with swastikas embroidered on their hats.

"*Sehr* handsome, *ja?*" she said, pointing at the men, and we nodded and prodded each other under the table.

Her house was small and made of stone, her food simple. Her legs were stocky and her laughter nervous. I knew she wanted something from us, but I could not tell what. For hours we sat there as she showed us her embroidery and photographs and spoke to us in streams of German we couldn't understand, mixed in with bits of English.

"Address telephone," she said at one point. "You *und* you."

Dutifully, we wrote them down.

"*Und* America," she said when she saw I'd written my address in Paris, so I wrote down my parents' address as well.

"Stay," she commanded when it grew dark and we got up to leave. "Stay stay stay!" She stood and flapped her arms up and down like a plump, anxious bird or a child winding up for a tantrum.

"No," we said nervously, "no, but thank you, *danke.*"

She flew into a panic then, ran around the house collecting things in a basket to send off with us: a red glass cup, a piece of lace, sausages, bread, a spool of thread.

"No," we said, "don't give us all that, really."

But she pressed the basket into our hands.

That night at the youth hostel, I peered into the mirror in the bathroom and wondered what she'd seen. Who was this woman who charged over to us in the bus and took us home as if she'd been waiting for months for our arrival? Why was she giving us things? Why had she shown us her relatives but ignored the swastikas on their hats?

Uncomfortably, I saw pieces of myself in her — in her longing and frenzy, her desire to take strangers home, collect objects in a basket, comb over photographs pointing out only what she wanted to see. In her effort, especially, to find, in the world of daily things, small footholds of meaning, a place to rest. And then I saw her relatives again in their uniforms, and my own face which may or may not have announced me as Jewish, my skin taut and open from the bath. Perhaps what she was saying was quite simple: Look — my people, the faces I love. Handsome, *ja?* Or maybe she was saying, Yes, here are my relatives who were Nazis, but years have passed and I'd like to feed you now. Whatever she wanted me to see, I know I could see only one thing: men made faceless by the overbearing symbols on their hats.

After we left (I later found out), she picked up her phone and placed a call to my parents overseas. When they answered, she said, "Daughter, *wunderbar,*" and my parents panicked, knowing only that I was traveling, thinking I might be hurt or dead. For months after I got back to Paris, I received postcards from her, written in German, signed with hearts and smiles. I never answered, too unsure of what she wanted. War guilt, said my French friends. After a while, the postcards stopped.

Did the woman from Baden-Baden ever ride the bus to the baths, untie her brown shoes, take off her thick wool skirt, unpeel her stockings, and sit on a bench, hosed in her own body, her own flesh, still with herself for a moment? Did she always scan the bus for strangers to take home — girls to mother, Jews or Americans to look at her photographs, mouths to feed, ears that could hear her sounds but not begin to understand? War guilt, perhaps (could she tell we were Jewish?), but I think that's only one part of the picture. Really I have no idea who I was to that woman, and I cannot describe in any simple way who she was to me. I know I felt scrubbed and naked that afternoon, missing a layer of skin. She tried to give me gifts; I said no. Later she wrote to me; I didn't answer. Daughter *wunderbar.* A call from across the ocean. This is not a story I can make clearer. That night I slept clean, tired and slightly less sure of my place in the world.

2

And then I was thirty, and my mother was fifty-eight. For three weeks we had been traveling together in Turkey, the country where my mother's parents were born and grew up. On this, our last day, we had come to a *hamam,* a Turkish bath, down an alley in a gray, ordinary section of the city of Ankara. This building, unlike the bathhouse in Baden-Baden, was plain on the outside — beige stucco with a nicked brown door. Inside, we left our clothes in a small room with a key, put on plastic clogs, and walked into a huge marble chamber dense with steam. My mother was naked and, without her glasses, nearly blind. On this trip she had seemed both old and young to me — young as we met children and scrambled after them down hills, through tunnels, into abandoned churches; old in the deepening fan of lines around her eyes, the frailty of her shoulders, the way she told me she felt invisible when we walked down the street and the men called out to me: Pretty girl, come have tea, hello American girl!

I crouched in a corner on the floor, held a plastic jug under the spigots of a squat marble sink, and poured hot and cold water over myself. I watched a Turkish woman lead my mother out across the floor. My mother groped forward, extended her foot to test for level ground. The woman took her firmly by her arm and laid her down across the *gobek tası,* or navel stone — an octagonal marble platform in the middle of the room. Above it, a dome rose like a pregnant belly, studded with round windows. From here (I, too, without my glasses, the world a little blurry) I might have been looking at a painting: two women in a bath, my mother and a stranger, their skin steamed and rosy in the light that filtered through the windows in the roof. My mother might have been a woman my own age, or this might have been not Ankara but Istanbul, where my grandmother used to visit the baths.

For Muslims, I had read, running water has mystical properties. And for Jews? For my Sephardic grandmother? Sitting in the half-light of the bath, I pictured my grandmother as a first-time bride in Istanbul. Her name before she was married the first time was Rebecca Cohen; then Rebecca Baruch, and later Rebecca Levy, like a spell with three parts. Like the Muslims, the Jews in Turkey sent the bride to the *hamam* for a ritual bath before her wedding. My grandmother would have been around nineteen the year she married Moses Baruch, a man who she told me (in the winding stories she spun the year before she died) worked in a cheese factory. I've seen a picture of her at this age, and it must be said that she was unusually beautiful, with a strong chin, a proud gaze, thick eyebrows, and luxuriant, wavy brown hair.

Two days before my grandmother's wedding, she would have had her hair, hands, and nails dyed red with henna sent by her groom, Moses, on a copper tray rimmed with candles. Her family would have rented the whole *hamam* for her ritual bath, or if they couldn't afford to rent the whole place, they would have used the Jewish corner. My grandmother's mother would have gone with her, along with her sisters, her aunts, her friends, perhaps even her close friend Suzanne Behar, who would later become the first wife of my grandfather Samuel Levy, the man my grandmother would marry after Moses Baruch and Suzanne Behar both died.

In the bath, my grandmother, her sisters, mother, friends, and aunts would strip off their clothes and chatter in Ladino — the archaic Spanish spoken by Sephardic Jews. Or they would sing, perhaps, in Turkish, Ladino, or French. I can picture my grandmother at the center of it all, gulping down the attention, singing the loudest, arching her body down onto the navel stone in the middle of the *hamam*. Was she scared that day, smeared with henna the color of dried blood, preparing her body for sex? If she was, I doubt she showed it; my grandmother had a talent for disguise.

She would have brought a package with her, a *bogo de banyo* from her future husband. The gift would have arrived wrapped in fabric embroidered with artichokes and tulips — a cloth valued for its reversibility, perfect inside and out with nothing to hide, like a good wife. Inside, a set of towels to cover the shoulders, the head, the torso. Also a *tasa de banyo* — a brass bowl for rinsing the body; and wooden clogs inlaid with mother-of-pearl; and combs, soaps, and perfumes; and money to pay for the bath.

Before my grandmother's ritual immersion, the women throw sugar cubes in the water. For a sweet life, Rebecca. (Would her life turn out sweet? Much bitterness and loss inside it; spurts of laughter, too.) She squats, tips her head back, and they cluster around her and douse her with water from the sink. As she stands up, someone (her mother? her sister?) breaks a yeast cake over her. A blessing. To life. To children (she will bear five). And with a giggle, some knowing looks, and a slap on the behind: to love.

I remembered my grandmother with her Jean Naté bath splash, and how, in her last days, when she had one leg and spoke in a torrent of Ladino, French, English, and Turkish, she still loved a good bath, the towels plumped and fresh, her Avon products left over from her days as an Avon lady in Florida, when she charmed her customers with songs. I remembered how exacting she was when she taught me to embroider; the cloth had to look as good on its underside as on its top. At home my parents keep matchbooks in a brass dish my grandfather said was for scooping water at the bath. A disgusting place, he said, drawing out the syllables — *deee-scoost-sting*. Unclean, where bad things happened. Later I learned from my mother that my grandfather's brother was gay and frequented the baths in Istanbul, bringing shame on the family.

My grandfather, as I remember him, was strict, practical, and wary of pleasure; it was hard to imagine him here. But my grandmother loved bodies, her own and other people's. As I watched my mother being bathed, I remembered the day, as a child, that I looked under my grandmother's couch pillows for drawing paper (everything tucked away and hidden in her house) and found, instead, calendar foldouts of naked women, plump, pink, and glistening, and how she laughed and mock-slapped me when I held them up.

"Don't be ashamed," she said, "of a person's body. It's a beautiful thing. What you think you're doing looking in that couch, you? You give me those, you wise guy!" *Bee-yooo-tee-ful,* her voice prancing up and down.

I watched my mother lying on the marble, her body so much like mine except that her stomach was rounder, her nipples darker, for she'd lived twenty-eight years longer than I and had given birth twice. The water as I poured it over myself was either too cold or too hot, but the marble was gray-veined and smooth and I crouched in my corner and listened to women speak in a rising, falling melody I couldn't understand. During our three weeks in this country where almost everyone was Muslim, we'd seen mostly women beneath veils, hanging back in doorways or courtyards. Here the bathing women were naked, and the staff wore tiny bikini underwear and wet brassieres. Watching them chat and drink tea from fluted glasses, I glimpsed how little I knew of the lives of anyone here, how much went on beneath veils, behind doors and windows.

And then my mother was being led back to our sink, and I was being led out to the navel stone, and a woman with a cheerful face and beige lace bra was leaning over me, scrubbing me roughly with her loofah mitt.

With my eyes shut, I might have been twenty years old in Baden-Baden; this might have been a woman in nurse's uniform; they had the same strong hands. Or I might have been four years old, this woman my mother or grandmother, for she was scrubbing me as hard as if I were coated in playground grime and she had no shame, working over my breasts, down my belly, pushing apart my thighs so she could slide her mitt between my legs.

I did not protest, not even to myself. I had no visions, here, of water turning to gas. This was the country that had welcomed my ancestors when Spain expelled them in 1492 and had taken in thousands of Jews during the Holocaust. At twenty, I'd gone to Germany because the train fare was cheap and I was in the neigh-

borhood, but I'd come to Turkey looking for something like recognition or knowledge, home or safety; this was, after all, a place
I was linked to in my blood. Was it fair to feel that history as I
barely skimmed the surface of a country for three weeks? I
couldn't help it; I saw my grandfather's hooded brown eyes in the
eyes of a shopkeeper in the Grand Bazaar, saw my mother's and
my own face in the faces of the girls we met in the streets. I heard
Hebrew rhythms, even, in the wails of the mosques' calls to prayer
and saw Stars of David carved on village walls.

Did it matter that Muslims also made use of the six-pointed star,
so that origins were impossible to fix? Did it matter that I was cared
for in Germany, taken into a stranger's home, given gifts? It would
have been easier, less foggy, to experience the bath in Baden-Baden
as a cold, efficient death-place, and the bath in Ankara — with its
navel stone and pregnant roof — as a place of continuity and birth.
But it wasn't like that. I may have imagined death as I lay swaddled
like a baby in Baden-Baden, but I was thirty in Ankara and that
much closer to actual death, threads of gray speeding prematurely
through my hair. I was washed by a round woman who may have
looked cheerful but was probably tired, doing her job. While we
were in Turkey, two Dutch women were abducted by their bus
driver, raped, then killed. And what of the country's history and
present state — the Armenian genocide, and the fact that on our
trip we didn't travel to Turkey's southeast corner because of what
the tourist bureau called "trouble with the Kurds"?

When the woman finished washing me, she, like the German
woman, held up the mitt to show me how pieces of myself were
clinging to the loofah — a snake's skin, my own grubby debris.
Then she left me alone and I lay on the navel stone distant from
myself, a body shucked of its husk, a mind far from its body. I
wished, then, that my mother had her glasses on so she could see
me lying as she had lain a few minutes before, as her mother had
lain more than seventy years ago. In the distance I could feel my
mother's presence, and my grandmother's. Could this be a link,
some kind of echo — vexed and inside my own head, perhaps, but
an echo nonetheless? I wasn't sure. I lay there pressed against the
stone of a country I could recognize only in fragments — a brass
bowl, embroidery perfect on both sides, *borek* pastries like the ones
my grandmother used to make, their edges frail and flaky as my
own shed skin.

EDWARD HOAGLAND

A Peaceable Kingdom

FROM PRESERVATION

IT'S TOO GOOD to be true, I've always thought, for the past twenty-eight years, when spring rolls around once again and I drive up to my warm-weather home, now the only occupied house on a four-mile stretch of dirt road that crosses a mountain notch in northeastern Vermont. A two-story frame dwelling, painted blue-gray and nearly a hundred years old, built by the first family who cleared these sparse fields. They had forty acres, ten or twelve cows, and three other families for neighbors, two living in log cabins that have since fallen in — enough kids for a one-room school, which later was moved next door, when that family's original house burned and they needed a new one. My predecessors had thrown together a log cabin at first; a barge-shaped depression in the woods still marks where it was. Then, when they decided to stay, they dug a cellar hole here with a horse-drawn scoop, split some granite boulders at the base of the cliff for blocks of stone to line it with, and set up a sawmill to cut floorboards of spruce. Sand from the stream was used for the plastering, and they planted apple trees and a black cherry tree, and four oaks, now nice and big, in front.

The farming ceased about forty years ago. The man I bought the house from was supporting himself by brewing corn whiskey and bathtub beer and shooting deer out of season for meat. He died too soon from drinking too much, and his British war-bride wife afterward, though she was a favorite person of mine and planted many of the flower beds I continue to enjoy. The lack of electric and phone lines had made them eager to move, and indeed explains why this mountain road has never been as unpopulated as it is now, and why beyond my house it is being abandoned "to the Indians," as the town authorities say.

What I do when I arrive is air and sweep the house, load the woodstove, turn the water on, browse my bookshelves for a glimpse of old friends, and check to see if the local ermine spent the winter inside, clearing the place of the few pairs of white-footed mice that otherwise might have chewed my socks. Thus I prefer to find her hairy little twists of dung over anybody else's. Chipmunks, when they wake from semi-hibernation, may seek entry also.

I open the four birdboxes that hang on trees to clear out squirrel nests — if any red squirrels had sheltered there through the snowy months — hoping that now tree swallows will come instead. I climb into the hayloft of the barn to see if a bear slept out the season in the mounds of hay, or merely some raccoons, and look, too, for the phoebes, early arrivals that nest under my eaves, then listen for white-throated sparrows, ovenbirds, yellowthroats, wood thrushes, robins, winter wrens, rose-breasted grosbeaks, chestnut-sided warblers, mourning warblers, and black-throated green, and black-throated blue, and black-and-white warblers. Cedar waxwings, indigo buntings, flickers, and goldfinches will be arriving. A certain apple-tree limb is where the hummingbirds will nest.

If the large mother coon has survived the winter, she will probably be using the hollow maple as a den tree. By putting my ear next to it, I may hear her kits. The ermine (now an ordinary brown weasel) that protected my woolens has meanwhile moved from the house to nest among the timbers of the barn. Investigating clues perhaps left by the bear in the hayloft, I'll hear her burbling expressions of alarm. The mother woodchuck hibernates under the chicken coop and reappears as soon as the grass does; and if I'm lucky, I'll see a migrating trio of black ducks sneak in at dusk for a night's rest — out of the hurly-burly of the lakes nearby — in my high-up, hidden frog pond. They'll eat some water greens at dawn and then be gone. Bears will have already clipped off the young spring sedges at water level. Sedges are among the first foods bears taste; or they trudge to the fir woods a few hundred yards downhill, where some deer have generally wintered, to find out if any died. I look for antlers the living bucks have dropped, but bears sniff for a carcass they can eat, though they will gobble deer droppings, too, in this hungry time, and search for last fall's sprouted beechnuts on the ground.

The lawn under my oaks, mossy and mushroomy, doesn't need much mowing. The apple trees mainly feed the wildlife, and I bush hog the fields only often enough to keep them open. The stream was dammed seventy-five years ago for homegrown experiments with water power, but flows just as it wishes now, and moose, deer, and coyotes drink from it instead of cows. I sometimes do, too, or kingfishers, ravens, or woodcock make use of it, and a great blue heron hunts mice and frogs alongside. I had the frog pond dug, hiring a bulldozer for the purpose of filling the air with song. Spring peepers and wood frogs start up in April. Then tree frogs, green frogs, pickerel frogs, and of course toads — my favorite serenaders of all — join in. As the lush orchard grass and the thick raspberry patch sloping away from the old barn have lost their soil nutrients from half a century's worth of cow manure from the animals that were stabled there, fireweed and other hardscrabble plants replaced them, and what had been a teeming colony of earthworms became scarcer. This was tough on the colony of garter snakes living underneath my house, which had fed on them. But the frogs, increasing tenfold, took up some of the slack as a food source.

These garter snakes, just twenty miles short of Canada, are blacker than the same species in southern Vermont because they need to absorb as much heat as possible during the brief summer season in order to digest what they eat; the sun is their engine. The woodchucks are blacker, too, not to accumulate heat but as camouflage: in these northern forests dark fur shows up less. The bears are black, the moose are black, the porcupines dark. The deer in their red summer coats look quite odd, as in fact they should, because they followed the white men north.

In the house, I load the flashlights, put candles around, fill the kerosene lamps, and look to see if anything has been pilfered over the winter — pipe wrenches, a fire extinguisher, boots, blankets, or possibly my ax? Secondhand books sell hereabouts for a dollar a box, so no one steals books, though somebody once purloined the magnifying glass that went with my *Oxford English Dictionary*. And, once, my field glasses were lifted, just before hunting season started, yet then were left on my woodpile during December. The next year, when it happened again, they weren't returned — this being such an impoverished area that woodpiles, too, are sometimes stolen. A furniture factory is the principal local employer, using the yellow birch and rock maple that people log around here when they aren't cutting pulpwood. Unemployment is so high it keeps wages low. Other people truck milk to Massachusetts, or cattle to the hamburger slaughterhouses down there. Where you see goshawks, red-tailed and broad-winged hawks, and peregrine falcons, you don't notice ads in the paper saying "Help Wanted."

My windows and rooms are small, as befits the cold climate most of the year. On some of the richest days, when a moose stalks by or a bear is blueberrying or munching hazelnuts outside, I think of my house as a bathysphere suspended in the wilderness. Nevertheless, it's comfortable — the floors painted russet, the furniture homey, the walls nearly covered with pictures I've taped up over the last quarter century. I'm partly surrounded by an eight-thousand-acre state forest, to which I'm leaving my land as a minor addition, except for the house, which will belong to my daughter. Big Valley Brook, Stillwater Swamp, May Pond, Boiling Spring, and Moose Mountain are spectacles that live in my head, yet I can walk to. If the weather muscles in, I chop four hours' worth of wood. I hear an owl; I hear the ravens; I hear a redstart.

Gardeners and trout fishermen got busy outdoors around mid-April, if the high water permitted, and the kids in town started shagging fungoes or fishing Kids' Brook, a stretch of stream near the fairgrounds so easy that it's lent to them. For me, spring had begun a month earlier, when a big male bobcat's tracks looped down off Moose Mountain into my wooded notch and intersected in a romancing scrawl with the solitary lady bobcat who shares the area with me. When the snow is gone, of course, her movements become more of a mystery, but my dog has treed her. On other rare occasions I notice her prints beside the pond or hear a rabbit scream at night, utterly suddenly, caught from ambush.

Then on the last day of March a bear that dens near my house left her little cave to enjoy what was perhaps her first drink in four months. Going a hundred feet so she could lap the trickling meltwater in a brook, her tracks showed that she made an immediate return trip to sleep some more. On Tax Day she was still in her den, her head protruding dozily, but the next day she descend-

ed a quarter mile to a patch of swamp to eat some cattails, with
yearling-sized tracks accompanying her. The presence of the grown
cub meant that, in the bearish biennial ritual, a male would probably come visit us in June so she could have new cubs next winter.

Among certain Indian tribes, a family used to inherit a given
cluster of bear dens and the winter nutrition to be gained by killing
the occupants in prudent rotation. Though I avail myself of the
local supermarket, I'm just as protective: don't mess with my bears.
And the dog doesn't. Wally is a sheepdog and patrols the meadow
aggressively but regards the forest as foreign territory. On the
other hand, when the county airstrip comes to life and low-flying
Cessnas angle over, he is inspired to defend the perimeter of our
empty field from these roaring eagles with a pell-mell frenzy, as if
we had a bevy of lambs that they might grab. Then, after chasing
a plane away, he'll cock his leg and pee triumphantly against a tree,
the same as when his adversary has been a wandering fox or
coyote, so it will know next time who it must reckon with.

He'll also mark a rabbit's trail, a squirrel's roost, a mouse's nest
for later reference when he hunts, although I doubt he is one
tenth as efficient at that occupation as a fox. In June, I'll lie in
the field at dusk and listen to a vixen's hectic rustle as she gleans
a stomachful of meadow mice, deer mice, shrews, moles, night
crawlers, and such to take back to her burrow and vomit for her
pups. And I remember how quickly a woodchuck that had grown
feisty from taunting Wally at the mouth of its hole fell prey to a
lank coyote that rambled through. The coyote carried the body
off, but stopped, dropped it, and performed an unexpected sort
of victory dance, stiff legged, around the corpse.

"Joy walking" is what deer hunters call what I do in the woods
because I bring no gun. For Wally, as well, our outings are a matter
of glee, not necessity. He'd rather simply haul home a dehorned
head or a gut pile a poacher has left than hunt for more than a
few minutes himself. Carrion tastes, I suspect, a bit winy, cheesy,
anchovy and green olivey, béarnaise and sour-creamy (which may
be why we late primates try so hard to approximate the piquancy
of fermentation with sauces). Wally drinks from muddy puddles
and nibbles green sprouts as a further change from piped-in water
and dog kibble before curling at my head as a sentinel when we
camp out.

Wally celebrated spring around Tax Day by running down to the pond alone for his first swim: this when the wood frogs and song sparrows had just started to sing. I was lolling in a patch of sunny grass, watching a pair of robins, listening to a kinglet and a phoebe, but, lest my delight seem unadulterated, also picking off my first tick of the season. Instead of forest lore, Wally has become adept at reading human beings (hunters are the only predators he flees), such as the precise moment every morning when he can jump on my bed without waking and angering me — or the extraordinary value I place on the welfare of the goofy parrot in the kitchen, versus the crows in the garden that he is encouraged to chase. They fly up into the basswood tree and razz him, then look for a hawk they can mob and mistreat.

JAMAICA KINCAID

In History

FROM CALLALOO

WHAT TO CALL the thing that happened to me and all who look
like me?

Should I call it history?

If so, what should history mean to someone like me?

Should it be an idea, should it be an open wound and each
breath I take in and expel healing and opening the wound again
and again, over and over, or is it a moment that began in 1492
and has come to no end yet? Is it a collection of facts, all true and
precise details, and, if so, when I come across these true and precise details, what should I do, how should I feel, where should I
place myself?

Why should I be obsessed with all these questions?

My history began like this: in 1492, Christopher Columbus
discovered the New World. Since this is only a beginning and I am
not yet in the picture, I have not yet made an appearance, the
word "discover" does not set off an alarm, and I am not yet con-
fused by this interpretation. I accept it. I am only taken by the
personality of this quarrelsome, restless man. His origins are sometimes obscure; sometimes no one knows just where he really comes
from, who he really was. His origins are sometimes quite vivid:
his father was a tailor, he came from Genoa, he as a boy wandered
up and down the Genoese wharf, fascinated by sailors and their
tales of lands far away; these lands would be filled with treasures,
as all things far away are treasures. I am far away, but I am not yet
a treasure: I am not a part of this man's consciousness, he does
not know of me, I do not yet have a name. And so the word

"discover," as it is applied to this New World, remains uninteresting to me.

He, Christopher Columbus, discovers this New World. That it is new only to him, that it had a substantial existence, physical and spiritual, before he became aware of it, does not occur to him. To cast blame on him now for this childlike immaturity has all the moral substance of a certificate given to a schoolgirl for good behavior. To be a well-behaved schoolgirl is not hard. When he sees this New World, it is really new to him: he has never seen anything like it before, it was not what he had expected, he had images of China and Japan, and, though he thought he was in China and Japan, it was not the China or Japan that he had fixed in his mind. He couldn't find enough words to describe what he saw before him: the people were new, the flora and fauna were new, the way the water met the sky was new, this world itself was new, it was the New World.

"If one does not know the names, one's knowledge of things is useless." This is attributed to Isidorus, and I do not know if this is the Greek Isidorus or the other Isidorus, the bishop of Seville; but now put it another way: to have knowledge of things, one must first give them a name. This, in any case, seems me to have been Christopher Columbus's principle, for he named and he named: he named places, he named people, he named things. This world he saw before him had a blankness to it, the blankness of the newly made, the newly born. It had no before — I could say that it had no history, but I would have to begin again, I would have to ask those questions again: What is history? This blankness, the one Columbus met, was more like the blankness of paradise; paradise emerges from chaos, and this chaos is not history; it is not a legitimate order of things. Paradise, then, is the arrangement of the ordinary and the extraordinary. But in such a way as to make it, paradise, seem as if it had fallen out of the clear air. Nothing about it suggests the messy life of the builder, the carpenter, the quarrels with the contractor, the people who are late with the delivery of materials, their defense which, when it is not accepted, is met with their back chat. This is an unpleasant arrangement; this is not paradise. Paradise is the thing just met when all the troublesome details have been vanquished, overcome.

Christopher Columbus met paradise. It would not have been

paradise for the people living there; they would have had the ordinary dreariness of living anywhere day after day, the ordinary dreariness of just being alive. But someone else's ordinary dreariness is another person's epiphany.

The way in which he wanted to know these things was not in the way of satisfying curiosity, or in the way of correcting an ignorance; he wanted to know them, to possess them, and he wanted to possess them in a way that must have been a surprise to him. His ideas kept not so much changing as evolving: he wanted to prove the world was round, and even that, to know with certainty that the world was round, that it did not come to an abrupt end at a sharp cliff from which one could fall into nothing; to know that is to establish a claim also. And then after the world was round, this round world should belong to his patrons, the king and queen of Spain; and then finding himself at the other side of the circumference and far away from his patrons, human and other kind, he loses himself, for it becomes clear: the person who really can name the thing gives it a life, a reality, that it did not have before. His patrons are in Spain, looking at the balance sheet: if they invest so much, will his journey yield a return to make the investment worthwhile? But he — I am still speaking of Columbus — is in the presence of something else.

His task is easier than he thought it would be; his task is harder than he could have imagined. If he had only really reached Japan or China, places like that already had an established narrative. It was not a narrative that these places had established themselves; it was a narrative that someone like him had invented, Marco Polo, for instance; but this world, China or Japan, in the same area of the world to him (even as this familiarity with each other — between China and Japan — would surprise and even offend the inhabitants of these places), had an order, and the order offered a comfort (the recognizable is always so comforting). But this new place, what was it? Sometimes it was just like Seville; sometimes it was like Seville but only more so; sometimes it was more beautiful than Seville. Mostly it was "marvelous," and this word "marvelous" is the word he uses again and again, and when he uses it, what the reader (and this is what I have been, a reader of this account of the journey, and the account is by Columbus himself) can feel, can hear, can see, is a great person whose small soul has been sundered by something unexpected. And yet the unexpected turned out to be the most ordinary things: people, the sky, the sun, the land, the water surrounding the land, the things growing on the land.

What were the things growing on the land? I pause for this. What were the things growing on that land, and why do I pause for this?

I come from a place called Antigua. I shall speak of it as if no one has ever heard of it before; I shall speak of it as if it is just new. In the writings, in anything representing a record of the imagination of Christopher Columbus, I cannot find any expectation for a place like this. It is a small lump of insignificance, green, green, green, and green again. Let me describe this landscape again: it is green, and unmistakably so; another person, who would have a more specific interest, a painter, might say it is a green that often verges on blue, a green that often is modified by reds and yellows and even other more intense or other shades of green. To me, it is green and green and green again. I have no interest other than this immediate and urgent one: the landscape is green. For it is on this green landscape that, suddenly, I and the people who look like me made an appearance.

I, me. The person standing in front of you started to think of all this while really focused on something and someone else altogether. I was standing in my garden; my garden is in a place called Vermont; it is in a village situated in a place called Vermont. From the point of view of growing things, that is the gardener's, Vermont is not in the same atmosphere as that other place I am from, Antigua. But while standing in that place, Vermont, I think about the place I am from, Antigua. Christopher Columbus never saw Vermont at all; it never entered his imagination. He saw Antigua, I believe on a weekday, but if not, then it would have been a Sunday, for in this life there would have been only weekdays or Sundays, but he never set foot on it, he only came across it while passing by. My world then — the only world I might have known if circumstances had not changed, intervened, would have entered the human imagination, the human imagination that I am familiar with, the only one that dominates the world in which I live — came into being as a footnote to someone just passing by. By the time Christopher Columbus got to the place where I am from, the place that forms the foundation of the person you see before you, he was exhausted, he was sick of the whole thing, he longed for his old home, or he longed just to sit still and enjoy the first few things that he had come upon. The first few things that he came on were named after things that were prominent in his thinking, his sponsors especially; when he came to the place I am from, he (it) had been reduced to a place of worship; the place I am from is named after a church. This church might have been an important church to Christopher Columbus, but churches are not important, originally, to people who look like me. And if people who look like me have an inheritance, among this inheritance will be this confusion of intent; nowhere in his intent when he set out from his point of embarkation (for him, too, there is not origin: he originates from Italy, he sails from Spain, and this is the beginning of another new traditional American narrative, point of origin and point of embarkation): "here is something I have never seen before, I especially like it because it has no precedent, but it is frightening because it has no precedent, and so to make it less frightening I will frame it in the thing I know; I know a church, I know the name of the church, even if I do not like or know the people connected to this church, it is more familiar to me, this church, than the very ground I am standing on; the ground has changed, the church, which is in my mind, remains the same."

I, the person standing before you, close the quotation marks. Up to this point, I and they that look like me am not yet a part of this narrative. I can look at all these events: a man setting sail with three ships, and after many, many days on the ocean, finding new lands whose existence he had never even heard of before, and then finding in these new lands people and their things and these people and their things, he had never heard of them before, and he empties the land of these people, and then he empties the people, he just empties the people. It is when this land is completely empty that I and the people who look like me begin to make an appearance, the food I eat begins to make an appearance, the trees I will see each day come from far away and begin to make an appearance, the sky is as it always was, the sun is as it always was, the water surrounding the land on which I am just making an appearance is as it always was; but these are the only things left from before that man, sailing with his three ships, reached the land on which I eventually make an appearance.

When did I begin to ask all this? When did I begin to think of all this and in just this way? What is history? Is it a theory? I no longer live in the place where I and those who look like me first made an appearance. I live in another place. It has another narrative. Its narrative, too, can start with that man sailing on his ships for days and days, for that man sailing on his ships for days and days is the source of many narratives, for he was like a deity in the simplicity of his beliefs, in the simplicity of his actions; just listen to the straightforward way many volumes featuring this man sailing on his ships begin: "In fourteen hundred and ninety-two . . ." But it was while standing in this other place, which has a narrative mostly different from the place in which I make an appearance, that I began to think of this.

One day, while looking at the things that lay before me at my feet, I was having an argument with myself over the names I should use when referring to the things that lay before me at my feet. These things were plants. The plants, all of them and they were hundreds, had two names: they had a common name — that is, the name assigned to them by people for whom these plants have value — and then they have a proper name, or a Latin name, and that is a name assigned to them by an agreed-on group of botanists. For a long time I resisted using the proper names of the things that lay before me. I believed that it was an affectation to say "eupatorium" when you could say "joe-pye weed." I then would only say "joe-pye weed." The botanists are from the same part of the world as the man who sailed on the three ships, that same man who started the narrative from which I trace my beginning. And in a way, too, the botanists are like that man who sailed on the ships: they emptied the worlds of things animal, mineral, and vegetable of their names, and replaced these names with names pleasing to them; the recognized names are now reasonable, as reason is a pleasure to them.

Carl Linnaeus was born on May 23, 1707, somewhere in Sweden. (I know where, but I like the highhandedness of not saying so.) His father's name was Nils Ingemarsson; the Ingemarssons were farmers. Apparently, in Sweden then, surnames were uncommon among ordinary people, and so the farmer would add "son" to his name or he was called after the farm on which he lived. Nils Ingemarsson became a Lutheran minister, and on doing so he wanted to have a proper surname, not just a name with "son"

attached to it. On his family's farm grew a linden tree. It had
grown there for generations and had come to be regarded with
reverence among neighboring farmers; people believed that mis-
fortune would fall on you if you harmed this tree in any way.
This linden tree was so well regarded that people passing by used
to pick up twigs that had dropped from it and carefully place
them at the base of the tree. Nils Ingemarsson took his surname
from this tree: Linnaeus is the Latinized form of the Swedish word
lind, which means linden. Other branches of this family who also
needed a surname drew inspiration from this tree; some took the
name Tiliander — the Latin word for linden is *tilia* — and some
others who also needed a surname took the name Lindelius, from
the same Swedish word *lind.*

Carl Linnaeus's father had a garden. I do not know what his
mother had. His father loved growing things in this garden and
would point them out to the young Carl, but when the young Carl
could not remember the names of the plants, his father gave him
a scolding and told him he would not tell him the names of any
more plants. (Is this story true? But how could it not be?) He grew
up not far from a forest filled with beech, a forest with pine, a
grove filled with oaks, meadows. His father had a collection of rare
plants in his garden (but what would be rare to him and in that
place, I do not know). At the time Linnaeus was born, Sweden —
this small country that I now think of as filled with well-meaning
and benign people interested mainly in the well-being of children,
the well-being of the unfortunate no matter their age — was the
ruler of an empire, but the remains of it are visible only in the
architecture of the main square of the capital of places like Estonia.
And so what to make of all this, this small detail that is the linden
tree, this large volume of the Swedish empire, and a small boy
whose father was a Lutheran pastor? At the beginning of this narrative, the narrative that is Linnaeus, I have not made an appearance yet; the Swedes are not overly implicated in the Atlantic
slave trade, not because they did not want to have a part in it, only
because they weren't allowed to do so; other people were better
at it than they.

He was called "the little botanist" because he would neglect his
studies and go out looking for flowers; if even then he had already
showed an interest in or the ability to name and classify plants, this

fact is not in any account of his life that I have come across. He went to university at Uppsala; he studied there with Olof Rudbeck. I can pause at this name, Rudbeck, and say rudbeckia, and say, I do not like rudbeckia. I never have it in my garden, but then I remember a particularly stately, beautiful yellow flower in a corner of my field garden, *Rudbeckia nitida,* growing there. He met Anders Celsius (the Celsius scale of temperature measurement), who was so taken with Linnaeus's familiarity and knowledge of botany that he gave Linnaeus free lodging in his house. Linnaeus became one of the youngest lecturers at the university. He went to Lapland and collected plants and insects native to that region of the world; he wrote and published an account of it called *Flora Lapponica.* In Lapland, he acquired a set of clothing that people native to that region of the world wore on festive occasions; I have seen a picture of him dressed in these clothes, and the caption under the picture says that he is wearing his Lapland costume. Suddenly I am made a little uneasy, for just when is it that other people's clothes become your costume? But I am not too uneasy, I haven't really entered this narrative yet, I shall soon. In any case, I do not know the Laplanders, they live far away, I don't believe they look like me.

I enter the picture only when Linnaeus takes a boat to Holland. He becomes a doctor to an obviously neurotic man (obvious only to me, I arbitrarily deem him so; no account of him I have ever come across has described him so) named George Clifford. George Clifford is often described as a rich merchant banker; just like that, a rich merchant banker, and this description often seems to say that to be a rich merchant banker is just a type of person one could be, an ordinary type of person, anyone could be that. And now how to go on, for on hearing that George Clifford was a rich merchant in the eighteenth century, I now am sure I have become a part of the binomial-system-of-plant-nomenclature narrative.

George Clifford had glass houses full of vegetable material from all over the world. This is what Linnaeus writes of it:

> I was greatly amazed when I entered the greenhouses, full as they were of so many plants that a son of the North must feel bewitched, and wonder to what strange quarter of the globe he had been trans-

ported. In the first house were cultivated an abundance of flowers from southern Europe, plants from Spain, the South of France, Italy, Sicily and the isles of Greece. In the second were treasures from Asia, such as Poincianas, coconut and other palms, etc.; in the third, Africa's strangely shaped, not to say misshapen plants, such as the numerous forms of Aloe and Mesembryanthemum families, carnivorous flowers, Euphorbias, Crassula and Proteas species, and so on. And finally in the fourth greenhouse were grown the charming inhabitants of America and the rest of the New World; large masses of Cactus varieties, orchids, cruciferea, yams, magnolias, tulip-trees, calabash trees, arrow, cassias, acacias, tamarinds, pepper-plants, Anona, manicinilla, cucurbitaceous trees and many others, and surrounded by these, plantains, the most stately of all the world's plants, the most beauteous Hernandia, silver-gleaming species of Protea and camphor trees. When I then entered the positively royal residence and the extremely instructive museum, whose collections no less spoke in their owner's praise, I, a stranger, felt completely enraptured, as I had never before seen its like. My heartfelt wish was that I might lend a helping hand with its management.

In almost every account of an event that has taken place sometime in the last five hundred years, there is always a moment when I feel like placing an asterisk somewhere in its text, and at the end of this official story place my own addition. This chapter in the history of botany is such a moment. But where shall I begin? George Clifford is interesting — shall I look at him? He has long ago entered my narrative; I now feel I must enter his. What could it possibly mean to be a merchant banker in the eighteenth century? He is sometimes described as making his fortune in spices. Only once have I come across an account of him that says he was a director of the Dutch East India Company. The Dutch East India Company would not have been involved in the Atlantic trade in human cargo from Africa, but human cargo from Africa was a part of world trade. To read a brief account of the Dutch East India trading company in my very old encyclopedia is not unlike reading the label on an old can of paint. The entry mentions dates, the names of Dutch governors or people acting in Dutch interest; it mentions trade routes, places, commodities, incidents of war between the Dutch and other European people; it never mentions the people who lived in the area of the Dutch trading factories. Places like Ceylon, Java, the Cape of Good Hope, are emptied of their people as the landscape itself was emptied of the things they were familiar with, the things that Linnaeus found in George Clifford's greenhouse.

"If one does not know the names, one's knowledge of things is useless." It was in George Clifford's greenhouse that Linnaeus gave some things names. The Adam-like quality of this effort was lost on him. "We revere the Creator's omnipotence," he says, meaning, I think, that he understood he had not made the things he was describing, he was only going to give them names. And even as a relationship exists between George Clifford's activity in the world, the world as it starts out on ships leaving the seaports of the Netherlands, traversing the earth's seas, touching on the world's peoples and the places they are in, the things that have meant something to them being renamed and a whole new set of narratives imposed on them, narratives that place them at a disadvantage in relationship to George Clifford and his fellow Dutch, even as I can say all this in one breath or in one large volume, so too then does an invisible thread, a thread that no deep breath or large volume can contain, hang between Carolus Linnaeus, his father's desire to give himself a distinguished name, the name then coming from a tree, the linden tree, a tree whose existence was regarded as not ordinary, and his invention of a system of naming that even I am forced to use?

The invention of this system has been a good thing. Its narrative would begin this way: in the beginning, the vegetable kingdom was chaos; people everywhere called the same things by a name that made sense to them, not by a name that they arrived at by an objective standard. But who has an interest in an objective standard? Who would need one? It makes me ask again what to call the thing that happened to me and all who look like me? Should I call it history? And if so, what should history mean to someone who looks like me? Should it be an idea, should it be an open wound and each breath I take in and expel healing and opening the wound again and again, over and over, or is it a long moment that begins anew each day since 1492?

WILLIAM MAXWELL

Nearing Ninety

FROM THE NEW YORK TIMES MAGAZINE

OUT OF THE corner of my eye I see my ninetieth birthday approaching. It is one year and six months away. How long after that will I be the person I am now?

I don't yet need a cane, but I have a feeling that my table manners have deteriorated. My posture is what you would expect of someone addicted to sitting in front of a typewriter, but it was always that way. "Stand up straight," my father would say to me. "You're all bent over like an old man." It didn't bother me then and it doesn't now, though I agree that an erect carriage is a pleasure to see, in someone of any age.

I have regrets but there are not very many of them and, fortunately, I forget what they are. I forget names, too, but it is not yet serious. What I am trying to remember and can't, quite often my wife will remember. And vice versa. She is in and out during the day, but I know she will be home when evening comes, and so I am never lonely. Long ago, a neighbor in the country, looking at our flower garden, said, "Children and roses reflect their care." This is true of the very old as well.

Though there have been a great many changes in the world since I came into it on August 16, 1908, I try not to deplore. It is not constructive and there is no point in discouraging the young by invidious comparisons with the way things used to be.

I am not — I think I am not — afraid of dying. When I was seventeen I worked on a farm in southern Wisconsin, near Portage. It was no ordinary farm and not much serious farming was done there, but it had the look of a place that has been lived in, and loved, for a good long time. I was no more energetic than most adolescents, but the family forgave my failures and shortcomings and simply took me in, let me be one of them. The farm had come down in that family through several generations, from the man who had pioneered it to a woman who was so alive that everything and everybody seemed to revolve around her personality. She lived well into her nineties and then one day told her oldest daughter that she didn't want to live anymore, that she was tired. Though I was not present but only heard about it in a letter, this remark reconciled me to my own inevitable extinction. I could believe that enough is enough. One must also, if possible, reconcile oneself to life. To horrors (the number of legless peasants in Cambodia) that if you allowed yourself to think about them more than briefly would turn your heart to stone.

Because I actively enjoy sleeping, dreams, the unexplainable dialogues that take place in my head as I am drifting off, all that, I tell myself that lying down to an afternoon nap that goes on and on through eternity is not something to be concerned about. What spoils this pleasant fancy is the recollection that when people are dead they don't read books. This I find unbearable. No Tolstoy, no Chekhov, no Elizabeth Bowen, no Keats, no Rilke. One might as well be —

Before I am ready to call it quits, I would like to reread every book I have ever deeply enjoyed, beginning with Jane Austen and Isaac Babel and Sybille Bedford's *The Sudden View* and going through shelf after shelf of the bookcases until I arrive at the autobiographies of William Butler Yeats. As it is, I read a great deal of the time. I am harder to please, though. I see flaws in masterpieces. Conrad indulging in rhetoric when he would do better to get on with it. I would read all day long and well into the night if there were no other claims on my time. Appointments with doctors, with the dentist. The monthly bank statement. Income tax returns. And because I don't want to turn into a monster, people. Afternoon tea with X, dinner with the Y's. Our social life would be a good deal more active than it is if more than half of those I care about hadn't passed over to the other side. However, I remember them. I remember them more, and more vividly, the older I get.

I did not wholly escape the amnesia that overtakes children around the age of six, but I carried along with me more of my childhood than, I think, most people do. Once, after dinner, my father hitched up the horse and took my mother and me for a sleigh ride. The winter stars were very bright. The sleigh bells made a lovely sound. I was bundled up to the nose, between my father and mother, where nothing, not even the cold, could get at me. The very perfection of happiness.

At something like the same age, I went for a ride, again with my father and mother, on a riverboat at Havana, Illinois. It was a sidewheeler and the decks were screened, I suppose as protection against the mosquitoes. Across eight decades the name of the steamboat comes back to me — the *Eastland* — bringing with it the context of disaster. A year later, at the dock in Chicago, too many of the passengers crowded on one side of the boat, waving good-bye, and it rolled over and sank. Trapped by the screens every-where, a great many people lost their lives. The fact that I had been on this very steamboat, that I had escaped from a watery grave, I continued to remember all through my childhood.

I have liked remembering almost as much as I have liked living. But now it is different, I have to be careful. I can ruin a night's sleep by suddenly, in the dark, thinking about some particular time in my life. Before I can stop myself, it is as if I had driven a mineshaft down through layers and layers of the past and must explore, relive, remember, reconsider, until daylight delivers me.

I have not forgotten the pleasure, when our children were very young, of hoisting them onto my shoulders when their legs gave out. Of reading to them at bedtime. Of studying their beautiful faces. Of feeling responsible for their physical safety. But that was more than thirty years ago. I admire the way that, as adults, they have taken hold of life, and I am glad that they are not material-istic, but there is little or nothing I can do for them at this point, except write a little fable to put in their Christmas stocking. Our grandchild is too young to respond to any beguiling but his mother and father's. It will be touch and go whether I live long enough for us to enjoy being in each other's company.

"Are you writing?" people ask — out of politeness, undoubtedly. And I say, "Nothing very much." The truth but not the whole truth — which is that I seem to have lost touch with the place that stories and novels come from. I have no idea why.

I still like making sentences.

Every now and then, in my waking moments, and especially when I am in the country, I stand and look hard at everything.

JOHN MCPHEE

Silk Parachute

FROM THE NEW YORKER

WHEN YOUR MOTHER is ninety-nine years old, you have so many memories of her that they tend to overlap, intermingle, and blur. It is extremely difficult to single out one or two, impossible to remember any that exemplify the whole.

It has been alleged that when I was in college she heard that I had stayed up all night playing poker and wrote me a letter that used the word "shame" forty-two times. I do not recall this.

I do not recall being pulled out of my college room and into the church next door.

It has been alleged that on December 24, 1936, when I was five years old, she sent me to my room at or close to 7 P.M. for using four-letter words while trimming the Christmas tree. I do not recall that.

The assertion is absolutely false that when I came home from high school with an A-minus she demanded an explanation for the minus.

It has been alleged that she spoiled me with protectionism, because I was the youngest child and therefore the most vulnerable to attack from overhead — an assertion that I cannot confirm or confute, except to say that facts don't lie.

We lived only a few blocks from the elementary school and routinely ate lunch at home. It is reported that the following dialogue and ensuing action occurred on January 22, 1941:

"Eat your sandwich."

"I don't want to eat my sandwich."

"I made that sandwich, and you are going to eat it, Mister Man.

You filled yourself up on penny candy on the way home, and now you're not hungry."

"I'm late. I have to go. I'll eat the sandwich on the way back to school."

"Promise?"

"Promise."

Allegedly, I went up the street with the sandwich in my hand and buried it in a snowbank in front of Dr. Wright's house. My mother, holding back the curtain in the window of the side door, was watching. She came out in the bitter cold, wearing only a light dress, ran to the snowbank, dug out the sandwich, chased me up Nassau Street, and rammed the sandwich down my throat, snow and all. I do not recall any detail of that story. I believe it to be a total fabrication.

There was the case of the missing Cracker Jack at Lindel's corner store. Flimsy evidence pointed to Mrs. McPhee's smallest child. It has been averred that she laid the guilt on with the following words: "'Like mother, like son' is a saying so true, the world will judge largely of mother by you." It has been asserted that she immediately repeated that proverb three times, and also recited it on other occasions too numerous to count. I have absolutely no recollection of her saying that about the Cracker Jack or any other controlled substance.

We have now covered everything even faintly unsavory that has been reported about this person in ninety-nine years, and even those items are a collection of rumors, half-truths, prevarications, false allegations, inaccuracies, innuendos, and canards.

This is the mother who — when Alfred Knopf wrote her twenty-two-year-old son a letter saying, "The readers' reports in the case of your manuscript would not be very helpful, and I think might discourage you completely" — said, "Don't listen to Alfred Knopf. Who does Alfred Knopf think he is, anyway? Someone should go in there and k-nock his block off." To the best of my recollection, that is what she said.

I also recall her taking me, on or about March 8, my birthday, to the theater in New York every year, beginning in childhood. I remember those journeys as if they were today. I remember *A Connecticut Yankee*. Wednesday, March 8, 1944. Evidently, my father had written for the tickets, because she and I sat in the last row of the second balcony. Mother knew what to do about that. She gave me for my birthday an elegant spyglass, sufficient in power to bring the Connecticut Yankee back from Vermont. I sat there watching the play through my telescope, drawing as many guffaws from the surrounding audience as the comedy on the stage.

On one of those theater days — when I was eleven or twelve — I asked her if we could start for the city early and go out to La Guardia Field to see the comings and goings of airplanes. The temperature was well below the freeze point and the March winds were so blustery that the wind-chill factor was forty below zero. Or seemed to be. My mother figured out how to take the subway to a stop in Jackson Heights and a bus from there — a feat I am unable to duplicate to this day. At La Guardia, she accompanied me to the observation deck and stood there in the icy wind for at least an hour, maybe two, while I, spellbound, watched the DC-3s coming in on final, their wings flapping in the gusts. When we at last left the observation deck, we went downstairs into the terminal, where she bought me what appeared to be a black rubber ball but on closer inspection was a pair of hollow hemispheres hinged on one side and folded together. They contained a silk parachute. Opposite the hinge, each hemisphere had a small nib. A piece of string wrapped round and round the two nibs kept the ball closed. If you threw it high into the air, the string unwound and the parachute blossomed. If you sent it up with a tennis racket, you could put it into the clouds. Not until the development of the ten-megabyte hard disk would the world ever know such a fabulous toy. Folded just so, the parachute never failed. Always, it floated back to you — silkily, beautifully — to start over and float back again. Even if you abused it, whacked it really hard — gracefully, lightly, it floated back to you.

MARY OLIVER

Building the House

FROM SHENANDOAH

1

I KNOW a young man who can build almost anything — a boat, a
fence, kitchen cabinets, a table, a barn, a house. And so serenely,
and in so assured and right a manner, that it is joy to watch him.
All the same, what he seems to care for best — what he seems
positively to desire — is the hour of interruption, of hammerless
quiet, in which he will sit and write down poems or stories that
have come into his mind with clambering and colorful force. Truly
he is not very good at the puzzle of words — not nearly as good
as he is with the mallet and the measuring tape — but this in no
way lessens his pleasure. Moreover, he is in no hurry. Everything
he learned, he learned at a careful pace — will not the use of
words come easier at last, though he begin at the slowest amble?
Also, in these intervals, he is happy. In building things, he is his
familiar self, which he does not overvalue. But in the act of writing
he is a grander man, a surprise to us, and even more to himself.
He is beyond what he believed himself to be.

I understand his pleasure. I also know the enclosure of my skills,
and am no less pert than he when some flow takes me over the
edge of it. Usually, as it happens, this is toward the work in which
he is so capable. There appears in my mind a form; I imagine it
from boards of a certain breadth and length, and nails, and all in
cheerful response to some need I have or think I have, aligned
with a space I see as opportunistic. I would not pry my own tooth,
or cobble my own shoes, but I deliberate unfazed the niceties of

woodworking — nothing, all my life, has checked me. At my side at this moment is a small table with one leg turned in slightly. For I have never at all built anything perfectly, or even very well, in spite of the pleasure such labor gives me. Nor am I done yet, though time has brought obstacles and spread them before me — a stiffness of the fingers, a refusal of the eyes to switch easily from near to far, or rather from far to near, and thus to follow the aim of the hammer toward the nail head, which yearly grows smaller, and smaller.

Once, in fact, I built a house. It was a minuscule house, a one-room, one-floored affair set in the ivies and vincas of the backyard, and made almost entirely of salvaged materials. Still, it had a door. And four windows. And, miraculously, a peaked roof, so I could stand easily inside, and walk around. After it was done, and a door hung, I strung a line from the house so that I could set a lamp upon the built-in table, under one of the windows. Across the yard, in the evening with the lamplight shining outward, it looked very sweet, and it gave me much satisfaction. It seemed a thing of great accomplishment, as indeed, for me, it was. It was the house I had built. There would be no other.

The labor of writing poems, of working with thought and emotion in the encasement (or is it the wings?) of language is strange to nature, for we are first of all creatures of motion. Only secondly — only oddly, and not naturally, at moments of contemplation, joy, grief, prayer, or terror — are we found, while awake, in the posture of deliberate or hapless inaction. But such is the posture of the poet, poor laborer. The dancer dances, the painter dips and lifts and lays on the oils; the composer reaches at least across the octaves. The poet sits. The architect draws and measures, and travels to the quarry to tramp among the gleaming stones. The poet sits, or, if it is a fluid moment, he scribbles some words upon the page. The body, under this pressure of nonexisting, begins to draw up like a muscle, and complain. An unsolvable disharmony of such work — the mind so hotly fired and the body so long quiescent — will come sooner or later to revolution, will demand action! For many years, in a place I called Blackwater Woods, I wrote while I walked. That motion, hardly more than a dreamy sauntering, worked for me; it kept my body happy while I scribbled. But sometimes it wasn't at all enough. I wanted to build, in the other way, with the teeth of the saw, and the explosions of the hammer, and the little shrieks of the screws winding down into their perfect nests.

2

I began the house when I returned one spring after a year of teaching in a midwestern city. I had been, for months, responsible, sedate, thoughtful, and, for most of my daylight hours, indoors. I was sick for activity. And so, instead of lingering on the porch with my arrangement of tools, banging and punching together some simple and useful thing — another bookshelf, another table — I began the house.

When anything is built in our town, it is more importantly a foundation than a structure. Nothing — be it ugly, nonconforming, in violation of bylaws or neighbors' rights — nothing, once up, has ever been torn down. And almost nothing exists as it was originally constructed. On our narrow strip of land we are a build-up, add-on society. My house today, crooked as it is, stands. It has an undeniable value: it exists. It may therefore be enlarged eventually, even unto rentable proportions. The present owners of the property would not dream of discarding it. I can see from the road, they have given it a new roof and straightened out some doubtful portions of the peaked section. To one end of the peak they have attached a metal rod which holds, in the air above the house, a statue of a heron, in the attitude of easy flight. My little house, looking upward, must be astonished.

The tools I used in my building of the house, and in all my labor of this sort, were a motley assortment of hand tools: hammer, tack hammer, drivers of screws, rasps, planes, saws small-toothed and rip, pliers, wrenches, awls. They had once belonged to my grandfather, and some of them to my great-grandfather, who was a carpenter of quality, and used the finer title cabinetmaker. This man I know only from photographs and an odd story or two: for example, he built his own coffin, of walnut, and left it, to be ready when needed, with the town mortician. Eventually, like the tiniest of houses, and with his body inside, it was consumed by flame.

These tools, though so closely mine, were not made therefore easy for me to use. I was, frankly, accident-prone; while I was making anything, my hands and shins and elbows, if not other parts of my body, were streaked with dirt and nicks. Gusto, not finesse, was my trademark here. And often enough, with these tools, I would come to a place where I could not wrest some necessary motion from my own wrists, or lift, or cut through. Then I would have to wait, in frustration, for a friend or acquaintance, or even a stranger — male, and stronger than I — to come along, and I would simply ask for help to get past that instant, that twist of the screw. Provincetown men, though they may seem rough to the unknowing, are as delicious and courteous as men are made. "Sure, darling," the plumber would say, or the neighbor passing by, or the fisherman stepping over from his yard, and he would help me, and would make a small thing of it.

3

Whatever a house is to the heart and body of man — refuge, comfort, luxury — surely it is as much or more to the spirit. Think how often our dreams take place inside the houses of our imaginations! Sometime these are fearful, gloomy, enclosed places. At other times they are bright and have many windows and are even surrounded by gardens combed and invitational, or unpathed and wild. Surely such houses appearing in our sleep-work represent the state of the soul, or, if you prefer it, the state of the mind. Real estate, in any case, is not the issue of dreams. The condition of our true and private self is what dreams are about. If you rise refreshed from a dream — a night's settlement inside some house that has filled you with pleasure — you are doing okay. If you wake to the memory of squeezing confinement, rooms without air or light, a door difficult or impossible to open, a troubling disorganization or even wreckage inside, you are in trouble — with yourself. There are (dream) houses that pin themselves upon the windy porches of mountains, that open their own windows and summon in flocks of wild and colorful birds — and there are houses that hunker upon narrow ice floes adrift upon endless, dark waters; houses that creak, houses that sing; houses that will say nothing at all to you though you beg and plead all night for some answer to your vexing questions.

As such houses in dreams are mirrors of the mind or the soul, so an actual house, such as I began to build, is at least a little of the inner state made manifest. Jung, in a difficult time, slowly built a stone garden and a stone tower. Thoreau's house at Walden Pond, ten feet by fifteen feet under the tall, arrowy pines, was surely a dream-shape come to life. For anyone, stepping away from actions where one knows one's measure is good. It shakes away an excess of seriousness. Building my house, or anything else, I always felt myself becoming, in an almost devotional sense, passive, and willing to play. Play is never far from the impress of the creative drive, never far from the happiness of discovery. Building my house, I was joyous all day long.

The material issue of a house, however, is a matter not so much of imagination and spirit as it is of particular, joinable, weighty substance — it is brick and wood, it is foundation and beam, sash and sill; it is threshold and door and the latch upon the door. In the seventies and the eighties, in this part of the world if not everywhere, there was an ongoing, monstrous binge of building, or tearing back and rebuilding — and carting away of old materials to the (then-titled) dump. Which, in those days, was a lively and even social place. Work crews made a continual effort toward bull-dozing the droppings from the trucks into some sort of order, shoving at least a dozen categories of broken and forsaken materials, along with reusable materials, into separate areas. Gulls, in flocks like low white clouds, screamed and rippled over the heaps of lumber, looking for garbage that was also dumped, often in no particular area. Motels, redecorating, would bring three hundred mattresses in the morning, three hundred desks in the afternoon. Treasures, of course, were abundantly sought and found. And good wood — useful wood — wood it was a sin to bury, not to use again. The price of lumber had not yet skyrocketed, so even new lumber lay seamed in with the old, the price passed on to the customer. Cutoffs, and lengths. Pine, fir, oak flooring, shingles of red and white cedar, ply, cherry trim, also tar paper and insulation, screen doors new and old, and stovepipe old and new, and bricks, and, more than once, some power tools left carelessly, I suppose, in a truck bed, under the heaps of trash. This is where I went for my materials, along with others, men and women both, who simply roved, attentively, through all the mess until they found what they needed, or felt they would, someday, use. Clothes, furniture, dolls, old highchairs, bikes; once a metal bank in the shape of a dog, very old; once a set of copper-bottomed cookware still in its original cartons; once a bag of old Christmas cards swept from the house of a man who had died only a month or so earlier, in almost every one of them a dollar bill.

Here I found everything I needed, including nails from half-full boxes spilled into the sand. All I lacked — only because I lacked the patience to wait until it came along — was one of the ridge beams; this I bought at the local lumber company and paid cash for; thus the entire house cost me $3.58.

Oh, the intimidating and beautiful hardwoods! No more could I cut across the cherry or walnut or the oak than across stone! It was pine I looked for, with its tawny pattern of rings, its crisp knots, its willingness to be broken, cut, split, and its fragrance that never reached the air but made the heart gasp with its sweetness. Plywood I had no love of, though I took it when found and used it when I could, knowing it was no real thing, and alien to the weather, and apt to parch and swell, or buckle, or rot. Still, I used it. My little house was a patchwork. It was organic as a garden. It was free of any promise of exact inches, though at last it achieved a fair if not a strict linearity. On its foundation of old railroad ties, its framing of old wood, old ply, its sheets of tar paper, its rows of pale shingles, it stood up. Stemming together everything with sixpenny nails, eightpenny nails, spikes, screws, I was involved, frustrated, devoted, resolved, nicked and scraped, delighted. The work went slowly. The roof went on, was shingled with red cedar. I was a poet, but I was away for a while from the loom of thought and formal language; I was playing. I was whimsical, absorbed, happy. Let me always be who I am, and then some.

When my house was finished, my friend Stanley Kunitz gave me a yellow door, discarded from his house at the other end of town. Inside, I tacked up a van Gogh landscape, a Blake poem, a photograph of Mahler, a picture M. had made with colored chalk. Some birds' nests hung in the corners. I lit the lamp. I was done.

4

There is something you can tell people over and over, and with feeling and eloquence, and still never say it well enough for it to be more than news from abroad — people have no readiness for it, no empathy. It is the news of personal aging — of climbing, and knowing it, to some unrepeatable pitch and coming forth on the other side, which is pleasant still but which is, unarguably, different — which is the beginning of descent. It is the news that no one is singular, that no argument will change the course, that one's time is more gone than not, and what is left waits to be spent gracefully and attentively, if not quite so actively. The plumbers in town now are the sons of our old plumber. I cut some pine boards for some part of an hour, and I am tired. A year or so ago, hammering, I hit my thumb, directly and with force, and lost the nail for a half year. I was recently given a power drill, which also sets and removes screws. It could be a small cannon, so apprehensive am I of its fierce and quick power. When I handle it well (which to begin with means that I aim it correctly), difficult tasks are made easy. But when I do not, I hold an angry weasel in my hand.

I hardly used the little house — it became a place to store some garden tools, boxes of this or that. Did I write one poem there? Yes, I did, and a few more. But its purpose never was to be shelter for thought. I built it *to build it,* stepped out over the threshold, and was gone.

I don't think I am old yet, or done with growing. But my perspective has altered — I am less hungry for the busyness of the body, more interested in the tricks of the mind. I am gaining, also, a new affection for wood that is useless, that has been tossed out, that merely exists, quietly, wherever it has ended up. Planks on the beach rippled and salt-soaked. Pieces of piling, full of the tunnels of shipworm. In the woods, fallen branches of oak, of maple, of the dear, wind-worn pines. They lie on the ground and do nothing. They are travelers on the way to oblivion.

The young man now — that carpenter we began with — places his notebook carefully beside him and rises and, as though he had just come back from some great distance, looks around. There are his tools, there is the wood; there is his unfinished task, to which, once more, he turns his attention. But life is no narrow business. On any afternoon he may hear and follow this same rhapsody, turning from his usual labor, swimming away into the pleasures, the current of language. More power to him!

For myself, I have passed him by and have gone into the woods. Near the path, one of the tall maples has fallen. It is early spring, so the crimped, maroon flowers are just emerging. Here and there slabs of the bark have exploded away in the impact of its landing. But, mostly, it lies as it stood, though not such a net for the wind as it was. What is it now? What does it signify? Not Indolence, surely, but something, all the same, that balances with Ambition. Call it Rest. I sit on one of the branches. My idleness suits me. I am content. I have built my house. The blue butterflies, called azures, twinkle up from the secret place where they have been waiting. In their small blue dresses they float among the branches, they come close to me, one rests for a moment on my wrist. They do not recognize me as anything very different from this enfoldment of leaves, this wind-roarer, this wooden palace lying down, now, upon the earth, like anything heavy, and happy, and full of sunlight, and half asleep.

TIM ROBINSON

Orion the Hunter

FROM THE RECORDER

for John Moriarty

I READ TOO MUCH, remember little, understand nothing —
nothing to its core, that is; on the outer surfaces of knowledge I
handle myself well enough, browsing with a goat's eclecticism. Piles
of books by my bed, tottering like the jungle cities I used to dream
of as a teenager, occasionally fall by night and frighten my little
terrier bitch asleep in her basket.

The following happened at some late hour. The dog went to the
door — the bedroom opens onto the garden — and whined. After
a while I closed my book on the name of Chios, and got up to let
her out. A vertical blade of cold air entered. Small-eyed from print,
I peered through the gap. The leafless birch at the end of the lawn
was motionless, blanched by the shaft of light from the door.
Above, spanning the perfect blackness, hung a huge empty frame-
work of stars. My breath caught in my throat, as always when I'm
confronted. Orion the Hunter, a mile high, a thousand miles high.

Orion is at once the most overbearingly transcendent of constellations and the most immediately, most humanly identifiable. One
notices his belt first, three stars of equal magnitude evenly spaced,
slanting up the sky in a line almost exactly straight but just percep-
tibly upcurved too, like sequent notes of a scale, a hunting horn's
bright echoing challenge. Above that, a perfect (to my eye) Py-
thagorean 3:4:5 triangle, the longest side horizontal and marked
out by two bright stars, the vertex a little fainter, the whole tensed
across a wide sector of the night. As a child I learned from my
father that this was Orion's bow, raised and drawn, but star charts

now tell me it is his club or his shoulders. The hero's sword is a
line of dim stars depending from his belt, and his feet are two very
prominent stars. Farther down the sky to the east is the most
brilliant of all, Sirius, the Dog Star; I remember my father pointing
out how it followed its master through the night.

On my way back to bed I picked out a few reference books from
the shelves: Lemprière's *Classical Dictionary,* some modern equivalent of it, and Graves's crotchety old Penguins of Greek myths.

It seems that Sirius is not in fact Orion's dog; its legend is quite
separate, part of a horrible mutual engendering of monsters from
the most primitive level of myth. Echidna, half woman, half snake,
mates with Typhon and gives birth to Hell's three-headed watch-
dog Cerberus, the many-headed Hydra, the Chimaera, and Sirius,
a two-headed dog that later belonged to the robber Geryon and
itself sired two baleful creatures on its own mother, the Sphinx and
the Nemean Lion. Both Sirius and the lion were to be killed by
Heracles. All this from Hesiod's *Theogony* — but my father's word
prevails over this most ancient and therefore probably corrupt
source: a hunter needs a dog, and Sirius is Orion's, and always will
be. The bow, too, is not in the ancient sources, according to which
Orion flourishes his club at a flock of doves, the little constellation
of the Pleiades, fluttering just beyond his reach to the west. When
Odysseus, on the shores of the River of Ocean, fills a trench with
sacrificial blood and stands over it with drawn sword to keep back
the mighty dead who come to drink, he sees among them "the
giant hunter Orion, rounding up game on the meadows of aspho-
del, the very beasts his living hands had killed among the lonely
hills, armed with a club of solid bronze that could never be broken." The name Orion means "dweller on mountains."

What is this tale of the Pleiades? They were the seven virgin
companions of Artemis the Huntress, whom the gods turned into
doves to save them from Orion's pursuit. Orion had been hunting
with Artemis, and her brother Apollo was concerned for her chas-
tity too, and incited Mother Earth against him by telling her of
Orion's boast that he would kill off all beasts and monsters. Earth
sent a huge scorpion against Orion, who leaped into the sea and
swam toward Delos, where once he had slept with Eos, the god-
dess Dawn. Apollo pointed out the distant figure among the waves
to Artemis and told her that it was a villain who had seduced one

of her priestesses, and in her anger she shot an arrow through
Orion's head; then, grief-stricken, she asked Asclepius to cure him,
but Asclepius was destroyed by a thunderbolt from Zeus before he
could do so. Finally Artemis placed Orion's image in the stars,
where it is eternally pursued across the sky by the constellation
Scorpio.

Eos, I read, still blushes in remembering her affair with Orion.
Their meeting is part of another legend in which the hunting of
beasts is entangled with the violation of woman. Orion had promised to rid the island of Chios of wild beasts, in return for the king's
daughter Merope; but when he came to claim his reward, the king
put him off with false reports of other beasts to be killed. The
frustrated hunter got drunk, burst into Merope's room and raped
her, and then fell into a stupor on the shore. The vengeful king
found him there, and put out his eyes as he slept. The oracle later
told Orion that he could regain his sight by traveling east until he
faced Heleus, the sun, rising from the Stream of Ocean. So Orion
rowed out to sea, and followed the sound of hammers until he
came to Vulcan's forge, where he snatched up an apprentice,
Cedalion, to be his guide. Cedalion led him to the farthest ocean,
where Eos saw and fell in love with him — for he was "the hand-
somest of men" — and persuaded her brother Heleus to cure him.

What is one to make of this barbaric stuff? Searching for solace
in the brutal rigmaroles of the Orion legend, my mind went back
to a painting that arrested me once and made me stay and wonder,
as I was making my way, footsore and eye-sated, out of the Metro-
politan Museum of Art in New York: Poussin's *Landscape with Orion*.
I wished I had a clearer memory of it, or a reproduction. The
landscape radiates cool light like cumulus clouds from which dawn
is about to break. Cedalion is a tiny figure perched on Orion's
shoulder and bending to his ear with encouraging words. Vulcan
indicates the way ahead, a sheep track winding through a tender,
spacious countryside with noble trees in the middle distance and
a richly various mountain skyline; one imagines birdsong and
rippling streams. In the twilit sky Artemis observes the hero pro-
tectively from a pearly cleft in the clouds like the aperture of a
cowrie shell. Orion is huge but not monstrous, a splendid golden-
skinned figure of a man, striding forward in joyful expectation, his
arms swimming before him in the air. I may have misremembered

the details, but of this I am sure, that every form in the painting is opulent, restorative, pregnant with happiness and perhaps with reconciliation, between the terrible hunter and the peaceful hills, between gods and mortals, and even, without forcing the sense of the legend too much, between man and woman.

As I reached for a pen to make a note of this, I heard my little dog's excited voice from the shrubbery, more of a whimper than a bark, and then a deep baying that seemed to roll around some huge, unidentifiable volume of space. The door, which I had left slightly ajar for the dog when it should choose to come in, was pushed a little wider open. Something blackish disengaged itself from black night in the gap, and slipped inside. Every instinct in my body cried out that it was an animal — its scent immediately filled the room, as complicated as a thicket, with flowers and bitter berries and foxy dung beneath — but I could see that it was human: a slight, ragged, dark-visaged male. My breath stopped in my throat, but he showed he meant no harm by turning to leave his stick propped in a corner. He was so thin he looked as if he were edgeways-on even when he turned to me, and perhaps only four or five feet tall but so crooked and angular he might have been able to stretch up to the ceiling. I would have spoken, but he glanced at my mouth as if it were an unusual plant, and this silenced me. He looked around for a place for himself; I indicated the chair opposite the foot of the bed, but he settled down into the space between it and a lamp on the floor, entwining his fingers on one bent knee and resting his chin on them. His eyes were blue like old ice, but fixed, as if they were part of a frozen mass filling his skull. He was old; he might have been newly delivered out of the ages like a corpse given up by a glacier. It was difficult in the complicated half-lights of my various lamps to distinguish his tattered, thong-tied clothes from his skin, which was seamed and scarred; even the backs of his hands buckled in ridges as he flexed his fingers. His tawny, ash-streaked hair was tied back with a convolvulus stem that carried two or three dying blossoms of stained ivory. But there was wealth about him too, gleams of amber and quartz in the caverns of his sleeves. The perspective of the room seemed to have reorganized itself around him, as if his body were of such a density as to distort space; he lay at the bottom of a depth; I was clinging to the rim. I could make nothing of him; incompre-

hensibility was ingrained in him like a darkness. He projected
shadows round the room, wolf packs of them shifting in corners,
isolated scraps of spiderweb drifting across the ceiling. These
appearances were his language, I knew, as were the effluvia filling
my nostrils: spore-borne fungal damps, aromatic mist-globules
sprayed from trodden beechmast, hazy reek of grass fires beyond
the horizon; and even closer feelings: a sliver of muddy ice in my
mouth, a river-cold nugget of gold in my palm, the suck of a snail
pulled off my forehead. I could do nothing with these forcings of
my senses; I opened books — astronomy came to hand — and
flung my thoughts against him.

Orion, I began, mighty hunter! — and suddenly all the scents
and skin-touchings were withdrawn and the flickering shades became still and attentive — Can you conceive of the vastness of
space, and how you are honored in it? Consider the fundamental
datum of our cosmos, the speed of light, a hundred and eighty-six
thousand miles a second, large beyond imagination, but crucially
not infinite, whose finitude in fact gives scale to all things. Even at
that unsurpassable velocity, light takes six hundred and fifty years
to reach Earth from your left foot, the star called Rigel. That's how
many trillions of miles? Those numbers: quadrillions, sextillions! I
used to mouth them like mantras as a child, and last night I came
across them for the first time in years, in Walt Whitman: "I hold a
leaf of grass to be the journeywork of the stars . . . and the mouse
is a miracle to confound a quadrillion atheists!" What's the relationship of the leaf to the star? A poet friend once remarked on
the accuracy with which the sunbeam strikes the seed — being
ignorant of the sun's copious output of light in all directions,
falling indifferently on good grain or stony ground or, most of
it, on nothing, anywhere, ever. Unimaginable floods of photons
poured forth by distant suns, that we can see them! Do you know
anything of stars? Your eastern shoulder: Betelgeuse, noticeably
reddish on a clear night, a "red giant" in the star catalogues; four
hundred times the diameter of the sun, ten thousand times as
luminous, but a mere dot to us, being two hundred and seventy
light-years away. I'll tell you what the visibility of that dot implies. Betelgeuse emits so many photons that even when they have
spread out over the surface of a sphere two hundred and seventy
light-years in radius — that's one and a half million billion miles

— they are still dense enough for our eyes to detect them, so there must be several of them passing through each little area the size of the pupil of an eye every second. Imagine that spherical surface divided up into elements a tenth of an inch across, like a composite insect eye of a zillion facets, but introverted, focused on its own center, absorbing star-dazzle in its totality into retinal blackness! But the adjustment of star to eye is illusory: a nearer or brighter star would burn out the optic nerve, and there are uncountable fainter and farther ones peppering the void in bottomless gradations whose photons arrive too thinly for our senses. Do these abysses make you dizzy? They are as nothing to the background, the galaxy as a whole, the catherine wheel we see from within as the Milky Way, a hundred thousand light-years across, built of a hundred billion stars. Which itself is as nothing among the several hundred billion galaxies spattered throughout space and fading out of vision fifteen billion light-years away. Your stars are bright because they are comparatively near, they all belong to the same spiral of our galaxy as the sun; we call it the Orion Arm, you are part of our address. The familiar constellations are the nursery decorations of life, though that's their significance. Do you want to know how life begins, O Great Engenderer? It could be happening within you at this moment! Consider that vague smudge of light among the stars of your sword — or is it an ejaculation of your phallus? — the Orion Nebula, a cloud of matter millions of miles across, all of a glow from the birth of stars within it. Whorls of gas pulled in on themselves by their own gravity, condensing into spheres, pressures rising, atomic reactions beginning. And when stars have gone through their long evolution — almost as long as all the past — and ever more complex processes in them have built the heavier nuclei out of hydrogen, the simple primordial stuff, they collapse inward, and then explode, and suffuse space with carbon, nitrogen, iron, and the rest, the rich and rare. Rigel, a "bright supergiant," only twenty times as big as the sun but a hundred thousand times as luminous, an old star as stars go, is burning itself down to such a catastrophe. In the hearts of nebulae like yours, sheltered from the ultraviolet radiation that disinfects open space, these elements can settle in the microscopic grooves on grains of dust and combine themselves into molecules as complex even as amino acids, the keys to self-replication, to life itself.

The journeywork of the stars! Then all they have to do is fall with meteors onto a hospitable planet like ours, not too far from a decent star, and in no time at all — amoeba, birds of paradise, pyramids, computers! Perhaps it's all happened elsewhere a trillion times, perhaps it has only happened once, and that's why you have had to come here to learn about yourself. But note this: the distances from here to your several stars are quite various; I have the statistics. Your dog, Sirius, is the brightest star in our sky only because it is one of the nearest, just 8.8 light-years, that's no more than fifty million million miles. So your splendid outline is a trick of perspective. Viewed from the Pole Star, for instance, you do not exist. "Constellation" is the name of an act, the quintessentially human act of joining up the dots, leaping over the dark, stringing events into stories, stories into persons, persons into history. Before we came, stars unnamed bloomed and seeded and blew away like dandelion fluff. And we may not always be here to keep up the pretense of meaning. We could, out of shame at the brief trouble of thought, memory, and lust we have brought upon the earth, commit suicide. We have the means, we have the bombs, it needs only the will. I like to imagine a few uncomprehending survivors — descendants of prisoners forgotten in a salt mine, say — emerging into a world of calcined cities and caramelized nature; they explore, they come to understand that humanity has done away with itself, they creep back underground and immure themselves, to keep faith with our ultimate loss of faith. That could be how it ends. Or indefinitely elsewise, with slow trailing edges, stories petering out into points of suspension, constellations drifting out of shape. And afterward, just the dislocated clockwork bits of heaven ratcheting away, to no end, world without end. Or can you see better in the future? Einstein wondered if a traveler at the speed of light carrying a mirror would find himself reflected in it. What did you see, riding time into my quiet historical garden, O Dweller on the Mountains?

The figure opposite me remained absolutely silent and still. All the wild sensations had withdrawn into him and the room was left an empty geometry. Time must have flowed on, though, like a trickle of meltwater under a glacier, for in the end a signal came: a bark that rattled the windows like a cannon shot, from the end of the garden, or the end of the world, I couldn't tell which. The hunter stood, and stretched and yawned, took up his stick — it was a little bow, I saw, with a thin knotted thong for a string — and stepped out into the glow of dawn. Very slowly the room was emptied of strangeness, as if he were drawing after him long dim tatters, glittering streamers, dazzling billowy starry banners.

After a while my dog came in, momentarily turned the unreadable black roundels of her eyes and nose toward me, and hopped into her basket. And I lay down, stretching out my hand to her who sleeps beside me.

OLIVER SACKS

Water Babies

FROM THE NEW YORKER

WE WERE ALL water babies, all four of us. Our father, who was a swimming champ (he won the fifteen-mile race off the Isle of Wight three years in succession) and loved swimming more than anything else, introduced each of us to the water when we were scarcely a week old. Swimming is instinctive at this age, so, for better or worse, we never "learned" to swim.

I was reminded of this recently when I visited the Caroline Islands, in Micronesia, where I saw even toddlers diving fearlessly into the lagoons and swimming, typically, with a sort of dog paddle. Everyone there swims, nobody is "unable" to swim, and the islanders' swimming skills are superb. Magellan and other navigators, reaching Micronesia in the sixteenth century, were astounded at such skills and, seeing the islanders swim and dive, bounding from wave to wave, could not help comparing them to dolphins. The children, in particular, were so at home in the water that they appeared, in the words of one explorer, "more like fish than human beings." (It was from the Pacific Islanders that, early in this century, we Westerners learned the crawl, the beautiful, powerful ocean stroke that they had perfected — so much better, so much more fitted to the human form than the frog-like breaststroke chiefly used until that time.)

For myself, I have no memory of being taught to swim; I learned my strokes, I think, by swimming with my father — though the slow, measured, mile-eating stroke he had (he was a powerful man who weighed nearly eighteen stone) was not entirely suited to a little boy. But I could see how my old man, huge and cumbersome on land, became transformed — graceful, like a porpoise — in the water; and I, self-conscious, nervous, and also rather clumsy, found the same delicious transformation in myself, found a new being, a new mode of being, in the water. I have a vivid memory of a summer holiday at the seaside, in England, the month after my fifth birthday, when I ran into my parents' room and tugged at the great whale-like bulk of my father. "Come on, Dad!" I said. "Let's come for a swim." He turned over slowly and opened one eye: "What do you mean, waking an old man of forty-three like this at six in the morning?" Now that my father is dead, and I myself am sixty-three, this memory of so long ago tugs, makes me equally want to laugh and cry.

Adolescence was a bad time. I developed a strange skin disease: *Erythema annulare centrifugum,* said one expert; *Erythema gyratum perstans,* said another — fine, rolling, orotund words, but neither of the experts could do anything, and I was covered in weeping sores. Looking, or at least feeling, like a leper, I dared not strip at a beach or pool, and could only occasionally, if I was lucky, find a remote lake or tarn.

At Oxford, my skin suddenly cleared, and the sense of relief was so intense that I wanted to swim nude, to feel the water streaming over every part of me without hindrance. Sometimes I would go swimming, at dawn, at Parsons' Pleasure, a bend of the Cherwell, a preserve since the 1680s or earlier for nude bathing, and peopled, one felt, by the ghosts of Swinburne and Clough. On summer afternoons, I would take a punt on the Cherwell, find a secluded place to moor it, and then go swimming lazily for the rest of the day. Sometimes at night I would go for long runs on the towpath by the Isis, past Iffley Lock, far beyond the confines of the city. And then I would dive in and swim in the river, till it and I seemed to flow together, become one.

Swimming became a dominant passion at Oxford, and after this there was no going back. When I came to New York, in the mid-sixties, I started to swim at Orchard Beach, in the Bronx, and would sometimes make the circuit of City Island — a swim that took me several hours. This, indeed, is how I found the house I now live in: I had stopped about halfway around to look at a charming gazebo by the water's edge, got out and strolled up the street, saw a little red house for sale, was shown round it (still dripping) by the puzzled owners, walked along to the real estate agent and convinced her of my interest (she was not used to customers in swim trunks), reentered the water on the other side of the island, and swam back to Orchard Beach, having acquired a house in midswim.

I was exceedingly fond of lake swimming, too, and often rented a room in a dilapidated old hotel on Lake Jefferson, in upstate New York — a smallish (fifty-acre), somewhat shallow lake, where no one motorboated or water-skied, and where I could swim or float on my back all day without danger, in a realm beyond boundaries or time. Many of my happiest weekends were spent swimming in this little lake — many of my most productive weekends, too, for there is something about being in water and swimming that alters my mood, gets my thoughts going, as nothing else can. Theories and stories would construct themselves in my mind as I swam to and fro, or round and round Lake Jeff. Sentences and paragraphs would write themselves in my mind, and at such times I would have to come to shore every so often to discharge them. Most of *A Leg to Stand On* was written in this way, the paragraphs forming themselves during long swims at Lake Jeff and being discharged, every half hour or so, drippingly, onto paper. (My publisher was puzzled by the water smudges and the running ink on the manuscript, and insisted that I have it typed.)

I tended to swim outside — I was hardier then — from April through November, but would swim at the local Y in the winter. In 1976–77, I was Top Distance Swimmer at the Mount Vernon Y, in Westchester: I swam five hundred lengths — six miles — in the contest and would have continued, but the judges said, "Enough! Please go home." One might think that five hundred lengths would be monotonous, boring, but I have never found swimming monotonous or boring. Swimming gave me a sort of joy, a sense of well-being so extreme that it became at times a sort of ecstasy. There was a total engagement in the act of swimming, in each stroke, and at the same time the mind could float free, become spellbound, in a state like a trance. I never knew anything so powerfully, so healthily euphoriant — and I was addicted to it, am still addicted, fretful when I cannot swim.

Duns Scotus, in the thirteenth century, spoke of *"condelectari sibi,"* the will finding delight in its own exercise; and Mihaly Csikszentmihalyi, in our own time, speaks about "flow." There is an essential rightness about swimming, as about all such flowing and, so to speak, *musical* activities. And then there is the wonder of buoyancy, of being suspended in this thick, transparent medium that supports and embraces us. One can move in water, play with it, in a way that has no analogue in the air. One can explore its dynamics, its flow, this way and that; one can move one's hands like propellers or direct them like little rudders; one can become a little hydroplane or submarine, investigating the physics of flow with one's own body.

And, beyond this, there is all the symbolism of swimming — its imaginative resonances, its mythic potentials.

My father called swimming "the elixir of life," and certainly it seemed to be so for him: he swam daily, slowing down only slightly with time, until the grand age of ninety-four. I hope I can follow him, and swim till I die.

The Page Turner

FROM THE THREEPENNY REVIEW

THE PAGE TURNER appears from the wings and walks onstage, into the light, a few seconds after the pianist and the cellist, just as the welcoming applause begins to wane. By her precise timing the page turner acknowledges, not so much humbly as serenely, lucidly, that the applause is not meant for her: she has no intention of appropriating any part of the welcome. She is onstage merely to serve a purpose, a worthy purpose even if a bit absurd — a concession, amid the coming glories, to the limitations of matter and of spirit. Precision of timing, it goes without saying, is the most important attribute of a page turner. Also important is unobtrusiveness.

But strive though she may to be unobtrusive, to dim or diminish her radiance in ways known only to herself, the page turner cannot render herself invisible, and so her sudden appearance onstage is as exciting as the appearance of the musicians; it gives the audience an unanticipated stab of pleasure. The page turner is golden-tressed — yes, "tresses" is the word for the mass of hair rippling down her back, hair that emits light like a shower of fine sparkles diffusing into the glow of the stage lights. She is young and tall, younger and taller than either of the musicians, who are squarish, unprepossessing middle-aged men. She wears black, a suitable choice for one who should be unobtrusive. Yet the arresting manner in which her black clothes shelter her flesh, flesh that seems molded like clay and yields to the fabric with a certain playful, even droll resistance, defies unobtrusiveness. Her black long-sleeved knit shirt reaches just below her waist, and the fabric of her perfectly fitting black slacks stirs gently around her narrow hips and thighs. Beyond the hem of her slacks can be glimpsed her shiny, but not too conspicuously shiny, black boots with a thick two-inch heel. Her face is heart-shaped, like the illustrations of princesses in fairy tales. The skin of her face and neck and hands, the only visible skin, is pale, an off-white like heavy cream or the best butter. Her lips are painted magenta.

Of course she is not a princess or even a professional beauty hired to enhance the decor but most likely, offstage, a music student, selected as a reward for achievement or for having demonstrated an ability to sit still and turn the pages at the proper moment. Or else she has volunteered for any number of practical reasons: to help pay for her studies, to gain experience of being onstage. Perhaps she should have been disqualified because of her appearance, which might distract from the music. But given the principles of fair play and equal opportunity, beauty can no more disqualify than plainness. For the moment, though, life offstage and whatever the page turner's place in it might be are far removed from the audience, transported as they are by the hair combed back from her high forehead and cascading in a loose, lacy mass that covers her back like a cloak.

In the waiting hush, the page turner lowers her body onto a chair to the left and slightly behind the pianist's seat, the fabric of her slacks adjusting around her recalcitrant hips, the hem rising a trifle to reveal more of her boots. She folds her white hands patiently in her lap like lilies resting on the surface of a dark pond and fixes her eyes on the sheets of music on the rack, her body calm but alert for the moment when she must perform her task.

After the musicians' usual tics and fussing, the pianist's last-minute swipes at face and hair, the cellist's slow and fastidious tuning of his instrument, his nervous flicking of his jacket away from his body as if to let his torso breathe, the music begins. The page turner, utterly still, waits. Very soon, she rises soundlessly and leans forward — and at this instant, with the right side of her upper body leaning over the pianist, the audience inevitably imagines him, feels him, inhaling the fragrance of her breast and arm, of her cascading hair; they imagine she exudes a delicate scent, lightly alluring but not so alluring as to distract the pianist, not more alluring than the music he plays.

She stays poised briefly in that leaning position until with a swift movement, almost a surprise yet unsurprising, she reaches her hand over to the right-hand page. The upper corner of the page is already turned down, suggesting that the page turner has prepared the music in advance, has, in her patient, able manner (more like a lady in waiting, really, than an idle fairy-tale princess), folded down all the necessary corners so that she need not fumble when the moment arrives. At the pianist's barely perceptible nod, she propels the page in the blink of an eye through its small leftward arc and smooths it flat, then seats herself, her body drifting lightly yet firmly, purposefully, down to the chair. Once again the edge of her short shirt sinks into her waist and the folds of her slacks reassemble beguilingly over her hips; the hem of her slacks rises to reveal more of her shiny boots. With her back straight, her seated body making a slender black L shape, once again she waits with hands folded, and very soon rises, quite silently, to perform the same set of movements. Soon this becomes a ritual, expected and hypnotic, changeless and evocative.

The page turner listens attentively but appears, fittingly, unmoved by the music itself; her body is focused entirely on her task, which is a demanding one, not simply turning the pages at the proper moments but dimming her presence, suppressing everything of herself except her attentiveness. But as able as she proves to be at turning pages — never a split second late, never fumbling with the corners or making an excessive gesture — she cannot, in her helpless radiance, keep from absorbing all the visual energy in the concert hall. The performance taking place in the hall is a gift to the ear, and while all ears are fully occupied, satiated — the musicians being excellent, more than excellent, capable of seraphic sounds — the listeners' eyes are idle. The musicians are only moderately interesting to look at. The eyes crave occupation too. Offered a pleasure to match that of the ears, naturally the eyes accept the offering. They fix on the page turner — pale skin, black clothes, and gold tresses — who surely knows she is being watched, who cannot deflect the gaze of the audience, only absorb it into the deep well of her stillness, her own intent yet detached absorption in the music.

The very banality of her task lends her a dignity, adds a richness to her already rich presence, since it illustrates a crucial truth:

banality is necessary in the making of splendid music, or splendid anything for that matter, much like the pianist's probable clipping of his fingernails or the cellist's rosining of his bow, though such banalities are performed in private, which is just as well.

And then little by little, while the listeners' eyes yearn toward the page turner, it comes to appear that her purpose is not so banal after all, nor is she anything so common as a distraction. Instead it appears that she has an unusual and intimate connection with the music. She is not a physical expression of it, a living symbol; that would be too facile. More subtly, she might be an emanation of the music, a phantom conjured into being by the sounds, but her physical reality — her stylish clothes and shiny boots — contradicts this possibility, and besides, the audience has seen her enter minutes before the music began and can attest to her independent life. No, the connection must be this: though the pianist is clearly striking the keys and the cellist drawing the bow over the strings (with, incidentally, many unfortunate contortions of his face), it comes to seem, through the force of the audience's gaze, that the music is issuing from the page turner, effortlessly, or through some supernatural, indescribable effort, as she sits in her golden radiance and stillness. So that as the concert proceeds, the audience gazes ever more raptly at the page turner. By virtue of her beauty and their gaze, she has become an ineffable instrument — no longer a distraction but rather the very source of the music.

Though the concert is long, very long, the air in the hall remains charged with vitality, the seraphic sounds yielding an ecstasy for which the entranced listeners silently bless the page turner. But perhaps because the concert is long and the page turner is only human, not even a princess, she cannot maintain her aloof pose forever. Though not flagging in her task, without any lapse of efficiency, she begins to show her pleasure in the music as any ordinary person might: her eyelids tremble at a finely executed turn, her lips hint at a smile for a satisfying chord resolution. Her breathing is visible, her upper body rising and sinking with the undulations of the sounds swirling about her. She leans into the music, once or twice even swaying her body a bit. While undeniably pretty to watch, this relaxation of discipline is a sad portent. It suggests the concert has gone on almost long enough, that beauty cannot be endlessly sustained, and that we, too, cannot remain absorbed indefinitely in radiant stillness: we have our limits, even for ecstasy. Banality beckons us back to its leaden, relieving embrace. The ordinary, appreciative movements of the page turner are a signal that the concert will soon end. We feel an anticipatory nostalgia for the notes we are hearing, even for the notes we have not yet heard, have yet to hear, which will be the closing notes. The early notes of a concert lead us into a safe and luxuriant green meadow of sound, a kind of Eden of the ear, but there comes a point, the climax in the music's arc, when we grasp that the notes are curving back and leading us out of the meadow, back into silent and harsher weather.

And this impression of being led regrettably back to dailiness grows still stronger when now and then the pianist glances over at the page turner with a half-smile, a tacit acknowledgment related to some passage in the music, maybe to a little problem of page turning successfully overcome, a private performance within the public performance, which will remain forever unfathomed by the audience and for those instants makes us feel excluded. With their work almost over the performers can afford such small indulgences — a foretaste of the inevitable melancholy moment when audience and performers, alike excluded, will file out into their lives, stripped of this glory, relieved of its burden.

When the music ends, as it must, the page turner remains composed and still: unlike the musicians, she does not relax into triumphant relief. As they take their bows, they show intimate glimpses of themselves in the ardor of achievement, as well as a happy camaraderie — their arms around each other's shoulders — in which the page turner cannot share, just as she cannot share in the applause or show intimate glimpses of herself. She stands patiently beside her chair near the piano and then, with the same precise timing as at the start, leaves the stage a few seconds after the musicians, deftly gathering up the music from the rack to carry off with her, tidying up like a good lady in waiting.

The musicians reappear for more bows. The page turner does not reappear. Her service is completed. We understand her absence yet we miss her, as though an essential part of the lingering pleasure is being withheld, as though the essential instrument through which the music reached us has vanished along with the sounds themselves. We do not wish to think of what ordinary gestures she might now be performing off in the wings, putting the music away or lifting her hair off her neck with long staved-off weariness, released from the burden of being looked at. We cannot deny her her life, her future, yet we wish her to be only as she was onstage, in the beginning. We will forget how the musicians looked, but ever after when we revisit the music we will see the page turner — black clothes, golden hair, regal carriage — radiant and still, emitting the sounds that too briefly enraptured us.

LOUIS SIMPSON

Soldier's Heart

FROM THE HUDSON REVIEW

IT BEGINS in France in June of '44. Men are lying face down on the earth. The air is filled with sounds, shrieks that come out of the sky and terminate with an explosion. This may be a matter of seconds. If the sounds continue, the men will be seen scraping the surface of the earth with shovels and burying themselves in it until, like a species of animal, they vanish from sight. A head emerges now and looks around cautiously before disappearing again.

Or the men are walking up a road in two parallel lines, with an interval between every man and the one in front of him and the one behind. They are heavily burdened, with a pack on their back, and they are carrying rifles, machine guns, and mortars. If the shrieking from the sky begins, they will turn quickly out of the road and lie face down. Or they have spread out and are walking in an open field. An embankment runs across it — the railroad. There is a brief purring sound, then a rhythmic drumming. If you should happen to be with these men, it would sound as though the air were being torn. One of them falls. The others run forward and crouch in the shelter of the embankment.

Such is the life or death of an infantry soldier in France in the summer of 1944. These actions will be repeated many times . . . the scenery will change, from small fields separated by hedgerows to a flat landscape with windmills to a forest covered with snow. The soldiers will pass through villages. Now they are on the banks of a river, and rowing across in rubber boats. Finally they are among mountains.

I was discharged from the U.S. Army in 1945 and went home.

I returned to the university. I have a vague recollection of sitting with other students in a room — only a few around a long table. Some great book was being discussed; it was the course for upper-division students known as the Colloquium. I was reading furiously about . . . everything. When I was not reading I was writing stories, essays, poems. From what I have been told I would hardly stop to eat. The man with whom I shared an apartment on Morningside Heights told me that he would be making dinner, and would ask me if I wanted some, and I'd say no.

I had some success with all this typing — a short story was published in *Esquire*. I cannot bear to think of it — I do not recognize the young man who wrote it. It must have been the manic humor with which this tale about a man who ran a beauty salon was told that appealed to the editors.

What followed I do not know. One person had it that I lost my key to the apartment I was sharing, and was found lying unconscious outside the door. A friend would inform me in a letter that I had been wandering in the streets, and picked up by the police, and that I resisted violently. Both versions cannot be true — or were they referring to different episodes? Perhaps each of my informants brought to my "breakdown," as such things were called, his own idea of my character.

Shadows were moving around me. The blind man in the Bible said, "I see men as trees walking." So did I. The darkness cleared, and I was in a large room with barred windows, and saw men as they were.

I was in a hospital ward. It wasn't an army hospital, but Kings Park on Long Island. Why wasn't I in a veterans' hospital? I suppose that after the war they were too crowded, and the rest had to be put in other places. Or perhaps the members of my family did not know that there were such things as hospitals for veterans. The war had passed them by. My father died when I was a boy, and my mother was traveling in Latin America. She sold cosmetics and advised women how to make themselves beautiful — like the owner of the beauty salon in my story. The only other relatives I had were some aunts and an uncle. They did as they were told, signed the necessary papers, and I was sent to Kings Park.

What name have they given it now, the illness I had as a result of being shot at and shelled for months on end? I don't suppose many of our soldiers in the Gulf War have suffered from it — they were spared a long engagement. After Vietnam it was called "post-traumatic stress disorder." In World War II it was called "combat fatigue." In the Great War (I prefer that name, for the Great War was what people at the time thought it was) it was called "shell shock." In the Civil War it was "soldier's heart." This name strikes me as the best, for it describes an illness that involved my heart as much as my head. My heart would beat faster, I would tremble and sweat and, on occasion, pass out.

The patients in Kings Park Hospital saw very little of the doctors. There was one who came into the ward now and then, but I don't recall any conversation I had with him. None, surely, that lasted more than a minute. There were two women — one was a nurse, the other seemed to have had some training in psychology. Their main duty was to see that the patients were quiet or harmlessly busy playing cards or board games or reading a magazine. The female psychologist was intelligent and kind. There were also three guards. They were the ones who kept order. Much of the time, especially during the evening and night hours, they ran the ward.

Two of the guards were the kind Chekhov describes in "Ward No. 6." One was a scrawny man with a vacuous face. He showed me his right hand — the trigger finger was missing. He waggled the stump under my face with a sly smile. This, he gave me to understand, was why he had been excused from military service. The other guard was an older man, stocky and muscular, with a bullet head. He was dangerous — he liked to beat up the patients. He informed me that he was the one who had knocked out my front teeth when I was first brought to the ward. He seemed to think it was a joke I would like to share. The third guard was a black man.

One of the patients was a young black man — I don't think he was more than eighteen or nineteen years old. There may have been other black patients in the ward, but I don't remember any. This one, however, I remember very well. He came toward me one day carrying a newspaper. "You can read it," he said. "Read it for me." The stocky, bullet-headed guard was standing nearby. The young man turned toward him and hit him lightly on the chest. It wasn't a blow, scarcely more than a tap. The guard knocked him down. The other guard, the one with the missing trigger finger, came over, and the two of them stood over the boy and kicked him repeatedly in his sides and belly.

The next day the black guard told me that the young man had died. He asked me if I had seen what happened. I said I had — it was right in front of me. "Will you testify?" he asked. I said that I would. That evening the guard who had knocked the boy down and kicked him to death spoke to me. If there was an inquiry, and if I was called as a witness, and if I said anything about what happened, I would never leave the hospital.

I was not called, and I did not bear witness. If I had, I would surely have been killed, or these murderers would have seen to it that I spent the rest of my life in a hospital ward. Such was the treatment of patients at Kings Park Hospital in 1946. I have no doubt that such incidents are still occurring in hospitals, though not as frequently as they did at that time. I can imagine what being in prison must be like.

I received shock treatments, and later I was assigned to help the doctor, lifting each patient onto the table. I watched as the current passed through and the body convulsed. There has been much controversy over shock treatments — whether or not they did irremediable harm. Speaking only for myself, I think they brought me out of the fog in which I had been walking. They may also have destroyed areas of memory. It took me some years to remember episodes of my early life, and I have never been able to recall the months leading to my collapse.

The war itself I have recovered in bright patches. The areas immediately surrounding these remain dark. Perhaps they would have been so in any case — life in barracks and between battles can be dreary. In fact, by writing about the war I may have recalled it more clearly than most of my fellow soldiers. Writers are different — they don't forget.

One of the symptoms of my illness had been hearing voices. But one day — and this was after I came out of the fog and was quite calm and rational — looking out of the cage, the barred windows behind which we lived, at grass and trees and clouds, I heard a voice say, "Praise God, they resist, they resist!" I could say, I *thought* I heard a voice, but am not willing to hand over the victory to those who believe that they know what is real and what is not. Most doctors are of this mind. It is a rare psychoanalyst who, like Freud and Jung, reads works of imagination. They don't take such things seriously — they cannot afford to take them seriously — it would be disastrous in the line of work they have chosen.

Who was it who was resisting? Others like myself, I suppose. I believe with Shakespeare and Blake and Rimbaud that there are more things in heaven and earth than are dreamed of in the philosophy of those who serve the world, and who administer its institutions, and, by a fortunate concatenation, grow rich.

Being pronounced whole, more or less, and discharged from Kings Park, but with instructions to report to a government-appointed doctor at regular times, is not the end of this history. The more evident symptoms of my illness would disappear so that I was thought of by most people as a reasonable and level-headed man. But the cure would take time.

For some years after leaving the hospital I was subject to the sudden onsets I have mentioned: a heart that beat faster, and shaking, and sweating. I would imagine shells falling and hear the sound of guns. I could not stand being confined. I went to the theater to see the first run of *I Am a Camera,* and had to walk out during the first act, to breathe the air of Broadway. I was having dinner in a restaurant with a woman who supported the arts. I began eating swordfish, a thing I had never eaten, and just as she was saying something I thought foolish, I was overtaken by the palpitations and nausea, and had to rise and, without a word, walk out of the restaurant. I looked back once and saw her staring in astonishment.

Such was my social life. And I had the habits that remain with soldiers. One in particular: when I went walking I would keep an eye peeled for an enemy position. If there was an open field I would think, How are we going to get across that? I imagined lying again on a railroad embankment in Normandy, waiting to be told to go over it in spite of the bullets that were sweeping to and fro directly above me. That day I was sure I would be killed. Or I was in a graveyard in Holland with shells falling and the living getting mixed in with the dead. I was in the Ardennes, standing in a fox-hole among trees covered with snow and stamping my feet. They were freezing.

The university informed me that before I could return I had to be cleared by their doctor. He picked up a folder and said, "You aren't going to be so taken up with your music, are you?" The question was probably one of their tricks, to test my sanity. He spoke again, saying that I ought to go out in the world and "meet the common man." I was silent. I had seen the common man . . . his guts spilled in a road, his limbs strewn in a field. The doctor told me that he could not recommend my returning to the college. It was only on the way home that I realized he had been looking at the wrong folder. What would the musician, whose file it was, say when he was advised to give up writing poems and stories?

So I looked for work and found it, as a copyboy on a newspaper. If I stayed with it, I might someday be a reporter. But this didn't appeal to me. I didn't have the fascination with gossip that a reporter needs to have — whether it is about a quarrel between nations or about a politician and his mistress. Then I worked for an import-export firm as a packer, shipping seconds — damaged stockings or ballpoint pens with some small imperfection not visible to the eye — to Brussels, where such things were in demand. But this too did not appeal to me; to succeed in this kind of business you have to think about the money you can make, and I preferred to think about other things.

I went back to the university, but not by the front entrance. I slipped in by a side door, the School of General Studies, which wasn't so particular about whom they let in. I took courses that met in the evening and on Saturday, and I worked at writing. I was no longer intent on writing prose and becoming a novelist — all that typing. I was unable to imagine someone who had a life different from my own, to feel intensely about such a person, sustain an interest in his fate for days, weeks, months, even years. That was what novelists had to do. I lacked consistency — my mind went shooting off in all directions — and I lacked patience. I couldn't take any pleasure in writing about furniture, or lighting a cigarette, the kind of stuffing of which fiction consisted.

Unless it was written by a great author, a work of fiction had a fairly common plot, spun out for three or four hundred pages. But you could put everything that you felt and thought in the space of a poem. You could get it out of your system and put it behind you.

I had been granted a pension for my disability, and the checks for several months started coming all at once. I also had the GI Bill.

I would be able to go to Paris. In the winter of '44 I had been hospitalized briefly in Paris. After Germany surrendered, the regiment was stationed at Sens, and I was appointed managing editor of the regimental newspaper. The staff would take a truck to Paris to fetch the big rolls of newsprint. I saw enough of the city to want to see more of it after the war.

I traveled to France on the *Queen Mary* and registered as a student at the Sorbonne. There were other Americans taking the course in French Civilization and Culture, but we had our own agendas, writing or painting. In any case, frequenting the cafés between St.-Germain-des-Prés and Boul' Mich'.

I have told this story before, but artists may make several paintings of the same subject. Why shouldn't a writer tell a story again, seen in a different light? One night while I was in Paris I dreamed that I was walking with G Company along a strip of land with trees. There was water on each side. Suddenly shells began falling and I was lying prone. Bullets were sweeping the trees — a trunk a few inches above my head was slashed white. Someone close by was calling for his mother in Italian.

The next morning I wrote out the dream in ballad stanzas:

> This was the shining green canal
> Where we came two by two
> Walking at combat interval.
> Such trees we never knew . . .

As I wrote, I realized that it wasn't a dream but a memory . . . our first contact with the enemy. With this dream, other memories of the war began to return.

"Carentan, O Carentan," is well known, insofar as poetry is known in our time. It was set to music by a French composer, Aubert Lemeland, and played over the radio on the fiftieth anniversary of the landing of the Allied armies in Normandy — at the moment of the landing. This poem has also been set to music by the American composer Benjamin Lees. The strangest things come together if you live long enough. One moment you are lying prone with bullets flying around you, mortar shells falling, and a man a few feet away dying and calling, "Mamma mia!" Blood is running down your back. The next moment you are writing about it. And half a century has gone by.

I am both the man there and then and the one who is writing this. Buddhists speak of seeing your life as part of a pattern. I do not have to practice Buddhism in order to do this — it happens when I write.

The process of regaining my memory began with the dream about Carentan. And there were other passages of my life that had been lost — I had forgotten much of my life before the war. I pushed into memory as into some cloudy stuff. So I recovered the house in Jamaica where I lived when I was a child. I recovered the veranda with its climbing vine on which lizards crawled and croaked. The drawing room with the piano, the closet with Chinese and Russian objects, the Victrola with a handle that you wound, and the goldfish bowl on a stand. I was listening to a record on the gramophone, and moved back and knocked over the goldfish bowl. There were fragments of glass on the floor, and goldfish gasping and dying. I remembered how I wept.

Such events came back at a great distance, like a story that was read to me as a child. I pushed into the cloud of memory, and people and incidents reappeared, and were connected, and made sense.

Those who have had a break such as I have been describing live in fear of a relapse. You can never be sure . . . The fear affects your behavior in all sorts of ways. You are afraid of the stranger inside you, the one who emerged . . . murderous Mr. Hyde to your good-natured, sociable Dr. Jekyll. You are afraid of yourself . . . you don't know what he may do. As a result, you keep your feelings under lock and key.

An episode like this could destroy an artist — a composer of music, a painter, or a writer. For the essence of art is self-expression. The poet Rimbaud stopped writing when he was only nineteen and at the height of his powers. People wonder at this. I do not. I think he saw shades of the madhouse in front of him, and preferred to be a trader and gunrunner in Africa.

There are artists — van Gogh comes to mind — who have psychotic episodes but don't let this hold them back. They just let themselves go. The end in such cases may very well be self-destruction, but they get themselves expressed. Which would one prefer to be, the man who kept his emotions under strict control, gave up writing, painting, or composing, and lived on as a "well-adjusted" man, or the one who blazed out and spent the rest of his life in darkness?

But isn't there an alternative to either of these ways? The more you pay attention to the world outside the self and think about individuals and the things they do, the more interesting they become. It seems that they need to be expressed, and in expressing them you express the best part of yourself.

But it may take years to arrive at this. Those who have had the kind of break I have described fear a recurrence. A chance remark by a stranger strikes you to the heart . . . it is clear that he knows your weakness. The fear is accompanied by a feeling of shame. For it is a shameful thing to have been weak and at the mercy of others. I am reminded of what I have read about some of the prisoners in concentration camps. They felt ashamed. Of what? Of their suffering. It is a shameful thing to be weak. Their tormenters played upon this feeling . . . they deserved what was coming to them.

Some people after the war argued that the Jews were to blame for not defending themselves — they conspired with their executioners! Hannah Arendt spoke for this point of view. The Nazis would have been pleased: wasn't it just what they had been saying, that Jews were an inferior race? The fact is that some Jews defended themselves as well as they could. But if you are standing with your parents, and your wife and children, under the eyes of men armed with machine guns, what are you to do? What would Hannah Arendt have done? Torn a gun from the hands of the guards? And what if you believed, as those Jews did, that it was a sin to shed blood?

I relived the war almost every night in my dreams. This continued for years. After Miriam and I were married, she woke one night to sounds that were coming from different parts of the room: sounds of battle, shelling and gunfire. They were coming from me! I was projecting them like a ventriloquist.

I dreamed of encounters with the Germans that I never had. But I had anticipated such meetings as — this was my job — I walked alone among trees or over fields, carrying a message from G Company to Battalion. Or I dreamed about horrors . . . the field in Holland I had to walk through night after night. It was strewn with the dead bodies of German infantry and American paratroopers who had shot each other at close range. The bodies changed, putrefying and swelling. I had to walk around arms and legs and faces shining with corruption.

I used to think that having such dreams was a thing to be ashamed of. For what had I suffered in comparison with others? When I thought of them, the dead, and those who were in wheelchairs, or blinded, or insane, had I really known war at all? What have we to complain of who have only known "soldier's heart"? Nothing, sir, nothing at all.

Some years ago a man from Czechoslovakia came to interview me. He said he was conducting interviews with writers who had seen combat during the Second World War. I told him about the dreams I had about the war — at first almost every night. In recent years they had been tapering off. "Yes," he said. He had been interviewing Russian soldiers, combat veterans. They had the same dreams. It was to be expected.

Why write about such things? Are they not better forgotten? After a war, the millions who have been through it want to forget. It was terrible, and sordid, and boring. Besides, everyone knows the things you do. But time passes and the number of those who remember is suddenly diminished. Who remembers the Great War?

When I was a teacher and the subject of war came up, I would write a name on the blackboard: Somme. Who, I would ask, had heard of it? None of the students would answer. Only one or two knew anything at all about the Great War. I would tell them that the Somme was a battle in that war, a terrible battle in which thousands were killed or wounded — sixty thousand casualties in the British army on the first morning alone. It was hell on earth, but the men who went through it consoled themselves with a thought: Generations will remember what we did here, it will never be forgotten. Yet not one of the young people in front of me had ever heard of it.

I have not forgotten the men I knew in the 101st Airborne Division. The men and women I worked with in universities were pale and unreal in comparison. They were hollow and filled with words. For the essential human virtue, courage, without which there is no other, I give you "point," the man walking up the road ahead of the company, his rifle held across his body at port arms.

What was I to think of the new breed of university professors, structuralists, poststructuralists, deconstructionists, who taught that experience had no meaning, that the only reality was language, one word referring to another, one "sign" to another, with no stop in any kind of truth? Who put the word "truth" in quotes?

It is right to remember such things as I have described — in the first place, because those who have lived and died before us should be remembered, insofar as it is possible. Otherwise our own lives seem worthless. In the second place, war is a permanent human condition, and men and women will have to face it. It may help them to know how people no stronger physically or mentally than they have faced it. In any case, everything that human beings do is interesting, when you think about it.

The war and its aftermath changed me. It gave me a respect and affection for the so-called common man that I have never lost. As if any life were common! The men I knew in the 101st, most of them, had no education beyond high school. And they weren't stunning physical specimens either, though they could carry a pack, trench tool, rifle or carbine, machine gun, tripod or ammunition boxes, for miles at a good pace.

> Most clearly of that battle I remember
> The tiredness in eyes, how hands looked thin
> Around a cigarette, and the bright ember
> Would pulse with all the life there was within.

They complained about it, of course. Then why were they willing to go through it? They were not indoctrinated like the Germans and Japanese and Italians with a belief in their racial superiority and a right to enslave other peoples. What most of them wanted was to get the fighting over with and go home . . . to the good life. The life of every day.

I was different from the men around me in one respect: the war gave me poetry. I had had what some would call a troubled childhood, though at the time, with the sea and sky of the Caribbean, I wasn't aware of being troubled. My parents were divorced when I was seven years old, and my mother left Jamaica and returned to the States. She disappeared and no one told me why. So I grew up as a rather lonely boy, though I had friends at school. My father died when I was sixteen. There was no place for me, so I left the island and came to New York, an entirely different world. There must have been a great deal of trouble in my mind, and no doubt this surfaced as rage when, after the war, I had my break.

But I shall leave the cause to professional explainers of the psyche. What the war and its aftermath gave me was the feeling that, since I had managed to survive, I owed no one anything for my existence — neither my parents nor the government. By moving my body some inches to the left or right, on more than one occasion I had saved my life. From now on it was my own, to do with as I liked.

I liked reading novels and poems. I could lose myself for hours, days even, in a story. And I had a driving need to write . . . a few lines for a poem, a paragraph of prose . . . anything! Even at the university there were very few who felt about such things as I did.

What did that matter? What if the only thing I could do was held in contempt by others, or met with indifference? Most people cared nothing about the kind of writing that mattered to me more than anything else. They were deaf to the music. So what! I was alive and doing what I liked.

DIANA TRILLING

A Visit to Camelot

FROM THE NEW YORKER

HERE WAS CAMELOT as I saw it and described it to my friends. At breakfast one morning in April of 1962 I read in the *Times* that there was to be a dinner for the Nobel Prize winners. I said to my husband, Lionel, "Here we go again. Lenny Bernstein." The story indicated that there were going to be guests in addition to the Nobel laureates. I concluded that that meant Lenny Bernstein and Julie Harris. What I was having, of course, was a terrible pang of jealousy, because these were the people who would be invited, and we would not. But, even as I was saying it, a quick wonderful thought ran through my head that perhaps we were going to be invited. I said nothing to Lionel about wishing that we had an invitation, and if he was suffering from a similar jealousy he hid it from me, too. And then one morning when the mail arrived, and Lionel asked me to come out to the hall, I could tell from his voice what was in the mail: a large square envelope marked in the corner "The White House."

Actually, I was worried about the expense, but there was no question that we were going to accept. I had a strong, simple feeling about the invitation, and it struck a sympathetic chord in Lionel. My father had come to America from Poland when he was a boy of eighteen, without a penny, and knowing no English. He peddled macaroons on the Staten Island Ferry while he learned the language, and now for his daughter to be invited to the White House — well, I owed him the acceptance of that invitation.

The invitation was for a Sunday night, April 29, and it said black tie. This made it perfectly clear what Lionel would wear, but what would I wear? With our old-fashioned notions, we decided that I should wear the simplest possible short evening dress, black, if I could find one, and covered up, not bare. I set out to find it, and there wasn't a short black evening dress in all New York. Then I called a salesgirl I knew at Hattie Carnegie and asked her what I could do. She was awfully pleasant and told me that she knew someone, Mac Weiss, who might have something for me at his shop. I went there, and I found not a short black evening dress at all but a black matte jersey dress with long tight sleeves. It was full length, but I was shown how the trains could be cut off and it could be made into a short dress, which I could wear with short white kid gloves. The problem seemed to entrance them. In fact, at one point the salesgirl whispered, "Mrs. Auchincloss is right in the next fitting room at this moment." Jackie's mother, of course.

The dress was a slinky tight thing, very theatrical, and something told me not to buy it without consulting Lionel. So I asked them to hold it, and the next day I took Lionel down to look at it. He didn't think it was at all the right thing. This troubled Mr. Weiss very badly, and he said, "I think I have one other dress that you didn't see," and he brought out a simple black crepe dress (that all my friends would be seeing for the next five years), with a little scarf attached to the shoulder which I could drop over my arms if I wanted them to be covered. And it made me look so thin — it was marvelous. It looked as if it had cost all of $19.95, if you weren't aware of the cut. It was $250. Mr. Weiss kept telling me how absolutely perfect it was, superb. Lionel was beaming, too. So this was how it was done, and I thought that I was all set and now all I had to worry about were the accessories.

And then that evening I picked up the *Times,* which I hadn't had a chance to read because I had been downtown shopping, and my eye lit on the social calendar of the Kennedys, and I saw that they were on their way to Palm Beach. They're going to Palm Beach, I thought furiously, and I'm going to their party, and they won't even be there. This impelled me to read the whole story, which said that they were going to be gone for ten days and then they would be back for the Nobel Prize winners' dinner on the twenty-ninth. And included in the news story were two sentences that, miraculously, I read: a directive had just that day been issued by the social office of the White House that although the party was to be on the black-tie level for men, it was on the white-tie level for ladies. The women guests, that is, were to wear long gowns and long white gloves. I had just taken my new dress out of its box and cut off the price tag. Hung it in the closet. Made it mine. But what I had bought was dead wrong.

We had just one week left before the party when my then sister-in-law Edna dragged me to a shop on Forty-eighth Street. A nasty, vulgar saleswoman came forward to ask what I wanted. I said I was looking for a long evening dress, and she said that all the shop's clothes were made to order. I hadn't even the strength to say thank you when I heard Edna say, "Yes, of course, but we thought that perhaps at this time of year you might have some of your model dresses left which you'd be willing to sell." The saleswoman examined her appraisingly. "Yes, we do," she admitted. She disappeared for a few minutes and then brought out just the dress I had been looking for — an all-seasons dress, champagne-colored, made of moiré taffeta printed in soft orange and green flowers. I forced myself to ask "How much?" before trying it on. It was $395, the saleswoman said, but since it was a model she might be able to do a little better on the price. Meanwhile, Edna was making gestures at me behind her back, and I knew just what she was trying to say, so I took a large gulp and murmured, "I hope you'll be able to give me a special price on this, because I'm going to wear it at the White House." The salesgirl didn't blink an eye. She said, "Oh, then I'm sure we can do even better. Just try it on first." I tried it on, and there were a few little things that needed altering. She disappeared for several minutes, and when she returned she said patriotically that the price would be $250, including the alterations.

All I had left to do was to have some slippers dyed to match. Edna had a lovely old evening bag that she lent me. She also lent me a mink stole. And I bought long white kid gloves that cost $22.

When Lionel first got our invitation, we had thought we might spend the whole weekend in Washington and stay at a hotel or motel. But our friend Thelma Anderson reminded us that she had a sister who lived just outside Washington, and who would be delighted to have us use her house to dress in. We welcomed that money-saving suggestion.

The twenty-ninth at last arrived, and we went down to Washington on the eleven-o'clock train. Dinner was scheduled for eight o'clock that evening, and we figured that that would give us plenty of time to get to Thelma's sister's house to dress without a rush. On our way down to Penn Station, we stopped at the Tip Toe Inn to buy sandwiches, to avoid the expense of the dining car. Lionel wanted to buy chairs in the club car, but I wouldn't let him. I was adamant: we would have a sleeper to come back in that night, but we would go down in a coach. So there we were, standing with a great big suitcase, in which were packed our evening clothes, and waiting for the gate to open, when suddenly a very seedy-looking man carrying a suitcase and a large raggedy bulging briefcase came up and asked, "Do you know where you get the eleven-o'clock train to Washington?" All of us did a doubletake. It was James Farrell.

Could there have been a more extraordinary sight? I thought of Yeats's "Fifteen apparitions have I seen; / The worst a coat upon a coat-hanger." He was wearing a suit that I think was supposed to be brown, but it was so shabby that you could no longer tell its color. His necktie was under his ear and a button was missing from his shirt front. Also, the shirt was filthy; he'd been wearing it for a week. I may be exaggerating a little, but I think his jacket was torn on the sleeve and that its buttons were hanging by a thread. He looked wild. We hadn't seen him for ages, and it flashed through both our minds: My God, has he been invited to the White House too? But an even worse thought was that we were going to have to ride all the way down to Washington with him, and it was going to be terrible. In fact, he'd already started to talk while we stood at the gate, and he was telling us that he'd begun volume nineteen in a series of twenty-five novels, not one of which had been published, and he quoted passages to us from the one he had just completed. In his bulging briefcase, he explained, he had all the royalty statements from his publishers. He felt that he was being very much cheated by the income-tax people, and he was going to Washington to take up the matter. I could hear Lionel heave a sigh of relief: he wasn't going to the White House; he was going to the Treasury Department.

He looked insane, sober but insane, but he couldn't have been sweeter. Well, this was what I got for not allowing Lionel to buy chairs in the club car. We were going to have to ride all the way to Washington with Jim Farrell! The gates finally opened, and Lionel and I started down the platform. We hadn't, of course, said anything about where we were going in Washington. When we got to the first coach car, we turned toward it, and he looked at us, surprised. "Oh, don't you have chairs?" Embarrassed, he explained that he was terribly sorry but he hadn't been sleeping well lately and was very tired. He had taken a chair because it would give him a chance to rest. I could feel humiliation racing through every inch of my husband's body. He was riding in a coach while this poor, bedraggled devil who looked as if he had not had a bed to sleep in for a year or a change in underwear for a month was traveling in a chair. But it was also a great relief; we wouldn't have to talk to him.

On the train, I'd begun to have a headache. I was well fortified with pills: aspirin, Bufferin, codeine, and also some pink pills that had been given me by the English novelist Pamela Hansford Johnson, the wife of C. P. Snow. We'd met at a dinner party, where I'd suddenly become ill and had to leave. She had followed me to the door and said, "You're having an attack of migraine, aren't you? I can tell. I'm vice president of the British Migraine Association. Here!" And she thrust a couple of pills into my hand. Of course, only in England could there be a migraine association. I asked what the pills were, and she said that when you have the aura of a migraine you take the first pill and, twenty minutes later, if you're not better you take a second pill. She had only two to spare. But they were marvelous, and really worked, and I had written to ask her to send me more. So on the train, when I got the aura, as she put it, I took one of them. As soon as I'd swallowed it, I got nervous: suppose I passed out in the middle of the dinner party? My headache was becoming quite severe, and I was alarmed because, if it followed its usual pattern, by eight o'clock I'd be very sick, and by nine I'd be throwing up. I dressed in agony. I was beginning to feel so sick and nervous that I couldn't bear the idea of trying to get through a party.

I had learned from an acquaintance that protocol required us to arrive at the White House by ten minutes to eight. At Thelma's sister Marilyn's house, Lionel asked where he could call for a hired car. But Marilyn and her husband wouldn't dream of letting us hire a car; they insisted that they themselves would drive us to the White House. It would be a forty-five-minute drive, and we protested vehemently, but they assured us that it would be fun for them, so at precisely ten minutes after seven we all piled into their station wagon, our host in his shirtsleeves, Marilyn in a housedress, the baby in the dirty play clothes she'd been wearing. The three of them got in the front of the car while Lionel and I arranged ourselves elegantly in the back. And I looked at Lionel and Lionel looked at me, and it was perfectly clear that the two of us were thinking the same thing: arriving like this, we wouldn't be allowed through the gate. Why couldn't our driver at least put on a jacket?

Still, we sat back and relaxed, and it suddenly came to me that my headache was all gone, and almost for the first time that day it occurred to me that I might even enjoy the evening. It was dusk, the fountains were playing, with lights on them. It had been a warm week in Washington, and flowers had burst into bloom on the White House grounds, so that you saw masses of color in the lowering light. People were beginning to gather to watch what was going on. It was like nothing I had ever witnessed, and it made my heart pound with excitement.

We drove up to the gate, and there was a row of army and navy people. Lionel handed his pass to a guard, and he received it without the slightest flicker of expression. He just checked off our names on a list and said, turning to Marilyn's husband, "Drive right up to the door." There we said, "Thank you so much for everything," and off they drove.

I took Lionel's arm. It was plainly indicated what we were supposed to do; nobody needed to tell us. Very slowly we walked through the portico. The entrance was lined on both sides with functionaries. There were also a great many military people in attendance, in their beautiful uniforms, and heaps of photographers taking pictures of the guests as they arrived, not asking their names; the sorting out would be done later. They took everybody's picture.

As we walked in, an aide came up and said, "The gentlemen please enter in that room, the ladies go to the dressing room, around to the right." In the dressing room, there were several maids and racks and racks of clothes, the women's wraps, and lavatories with mirrors, not unlike the dressing room on the mezzanine level of the Plaza Hotel in New York, but bigger. The moment I got in there, I knew it was going to be a wonderful party. There were two or three elderly women fixing their hair in front of the mirrors, and they beamed at me. One of them said, "Have you come far?" and I said, "From New York. Have you come far?" She replied that she had driven in the rain from Baltimore; I suppose it was from Johns Hopkins. They were wearing the most marvelous antique dresses, this little group of old ladies. One of them might have been eighty. She had on a taffeta dress with ruching around the neck and puffed sleeves. She looked exquisite, with beautiful jewelry that had probably been in her family forever. Nothing could have been a more wonderful introduction to the party than these women: they weren't young, they weren't smart — they were just lovely.

I came out of the dressing room and there was Lionel, waiting for me. Immediately an aide came up, introduced himself, and inquired, "May I ask your name?" When Lionel said, "Mr. and Mrs. Trilling," he said promptly, "Of course. Mr. and Mrs. Lionel Trilling." Obviously, he had memorized the entire guest list — I think there were about 180 of us altogether — and he couldn't have known in advance who was going to fall to him. Then he said to me, "Would you take my arm?" and held out his arm while Lionel fell back and walked two or three paces behind us. As we moved along, he asked me, "Does your husband prefer to be introduced as Mr., Dr., or Professor?" "He prefers to be called Mr. Trilling," I said. "Good," he said, and added, "I'll be your aide for the early part of the evening. You'll be told everything you have to do, so you needn't feel any constraint at all."

While he was talking to me, I saw that perhaps five yards ahead of us another couple was being ministered to in the same comforting fashion. There must have been eighteen or twenty such aides, each in charge of eight to ten people. But there was no pressure of any kind. Just the contrary.

He led me to a table, and an attendant checked a list and handed him a little envelope, saying, "Mr. Trilling will be seated at table 2. You, Mrs. Trilling, will be seated at table 6. You're both in the main dining room. This evening, we're going to be using both dining rooms, the State Dining Room and the Blue Room. President Kennedy will be in the State Dining Room, where your tables are. Mrs. Kennedy will be in the Blue Room." The predinner reception was being held in the East Room, and at the door stood another attendant, with a microphone. Our aide went up to him and said, "Mr. and Mrs. Lionel Trilling," and the aide at the door repeated into the microphone, "Mr. and Mrs. Lionel Trilling." From then on, I kept catching the names of people who were arriving and being announced. I'd have loved to be standing quietly by myself, listening to the names and trying to put them together with the faces to which they belonged, but that wasn't possible. My aide had returned and deposited us where Lionel and I belonged alphabetically, or near enough to it for easy correction. He took me up to Fredric March and introduced us. Like many accomplished actors, March had very smooth manners. He greeted me warmly. Then a kind of chain reaction got started in the reception room. One didn't speak to anyone without introducing him or her to the person with whom one had just been speaking. It seemed to happen automatically: we caught the procedure from the aides and carried it forward without being told to. It was the most enchanting performance, everybody introducing somebody to somebody else in the most charming way.

Immediately the room began to fill with waiters carrying huge trays loaded with everything that one could possibly desire to drink: manhattans, martinis, highballs, sherry, tomato juice, orange juice. There were no canapés, just drinks.

The room was now filling up with familiar names. Not familiar faces. I soon heard the attendant announce, "Mr. and Mrs. Arthur Schlesinger." Arthur saw me and waved and came over. He greeted me and introduced his wife, but he didn't seem relaxed and friendly, like everyone else. He appeared to be self-conscious, as if borne down by his official White House connection.

Meanwhile, out of the corner of my eye I had spotted Colonel John Glenn. He was talking to, of all people, Robert Frost, and there must have been six people huddled around them, trying to hear what they were saying. And then a little lady, just a wee thing, and the most enchanting-looking person, was being introduced to me — she looked to be about eighty-five, and her name was Mrs. Waterman. Later, I found out that her husband was in charge of the National Science Foundation. She said to me, "Oh, Mrs. Trilling, you're literary. Is there anyone here I'm supposed to know?"

She had a charming bird-like way of speaking, and I said, "Well, I haven't seen many writers, but that's Katherine Anne Porter over there in the white brocade dress and the white hair and the white pearls."

"Am I supposed to know her?" Mrs. Waterman inquired. "Because I don't want to."

I was dying for a cigarette, but I didn't see any woman smoking, and very few men were smoking. My headache was gone, but I was still afraid to drink, because that might bring it back. I held a cocktail in my hand, but I didn't dare touch it. A stupendous amount of liquor was flowing around. People felt so much at home that they were drinking just as they might at a cocktail party at the home of their closest friends. Bill Styron lit a cigarette, but I didn't myself dare to, so he kept giving me puffs of his.

Then suddenly I heard over the loudspeaker the name of Mr. James Farrell, and, sure enough, there he was. I don't know in whose charge he had been in those intervening hours since we had last seen him, but he was transformed. He had on an absolutely clean shirt, his suit was pressed and sparkling clean, every shirt stud was in place. He looked dreamy, and I felt horribly ashamed of us for not having wanted to tell him that we were going to the White House and asking whether that was where he was going, too. What was amazing was that he had had the delicacy not to ask us, for fear that we hadn't been invited and would feel bad.

Jimmy Baldwin looked elegant in his evening clothes, and we just waved to each other across the room. I caught a glimpse of John Dos Passos in the reception room, but I didn't see him again through the rest of the evening. With Frost, that about made up the literary contingent. I took note that Lionel was drinking an awful lot of martinis. But he was obviously enjoying himself. Long before we were put into the receiving line and the President made his appearance, everybody was saying to everybody else, "Isn't this a wonderful party?"

By now it must have been half past eight. Our aide explained that the President and Mrs. Kennedy were about to come in, and as soon as they did the receiving line would start moving forward. Everyone would be in alphabetical order, with the Nobel Prize winners first and then the other guests. "Please don't lose your places," he urged. "That's very important. The gentleman goes in front of the lady in the receiving line." He turned to Lionel. "We mean that."

At that moment, there was a great fanfare of trumpets — quite literally — and the band played "Hail to the Chief." Then in marched the color guard, and I heard a voice say, "The President and Mrs. Kennedy," and in they came, into the sudden stillness. They didn't come in slowly, or in any way regally. They moved almost hastily, as if they didn't want to be specially noticed. It's true that there had been the big fanfare for the entrance, but then, as individuals, they comported themselves with great modesty.

They had just come back from the Palm Beach vacation, and they were very suntanned. Jackie was a deep cocoa brown and she was wearing a sea-green chiffon dress, to the floor, but cut simply except that it had one bare shoulder. She wore green slippers to match her dress and no jewelry at all except some earrings, which were the most beautiful shade of green. She was a hundred times more beautiful than any photograph had ever indicated.

In photographs, her head always looked too large. But it wasn't at all that large in real life. She didn't have as bouffant a hairdo as I thought from her pictures, and she had a long and beautiful neck. Her dress really wasn't cut very elaborately, but it had millions of pleats. Hers was a charming figure rather than a perfect one, and she carried her clothes exquisitely. The President was handsome and exuded energy — I could feel it even at my distance from him. And one thing I noticed right away: among the Nobel Prize winners he had apparently changed the alphabetical order, so that the line was headed by Mrs. George Marshall, the widow of General Marshall — of the Marshall Plan. She was followed by Mrs. Ernest Hemingway, who had on what I thought was the most beautiful and appropriate dress at the party. After all, it was less than a year since Hemingway's death. She knew that she was going to be very much in the public eye. It was a black sheath, very tight to below her knees, where it went out in a flare, and the flared part had large crimson roses appliquéed on it — she was essentially in black but not in mourning. I should perhaps say here that I'd often seen pictures of her and had always thought she looked like a lady buyer, hard-bitten. But, actually, there was more tenderness in her face than I had expected; more pain. Her eyes were softer, more appealing, and the whole outline of her face was more blurred than was suggested in photographs.

The line began to move quite rapidly now, but people didn't stop drinking until they came to within a few feet of the President. Then they set down their drinks — there were lots of shelves and

little tables around the sides of the room. There were a few chairs
scattered about, but nobody used them; everyone was in motion.
By the time Lionel and I got to the President, the room was, of
course, almost empty. Lionel moved out ahead of me. He had
already put out his hand while his name was being announced, so
that he had the President's hand in his and the President was
saying, "It's very nice to see you, sir," when Lionel's name fully got
through to him.

"Oh, it's you," the President exclaimed. "I'm so glad to see you."
Lionel beamed, of course, and said, "Thank you." By this time,
Mrs. Kennedy had her hand out and Lionel was taking it. And she
said, "You know, I have a stepsister who won't have one idea in her
head unless you tell her it's all right to have it. She never says
anything unless you say it's all right for her to say it."

Lionel inquired who the stepsister was.

"Nina Auchincloss," Mrs. Kennedy replied. "She was a student
of yours."

Lionel couldn't place Nina Auchincloss, but he said, "That's
very nice of her." But he didn't stop there. I could see that he
wasn't being his usual shy self — he had had six martinis, I'd been
counting. And I thought, Oh, my God, what's coming next? He
was still holding Mrs. Kennedy's hand. "Wait till I tell you what they
said about you at Vassar," he said, smiling at her.

She began to laugh. "What?"

"Never mind," said Lionel. "Later, I'll tell you later."

At this point, the President dropped my hand and inquired of
Lionel, "What did they say at Vassar?"

"Later," Lionel repeated. I had myself now been moved on to
Mrs. Kennedy, but I saw that both the President and Mrs. Kennedy
were grinning; they were amused by Lionel.

I said, "Don't worry. What they said was very nice."

Mrs. Kennedy said, "Oh," but she looked at me as if to ask where
I had materialized from. What was I doing in her conversation with
Lionel? Lionel and I moved together toward the dining room, and
he said, "I'm going to die — I've never been so flattered in my
whole life."

In the dining room, we separated. I went to my table 6, Lionel
went to his table 2. The tables were round, quite close to each
other. The President's table was in the center, and he had Mrs.

Marshall on his right and Mrs. Hemingway on his left. Frost was at
the President's table, and so was Mrs. Smith, the President's sister.
While people were coming into the dining room, I had been able
to look at the place cards at my table. I had Pierre Salinger on my
right. On my left was a Dr. Stanley. On the other side of Dr. Stanley
was a woman I'd been talking to in the reception room, a very
charming and handsome woman with a great deal of social poise.
Her name was Mrs. Stratton, and I think she was the wife of the
president of MIT. I asked her if she had any idea who Dr. Stanley
was, and she told me that he had done important work on viruses.
She added that Mrs. Kerr, whose husband was president of the
University of California, and who was also sitting at our table,
would be able to tell me all about him. I looked at the cards and
saw that sitting on the other side of Mrs. Kerr would be James
Baldwin. That was a relief to me and apparently to him, too,
because when he got to the table and saw me there he said, "Oh,
you're here. Thank God, a familiar face."

The first thing Jimmy did was to look at the card next to him.
The place was still empty. "Who is Mrs. Kerr?" he asked me. "Didn't
she write a book, *Please Don't Eat the Daisies?*" I shook my head.
"Wife of the president of the University of California."

Soon Salinger came in, and Dr. Stanley, and we all sat until the
President came in, and then we all stood up again. It was plain
that he was trying not to draw too much attention to himself: he
walked in rapidly and sat down right away, no airs about it.

Dr. Stanley picked up my card. I said, "You haven't the vaguest
idea who I am. You scientists don't read." He loved my introducing
myself that way. He spent the entire dinner trying to persuade me
to stop smoking, telling me in horrendous detail about the cancer
I was heading into, and how I was going to rot inch by inch. It was
so relaxed in the dining room that I was able to smoke through
the entire meal. Nearly everybody was smoking, including most of
the women. But Dr. Stanley kept taking my cigarette out of my
mouth.

At one moment, he said, "What am I doing this for? I haven't
been able to stop my own wife from smoking. Why am I trying to
stop you? She's so nervous it's probably better for her to smoke
than not to." Of course, we were all tight. Everybody was tight.

Everybody at the table was having fun except the two of us on either side of Salinger. I must have launched fifty topics of talk, all of which fizzled out. Nothing we said to each other involved more than two sentences: my remark, his answer. Then we'd have to start all over again. Eventually, I found it interesting that it was so dull with him.

The dinner was delicious. The meal had been much delayed, yet the beef was absolutely perfect. The wines were French, and there was no end to the amount you could drink; you had barely set down your glass before it was filled again. With the dessert came champagne.

When the champagne was served, the President rose at his place and knocked on his glass. The dining room became instantly quiet while he made the tiniest bit of a speech. He said, "This is the most extraordinary collection of talent, of human knowledge, that has ever gathered at the White House, with the possible exception of when Thomas Jefferson dined alone."

He at once had the place in his hands; everyone adored it. He added a few other words and sat down. Coffee was served right at the table, and suddenly even Pierre Salinger became human. He said to me, "Cigars are moving slowly. If the President rises before they get to me, I won't have one. But I know all these waiters, and I'm not worried — they'll bring me a cigar."

The President rose, and everyone else rose too. He moved out of the room, stopping as he went to shake hands with friends as he chanced to see them. And then the old fraternization started all over again. People moved around talking to one another as they left the dining room, moving into the corridors, where strolling strings were playing. We had been instructed that there would be a short interval after the dinner, and that, after that, there would be a reading by Fredric March. But now we had about a half hour in which President and Mrs. Kennedy had retired — he had to catch his breath, and I guess she needed some time to herself as well. But the party continued on its own momentum.

Coming into the dining room we had run into Dr. and Mrs. J. Robert Oppenheimer. They were just ahead of us, and he turned and said, "You don't know my wife, do you?" She was a lovely-looking woman. Lovely but agonized-looking. My heart ached for the two of them. It was such a nice gesture on the part of President Kennedy wanting publicly to rehabilitate Oppenheimer after he had been treated as a security risk for nearly a decade. But his appearance was like that of a specter, a memento mori. He carried himself with great dignity, but that only made it worse. I remembered having heard that his wife was an acute alcoholic and drug addict. What a strain it must have been for her, with so much riding on the evening for him and all that liquor around.

Everywhere I looked there were enormous vases of flowers. The White House was like a fairyland — everything so elegant, easy, and gay, and the colors soft and varied. Wherever there was a table or a shelf or a fireplace, there were magnificent flowers in soft arrangements.

My aide gave me his arm and said, "Wouldn't you like to come into the East Room now and take your place? There's to be a reading. I want you to have a good seat, so let's go in now." He seated us plunk in the center of the third row. The President and Mrs. Kennedy had already come in and were seated right in front of us, where we could see them. They were in armchairs; we were in little gold chairs. And there was Mrs. Marshall and Mrs. Hemingway and Robert Frost and Vice President and Mrs. Lyndon Johnson, all in the row in front of us with the President. Throughout the evening, no notice had been taken of Johnson's entrance or his presence. I'd seen them, of course. Mrs. Johnson looked old and tired in that lively company. And Johnson himself had on the most awful dinner jacket. I think it was gray, and I don't know what it was made of, but it seemed to shimmer, as if he were a master of ceremonies in some cheap nightclub. Bobby Kennedy and his wife and the President's sister, Mrs. Smith, were also sitting in the front row just ahead of us. One of the things that struck me was Bobby Kennedy's good looks. He was infinitely better-looking than the President, but he didn't exude anything like his brother's power. Everything in his appearance was more delicate, and he looked very young, like an undergraduate. The President's face, on the other hand, radiated strength, power so compressed that you felt it was about to explode.

Fredric March read from three dead Nobel Prize winners, beginning with the introduction to Sinclair Lewis's *Main Street*. Next came some excerpts from Marshall's outline for what was to become his famous plan. Very handsome, very traditionally worded. The final reading was from Hemingway. March said, "I was going to read Ernest Hemingway's 'The Killers,' but Mrs. Hemingway felt that we were all of us too familiar with that, and that perhaps you would like to hear something that had been unpublished, so she went through her husband's unpublished works and selected a chapter from an unpublished novel."

This was intriguing, and he read it very well. But the chapter itself was so poor that one was pained for the man who had written it. When March finished, the President rose from his chair and walked over to Mrs. Hemingway; he virtually lifted her out of her seat and had her bow to the audience. She was having a tough time, poor woman, and I saw the President do something so nice. He squeezed her arm comfortingly. Then he went back to sit in his own place again.

During the reading, I had been sitting next to Katherine Anne Porter. She acted in the most annoying fashion. She fussed with her necklace, she fussed with her earrings, she fussed with every curl in her beautiful white hair. She had apparently spotted a woman who had kept her long gloves on, so she again put her own gloves on. Then she spotted a woman whose gloves were off and once more removed her own gloves. Then she saw someone who had only one glove on, and she copied that. Meanwhile, she was telling me how her life was being ruined by success — she was so hounded by newspaper people that she couldn't get any work done. What she needed that evening was the undeviating attention of a naval aide. She was used to being made much of by men; she must have felt rather frighteningly alone.

Everybody now stood up. No one actually rushed to the exit, but everyone sort of started to move in that direction. Lionel went over to talk to Robert Frost, but Lyndon Johnson moved in ahead of him, so Lionel waited. I stood at his side, waiting with him until Johnson had finished. After Lionel and Frost had talked for a moment, we moved toward the door. But just then I saw our aide approaching. "The President would like it very much if you and Mr. Trilling would join him upstairs," he said. By this time, I felt as if anything could happen, and I was scarcely surprised. Hadn't Lionel said that he'd tell him about Jackie at Vassar later? And it was only eleven o'clock — why should we go home? The party was just beginning.

Actually, I've never been a less important feature in our shared social life. I had nothing to do with this occasion except as Lionel's wife. Obviously, the President and Mrs. Kennedy knew who Lionel was. Most educated people were acquainted with Lionel's name, just as they knew the names of Katherine Anne Porter and James Baldwin. These were literary celebrities. But did they read the serious intellectual journals and know that I was a writer too? I didn't have to ponder the answer. It was no. The Styrons knew my work. So did Katherine Anne Porter and Farrell and Jimmy Baldwin. But neither of the Kennedys had ever heard of me, of that I'm almost certain. But I didn't let myself dwell on that aspect of the evening. I was delighted for Lionel, and I was enjoying myself thoroughly.

As my migraine had disappeared, I had drunk several glasses of champagne. I had even sipped some of the wines at dinner. I hadn't had six martinis, like Lionel — Lionel couldn't have been more pleasantly looped, perfect. Pretty soon, we were led into a large empty room, and the aide said, "This is the Oval Room. President Eisenhower worked here. The Kennedys don't use it that way; they use it for informal entertaining." There was a sofa in the middle of the room and another at right angles to it, and there were lots of occasional chairs grouped around the sofas very attractively, with little tables and lamps. There were flowers everywhere. The aide who led me in picked out a chair for me. He said that I ought to sit in that chair because it was the color of my dress. I asked if I could smoke. He said, "Of course," and he brought me an ashtray.

Immediately there sprang up before us, as if out of the ground, a waiter with a tray of full champagne glasses. I took a glass and then my aide said, "Just make yourself at home. The President will be here as soon as he's free downstairs. Have a good time." Lionel and I were now alone, sitting in the Oval Room of the White House, and we just looked at each other as though to say, "What in the world are we doing here?" We could scarcely talk to each other. We felt as if we were in a daydream.

At that moment, an aide came in with Rose Styron; a few paces behind them was Bill. They had the same mixed look of pleasure and bewilderment that we did. Rose and Bill struck me as being far more relaxed people than Lionel and I, but they weren't finding it much easier to talk; the whole situation was so extraordinary.

Then suddenly several people were led in. Robert Frost came in with Mrs. Smith, Bobby Kennedy came in with his wife, Ethel. Then Mrs. Kennedy came in, in a bit of a bustle. She was holding a glass of champagne in her left hand and she said, "Oh, hello." Lionel had sat down on one of the sofas, and I was sitting in a velvet chair next to it. Totally ignoring the Kennedys, Mrs. Kennedy came straight across the room to Lionel. They didn't count in *her* life, and she didn't care who knew it. The men had of course risen when she came into the room, and Rose Styron and I got up as well. There was a wooden chair, sort of in back of the sofa, and she pulled it out — it was a little wooden armchair — and she said, "Every time Lyndon Johnson sits on this chair, he breaks it. He's broken it three times so far. Now watch me. I'm going to sit on it, and, you'll see, it won't break under me. He doesn't know how to sit." She had brought the chair right next to Lionel and now she sat down in it, next to him.

"Now." She looked up at Lionel as he sat down once more. "What did they say about me at Vassar?"

Lionel laughed and replied, "They said that you were a serious student. A very devoted student. And quite shy."

Jackie repeated after him, "Shy. Yes, I am shy."

Lionel said, "I'm shy too." She looked at him, and they both burst out laughing. She knew that he was teasing her, and she liked it. I heard her say then, "Do you know who was here tonight?" And they began talking, and the conversation between them continued for the rest of the evening. Jackie's basic courtesy is sharply developed, and until a man came and sat down to talk specifically to me she was careful to try to guide some of her conversation with Lionel to include me. It's learned courtesy, totally conscious, not imperiled by champagne. But, once I was engaged in a conversation of my own, she fully directed herself to Lionel and never once gave a sign of having any interest in anyone else.

Not long after Jackie came in, the President came in, and with him were the undersecretary of defense and the deputy assistant secretary of state for inter-American affairs. We were fourteen or fifteen people altogether, and I began to understand that having this gathering in the Oval Room, although it included the President's family and some government people, was really Jackie's personal part of the evening. She had done her duty as a hostess, gone through the whole official occasion, and now it was her turn to have fun. In fact, I somehow had the impression that these little gatherings upstairs had become a kind of routine after large formal dinners, the price she demanded for having played her public part as conscientiously as she did.

And I felt the Kennedys had to accept Jackie's terms, because they realized that, for instance, the whole occasion we were having and the way the White House looked and how it ran were her doing — and this was not to mention the response of the public to her charm. She was their billion-dollar asset, and they were far too clever not to recognize it.

When Jackie first came into the room, she had pointed to a wooden rocker and said, "There's one in every room in the house. They're eyesores, aren't they?" She was referring to the rocker that was ordered for the President by his woman physician for his bad back. Jackie called it the President's health rocker and she said, "Do you know how much money is being made out of this? Do you know how many thousands of these rockers have been sold?"

At one moment, when there was a lull in the room and I thought that somebody ought to say something, I asked Jackie, "Did you have a good time on your trip?" I didn't mean her Palm Beach trip, and she understood that I meant a previous tour that she had been on. She looked at me and began a little smile, her eyes twinkling. She said, "I had a lovely time," and she said it in a tone that made it plain to me that she was repeating an official statement and that she hadn't had a good time at all.

At another point, she said something fairly startling about Khrushchev. In Vienna, a year earlier, she sat next to him at a state banquet. "I was sick with nervousness," she said. "I didn't know what I could talk about with him, and I kept asking Jack, 'What shall I say to him? What do I talk about?' I kept sitting there wondering what would be an innocent subject of conversation, and I decided to talk about animals. I said, 'I just love Russian dogs.' I asked him to send me one, and he did. Jack was furious with me for giving him such a diplomatic advantage." It was a marvelous story, but if it had got to the newspapers it would have been embarrassing for the President. "I still have that dog," she said. "It's around the White House grounds. But the problem is what to do with him. I want to mate him, but I haven't another Russian dog to mate him with, so I'd have to mate him with an American dog. I've been working on it, and I've been told that it won't take: a Russian dog and an American dog won't mate."

The President approached Lionel and pulled his chair — rocker — so close to him that they were really knee to knee.

"Well, what did they say about her at Vassar?" he asked Lionel.

Not at all awed, Lionel replied quietly, "They said that she was serious, a devoted student, a good student, shy." Jackie was just sitting there, watching Lionel's face.

"Shy, hmm," said the President. Nobody laughed; they were speaking quietly. I had the impression that the President was not thinking at all about Jackie or whether she had been shy at Vassar. He was looking at Lionel very sharply indeed. In teasing the President's wife, was he being impertinent to the President? Was he, in fact, that self-assured, and, if so, why? Was his report a literal report of what had been said to him about Jackie? From the answer to these questions the President would know how to place Lionel. All he said was "Linus Pauling was a lot of trouble today. He kept Caroline awake." And he told the famous story about how Caroline couldn't take her nap because of the noise on the picket line. "I don't mind his picketing the White House, but why does he have to picket right under the nursery window and keep the children awake?"

Then he got up from his rocker. He'd had his conversation with the Trillings, and now he moved on to somebody else. He joined the group around Frost, where the members of his family were seated. Then, sure enough, he went to a corner with Bobby and Salinger and the inter-American affairs man. It was plain that they were talking shop, and that for him the party was over. Jackie, however, was still having her party.

I could hear that Jackie had started to talk to Lionel about D. H. Lawrence. She said, "Is it true that *The Rainbow* is Lawrence's best book?"

Lionel said, "Some people may think so. Myself, I think *Women in Love* is better. What makes you think it's *The Rainbow?*"

"I was reading Compton Mackenzie's memoirs. He knew all of Lawrence's work, and he said that he thought *The Rainbow* was his best book." She added quickly, "Oh, I'm not sure I have that right. I think he said it was *The Rainbow.* Wait a minute." She jumped up and ran to the next room, which seemed to be a library, returning with the book in her hand. She leafed through it and quickly found the place — she knew how to handle books, how to find what she wanted in them. "Here it is," she said, and she read it aloud, and it was *The Rainbow* that Mackenzie had been praising. Lionel repeated that although he preferred *Women in Love, The Rainbow* was a great novel, and they kept on talking about Lawrence and about other writers. Jackie spoke very openly and unpretentiously, including her stepsister Nina in her conversation — Lionel had said he hadn't remembered her and wanted to be reminded. She spoke very charmingly, and said that she herself had wanted to audit one of Lionel's classes. She said Nina had been so insistent about being a student of Lionel's that she had almost made the family move to New York for just that reason. But Nina hadn't been accepted as a student; she had just audited his classes. She had been getting more and more pregnant. As soon as the baby was born, she had it in mind to go to Columbia and audit courses with Lionel three times a week.

I think it was here that I asked her in what way they were stepsisters. She assured me that she could never explain to anybody how her family worked, that everybody in it was a stepsister or stepbrother to everybody else. "There have been so many marriages in every part of the family — at Christmas it's a shambles. You don't know whom you have to send a card to, you don't know who your relatives really are."

Through all of this she was very open, in a crisp, modern manner: sure of herself and reliant on her own wit. But she must have made reference to her husband no fewer than a dozen times — how Jack had been very angry at her, how Jack had told her to stop reading in bed and put out the light. While Lionel was telling the President what they had said about Jackie at Vassar, Jackie herself kept looking at her husband, but with a deliberately blank expression.

We somehow knew that the party was over. She wanted it to continue, you could see that. She and Lionel were getting on so splendidly — Lionel really liked her, and she really liked him. It was now twelve-thirty.

The President was standing, and we all rose to leave. We all went over to him and shook hands with him, and I found myself saying what a lovely party it had been, and thank you very much, just as I would to any ordinary host. I had already said good night to Mrs. Kennedy and told her what a charming party it had been. I heard Lionel say to her, "I think you deserve great credit for this evening, everybody had such a wonderful time." She said, "You see, we used to have to come to the White House when Jack was a senator and the Eisenhowers were here. It was just unbearable. There would be Mamie in one chair and Ike in another. And on Mamie's right side would be the guest of honor, male, and on Ike's right side would be the guest of honor, female, and everybody stood, and there was nothing to drink. During that regime, there was never anything served to drink, and we made up our minds, when we came to the White House, that nobody was ever going to be as bored as that. We do try to make it a good party."

So there we said good night at the door. When we told the President what a wonderful party it had been, he replied that it had been very lovely to have us. He said that in a warm and personal way, but he was actually looking out the door. Jackie was at the party every moment of it, at least the upstairs part of it, and dying to go on some more. But he was tired and wanted to get to business. Or bed.

Bobby Kennedy led us to an elevator — I guess it was a private family elevator, large but not very sturdy-looking, and we all trooped into it. Bobby started to close the door when suddenly Jackie and Jack Kennedy came down the hall to see us off. It was a bit of a squeeze with so many of us, but Bobby stayed at his post to run it. Jackie said, "Oh, Bob, you can't crowd this many people into this elevator. Think of the headlines tomorrow morning, with all these distinguished people dead at the bottom of the shaft!" "It's all right, it's all right," Bobby replied. "Hold on, Mr. Frost!" He closed the gate. At our last sight of Jackie, she was waving to us. The car went down, and when we got downstairs we were led by Bobby to another portico, where our wraps were waiting for us. They'd been put there while we were upstairs.

"Are you staying at a hotel in Washington?" Bobby asked me. I said that we were going back to New York by the late-night train. He looked confounded. "The train?" he repeated, as if I had just told him that we were journeying to New York by tandem bicycle.

I assured him that I loved night trains, but he shook his head, unbelieving.

I don't know how we got to the train station — I suppose they had a car waiting for us. We could have danced our way, Lionel and I were so giddy. In fact, we did dance into the train station — I remember that. I had my left arm raised, Lionel had his right arm raised, and he was holding my hand while my mink stole trailed from our enfolded fingers. It was a kind of minuet we performed the length of the Union Station all the way to our train and our compartment.

JOHN UPDIKE

Lost Art

FROM THE NEW YORKER

IN THE THIRTIES and forties, when I was growing up, the cartoonist occupied a place in the cultural hierarchy not far below that of the movie star and the inventor. Walt Disney, Al Capp, Peter Arno — who, now, could attain their celebrity with just pen and ink? I cut my teeth on blocks and rubber toys depicting Disney characters, illiterately pondered oilcloth pages showing Donald Duck when he looked more like a gander, learned to read from a cardboard booklet telling the cautionary tale of the Three Little Pigs and the Big Bad Wolf, and climbed up through the comics section of the local paper into the slightly racier world of comic books and the single-image cartoons, usually captioned, in *Collier's*, *The Saturday Evening Post*, *Esquire*, and — much the best and most thought-provokingly adult — *The New Yorker*. Together, from chewable Disney artifact to decipherable Thurber scrawl, they formed a world that was realer to me than all but a few patches of the substantial world that had not been conjured up by cartoonists.

This world offers a child many sites for passionate involvement: the keyboard of a piano, for instance, or the workings of an automobile engine. By my teens, I had friends who were clever in one or the other realm; one boy, years before we got our drivers' licenses, could identify the make of car — cars were overwhelmingly of Detroit manufacture then — at a glance from a block or more away. He loved cars, and love breeds knowledge. I was able to identify all the cartoonists as they appeared in a magazine, which I rapidly leafed through upside down while my audience — usually an audience of one, and soon bored — confirmed me right side up. Like trees for an arborist, cartoons have personalities whose recognition the informed mind attains before any conscious sorting out of traits, just as we spot a known face, or even a certain swing of the body, at a distance that blurs all details.

I loved cartoons — almost any cartoon that met a modest standard of professional crispness — and studied them as if my salvation lay somewhere in their particularities of shading and penmanship. V. T. Hamlin, for instance, who drew the syndicated strip "Alley Oop," had a deliberate, grid-like style of cross-hatching that, mixed with the peculiar inverted proportions of his cavemen's legs and arms, signaled a special solidity in the progress of his dinosaur-studded panels. Hamlin, like Alex Raymond of "Flash Gordon" and Harold Foster of "Prince Valiant" and Milton Caniff of "Terry and the Pirates" and then "Steve Canyon," seemed to be operating well within his artistic capacities, as opposed to Chester Gould of "Dick Tracy" and Harold Gray of "Little Orphan Annie," who I felt were drawing at the very limit of their skills, with a cozy, wooden consistency; Gould, in his doubts that he had made this or that detail clear, would sometimes enclose an enlargement within a sharply outlined balloon, with an arrow and a label saying "2-Way Wrist Radio" or "Secret Compartment for Cyanide." Fontaine Fox of "Toonerville Folks" and Perry Cosby of "Skippy," on the other hand, worked with a certain inky looseness, a touch of impatience in their confident pen lines. This inky ease attained opulence in Al Capp's "Li'l Abner," the lines of which experienced a voluptuous thickening when limning the curves of Daisy Mae or Moonbeam McSwine. Capp and Caniff and Will Eisner, who drew the bloody, vertiginous "Spirit" comic books, were virtuosos; closer to a child's heart, and containing the essence of cartoon reality, were the strips of finite artistic means, like "Mutt and Jeff" and "Bringing Up Father" (Jiggs and Maggie) — holdovers from an earlier, vaudevillian era — and adventure strips whose implausibility was framed in an earnest stiffness of execution, such as "The Phantom" and "Mandrake the Magician." Strikingly minimal, in that pre-"Peanuts" era, was Crockett Johnson's "Barnaby," whose characters appeared in invariable profile and whose talk balloons were lettered not by hand but by mechanical typesetting. In my love of cartoons I sent away to cartoonists, care of their syndicates, begging for a free original strip; surprisingly many of them obliged. My sample "Barnaby" strip slowly shed, over the years, its glued-on lettering.

At a certain votive stage, I cut out favorite strips and made little long cardboard books of them, held together with those nail-like brass fasteners whose flat stem splits open, it always occurred to me, like a loose-jointed dancer's legs. In my passionate doting I cut cartoons out of magazines and pasted them in large scrapbooks, agonizing over which to choose when two were back to back — my first brush with editorial judgment. And of course I copied, copied onto paper and onto slick white cardboard, trying to master each quirk of these miniature universes. Li'l Abner's hair was always seen with the parting toward the viewer, and Mickey Mouse's circular ears were never seen on edge, and Downwind, in Zack Mosley's "Smilin' Jack," was always shown with face averted, and Smokey Stover, in Bill Holman's "Krazy Kat"-ish slapstick, kept saying "Foo" apropos of nothing and drove vehicles that were endlessly shedding their nuts and bolts. God — the heat, the quest, the bliss of it — was in the details. The way the letters of POW! or SHAZAM! overlapped, the qualities of the clouds that indicated explosions or thoughts, the whirling Saturns and stars that accompanied a blow to the head, the variations played upon the talk balloon, that two-dimensional irruption into the panel's three-dimensional space, invisible to its inhabitants and yet critical to their intercourse — all this had to be studied, imitated, absorbed. The studying occurred mostly on the floor, my head lifted up on my elbows but not very high. When I drew, too, my nose had to be close to the paper, though I was not generally nearsighted. But the *entering in* required close examination, as though I were physically worming my way into those panels, those lines fat and slender, those energetic zigzags, those shading dots I learned to call Benday.

A craft lore existed, of pen nibs, fine brushes, blue pencils, art-gum erasers, whiteout, and Higgins India ink (which came in broad-bottomed bottles that nevertheless could be knocked over, as several indelible stains on my family's carpets testified). The prestige of cartooning during the Depression and the forties was such that one did not have to travel farther than the variety store and the adjacent camera shop in the center of our small Pennsylvania town to find most of the necessary equipment. Bristol board (two- or three-ply, more flexible and ink-accepting than the slick posterboard children use in school), and a cardboard whose rippled surface would turn Conté crayon into halftones, and scratchboard, whose clayey top layer could be scraped to make white on black — for those one had to travel to the nearby city of Reading, where a number of art-supply stores, some combined with a framer's shop, offered their wares to the artsy-craftsy crowd. Black-and-white cartoons were reproduced by means of line cuts, which failed to register washes and penciled shadings. A great deal of technology went into creating the impression of gray; cross-hatching, stippling, and crayon textures could be done by hand, and then there were sheets of Benday in many patterns, to be laid on and selectively cut away. There was even a treated cardboard, Craftint, that, depending on which of two chemicals was brushed on, produced fine stripes or a crosshatch, thus supplying two degrees of halftone. My high school yearbook, for which I did many illustrations — more than anyone asked for — contains examples of this mechanical hatching, and of most of the other techniques my apprenticeship claimed acquaintance with.

I drew not for the sake of drawing but to get into metal — to have the work of my hand be turned into zinc cuts and by this means printed. The first cuts made from a drawing of mine — a Christmas card, perhaps, portraying the family dog, or a caricature done for the class-play program — were to me potent objects, a purchase on power. In the alchemical symbology of those gritty decades, and nowhere more so than in the gritty cities of Pennsylvania, metal was power — steel rails, iron beams, lead bullets, great greased knitting machines twittering with a thousand nickel-plated needles. The basement "machine shop," with a metal lathe, was commonplace in the town, and here and there an adept set up a gun shop in his backyard garage. The toy tanks and battleships and dive bombers that simulated the distant headlined war were metal, though of the cheapest "white" sort, which would bend and break in your hands. When you paid a school visit to the city newspaper, the linotypers would place in your palm a still hot lead slug bearing your name backward. When, in high school, I became a summer copyboy for the same newspaper, I saw how the comic strips arrived from the syndicates in the form of bundled paper matrices — a stiff pulpy colorless paper like that used in egg cartons — and how these rough (but legible, the reverse of a reverse) intaglios were filled with hot metal, and the cooled lead rectangles

were locked into forms and recast into curved plates, which were
bolted onto the rotary cylinders of the presses and thunderously
rolled to produce the daily comic pages. A cartoonist partook of
this process at the tentative, scratchy, inky outset, and then was
swept up and glorified by a massive, ponderous miracle of reproduction. To get a toehold in this metal world — that was my ambition, the height of my hope.

A 1950 issue of the soon defunct magazine *Flair* contained, in its
eccentric format, a booklet about the *Harvard Lampoon*, including
photographs of the young, crew-cut editors, the curious mock-
Flemish building, and some sample cartoons. Somewhere in the
concatenation of aspirations and inadvertences that got me to
Harvard, this story played a crucial part. Early in my freshman year,
I carried a batch of my cartoons down to the *Lampoon* building,
there where Mount Auburn Street meets Bow at an acute angle,
an ornate little brick flatiron fronted by a tower with a sort of cartoon face and, on its hat of roof tiles, a much stolen copper ibis.
In due course, some of my drawings were printed in the magazine, and I was accepted for membership. The *Lampoon*, I was too
ignorant an outsider to realize, was a social club, with a strong
flavor of Boston Brahminism and alcoholic intake; to me it was a
magazine for which I wanted to work. This I was allowed to do,
especially as the upperclassmen year by year graduated and the
various editorial offices fell to me. Though Harvard did little to
attract cartoonists, in fact there were four on the *Lampoon* in 1950
— Fred Gwynne, Lew Gifford, Doug Bunce, and Charlie Robinson
— who seemed to me much my betters in skill and sophistication.
Fred Gwynne, a multitalented giant who went on to become an
actor, best known for *Car 54, Where Are You?* and *The Munsters,* drew
with a Renaissance chiaroscuro and mastery of anatomy; Bunce
had a fine line, and Gifford, who made his career in television
animation, a carefree, flowing brush stroke years ahead of its time.
I tried to measure up to their examples, and cartooned abundantly
for the *Lampoon* — over half the artwork in some issues was mine
— but the budding cartoonist in me, exposed to what I felt were
superior talents, suffered a blight; my light verse and supposedly
humorous prose felt more viable. By graduation, I had pretty well
given up on becoming a cartoonist. It took too many ideas, and

one walked in too many footsteps. Writing seemed, in my inno-
cence of it, a relatively untrafficked terrain.

When I think of my brief cartooning heyday, I see myself at my
desk in my narrow room on the fifth floor of Lowell House,
working late at night under a hot gooseneck lamp. An undergraduate lives in a succession of rooms, and I drew in all of mine, but
this attic-like cubbyhole, occupied in my junior year, comes to
mind as *mon atelier.* My nose inches from the garishly illumined
bristol board, my lower lip sagging in the intensity of my concentration, a cigarette smoking in an ashtray near my eyes, I am
"inking in" — tracing the lightly penciled lines, trying to imbue
them with a graceful freedom while scarching out, in this final
limning, the contour being described. The nervous glee of drawing is such that I sometimes laugh aloud, alone. I would get so
excited by the process, so eager to admire the result, that I frequently smeared the still wet lines with my hand. This would put
me in mind of a tip I had read of in my high school days: a successful cartoonist advised aspirants to the art, "If you're not sure
the ink is dry, rub your sleeve over it." It had taken some days
before I realized that this was a joke, meant ironically.

Or, the precarious inking done, I am warily slicing, with a lethal
single-edge Treet razor blade, the boundaries of a patch of Benday,
or applying, with an annoyingly gummed-up little brush, whiteout
to an errant line or a stray blot. Years before, I had studied my
collection of begged comic strips, marveling at the frequency of
whiteout touches. Even professionals err. My soul hovers, five stories up, in the happiness of creation, the rapture of conjuring
something out of nothing. All around me, my fellow students are
silent, sleeping, or communing with the printed page; only I, in
this vicinity, am carving a little window into a universe that, an
hour ago, had not been there at all.

I dislike drawing now, since it makes me face the fact that I draw
no better, indeed rather worse, than I did when I was twenty-one.
Drawing is sacred to me, and I don't like to see it inferiorly done.
A drawing can feel perfect, in a way that prose never does, and a
poem rarely. Language is intrinsically approximate, since words
mean different things to different people, and there is no material
retaining ground for the imagery that words conjure in one brain
or another. When I drew, the line was exactly as I made it, just so,

down to the tremor of excitement my hand may have communicated to the pen; and thus it was reproduced. Up to the midpoint of my writing career, most strenuously in the poem "Midpoint," I sometimes tried to bring this visual absoluteness, this two-dimensional quiddity, onto a page of print with some pictorial device. But the attempt was futile, and a disfigurement, really. Only the letters themselves, originally drawn with sticks and styluses and pens, and then cast into metal fonts, whose forms are now reproduced by electronic processes, legitimately touch the printed page with cartoon magic.

JAMES WOOD

Real Life

FROM NEWS FROM THE REPUBLIC OF LETTERS

GOING TO the theater is generally unrewarding; even Ibsen in New York, this summer, was tedious. I watched a new production of *A Doll's House* with mounting dismay, and was reminded of mild, slippery Chekhov telling Stanislavsky in a quiet voice, as if it were something too obvious to say: "But listen, Ibsen is no playwright! . . . Ibsen just doesn't know life. In life it simply isn't like that."

No, in life it simply isn't like that. Outside the Broadway theater the traffic sounds like an army that is always getting closer but which never arrives, and the fantastic heat is sensual, and the air conditioners drip their sap, their backsides thrust out of the window like Alisoun who does the same in Chaucer, and everything is the usual chaotic obscurity. Nothing is clear. But inside, here is Ibsen didactically ordering life into three trim acts, and a cooled audience obediently laughing at the right moments and thinking about drinks at the interval — the one moment of Chekhovian life is that, in the lobby, the barman can be heard making too much noise putting out glasses. The clinking is disturbing Ibsen's simpler tune.

A Doll's House, of course, tells the story of a woman's subjection to and eventual escape from her husband. Ibsen is not entirely clumsy; he does not make Nora's husband, Torvald, monstrous so much as uncomprehending. And yet he cannot help neatly underlining how uncomprehending Torvald is, just in case we miss it. Nora deceives her husband in order to protect him. He discovers the deception and is furious. Toward the end of the play, Nora tells him that she is leaving him because she sees that she has never been more than his toy. She cries because he does not understand her complaint, and Ibsen hammers this home: "Why are you crying?" Torvald asks her. "Is it because I have forgiven you for your deception?" At this moment the audience snickered knowingly. Poor, foolish Torvald! Someone behind me, caught up in the play's melodramatic slipstream, whispered, "He is dreadful!"

Ibsen is like a man who laughs at his own jokes: he relishes too obviously the dramatic ironies of the situation. Ibsen's people are too comprehensible — we comprehend them not as we comprehend real people but as we comprehend fictional entities. He is always tying the moral shoelaces of his characters, making everything neat, presentable, knowable. Their secrets are of the formal, bourgeois, novelistic kind: a former lover, a broken contract, a debt, an unwanted relative, a blackmailer on the prowl. Ibsen's task is to drag these secrets to light and make them the engine of the drama. It is because Nora's "secret" — the fraudulent contract she signs to borrow money — is revealed that the play is set in motion.

But these are merely knowable secrets. Chekhov deals in true privacies. I sat in the theater and considered Chekhov's idea of art, a bashful, milky complication, not a solving of things. How does Chekhov make us feel, in *Uncle Vanya* or in the great stories, that his art is not hustling life into comprehensibility? One way is through a pioneering use of what is called stream of consciousness. He allows his characters to speak as if they are turning a mental stream of consciousness outward. The particular loveliness of Chekhov is that what people say to each other and think to themselves feels arbitrary, like life or like memory. And this is also why it so often strikes us as comic, for watching a Chekhov character is like watching a lover wake up in bed, half awake and half dreaming, saying something odd and private that means nothing to us because it refers to the receding dream. In life, at such moments, we often laugh, and say, "You're not making any sense, you know." Chekhov's characters have a similar dreaminess.

The key to the great freedom of Chekhov's characters lies in his use of how thought works, and how we put this into words. You can see this very beautifully in "The Steppe," Chekhov's first major story, which he wrote when he was twenty-eight. A small boy, Yegorushka, goes on a journey across the steppe. He is going to a new

boarding school, accompanied by two men — a trader and a priest.
As he watches a cemetery go by, the boy thinks to himself:

> From behind the wall cheerful white crosses and tombstones peeped
> out, nestling in the foliage of cherry trees and seen as white patches
> from a distance. At blossom time, Yegorushka remembered, the white
> patches mingled with the cherry blooms in a sea of white, and when
> the cherries had ripened the white tombs and crosses were crimson-
> spotted, as if with blood. Under the cherries behind the wall the boy's
> father and his grandmother Zinaida slept day and night. When Grand-
> mother had died she had been put in a long, narrow coffin, and five-
> copeck pieces had been placed on her eyes, which would not stay shut.
> Before dying she had been alive, and she had brought him soft poppy-
> seed bun rings from the market, but now she just slept and slept.

One sees here why Joyce admired Chekhov (and watching *A
Doll's House*, alas, one sees why Shaw admired Ibsen). "Before dying
she had been alive . . . but now she just slept and slept." This is
not only how a small boy thinks, but how all of us think about the
dead, privately: *Before dying, she had been alive*. It is one of those
obviously pointless banalities of thought, an accidental banality
that, being an accident, is not banal. Chekhov's genius was to see
how often we speak like this too. When the little boy cries (he
misses his mother), Father Christopher, the priest, comforts him.
But his solace has no dramatic "point," in the Ibsen sense. It
furthers no ideological argument. Indeed, in Chekhovian fashion,
it is not really solace at all. The priest is simply thinking aloud,
selfishly:

> Never mind, son . . . Call on God. Lomonosov once travelled just like
> this with the fishermen, and he became famous throughout Europe.
> Learning conjoined with faith yields fruit pleasing to God. What does
> the prayer say? "For the glory of the Creator, for our parents' comfort,
> for the benefit of church and country." That's the way of it.

Father Christopher is speaking in the same way that, a minute
before, the little boy was thinking: aimlessly.

The great innovation of the stream of consciousness is that it
allows absent-mindedness into fiction. Buried deep in their subjectivity, people forget themselves while thinking, and go on safaris
of detail. Or rather, they don't exactly forget themselves. They
forget how to act as purposeful fictional characters. They forget

what they are supposed to do. They mislay their scripts. They stop being actors and become people. Remember the virginal soldier in Chekhov's "The Kiss," who kisses a woman at a party and longs to tell his fellow soldiers about it? When he finally gets the chance, he is amazed that his anecdote takes only a few seconds. Because he has been hoarding his story, he "had imagined it would take until morning." The soldier forgets that he is in Chekhov's story, because he is so involved in his own. Think of how often Chekhov brings his characters out of their fantasies and into real life. How often in his fiction we encounter the formulation "And suddenly he realized that . . ." or "It was not until that moment that he knew . . ."

Some of this became clear as I sat watching *A Doll's House*. This, partly, is what Chekhov means by real life: he means real mental life, with its wrong turnings and cul-de-sacs and random, intimately treasured banalities. He lets his characters speak their minds. Isn't this what Henry James meant when he spoke of wanting to let his characters exist in the "irresponsible, plastic way"? Ibsen's characters are always stage actors. Chekhov's characters forget to be Chekhov's characters, and nothing could be more irresponsible than that.

Biographical Notes

ANWAR F. ACCAWI was born and raised in Magdaluna, a very small Lebanese village in the remote hills above the city of Sidon. He received his college education in the United States and afterward began writing stories about his life and old home for his children, who knew nothing of the old country. He has just begun publishing his essays and stories, and currently teaches at the University of Tennessee.

ANDRÉ ACIMAN was born in Alexandria and raised in Egypt, Italy, and France. Educated at Harvard, he teaches literature at Bard College and is the author of a memoir, *Out of Egypt* (1994). "Shadow Cities" is adapted from a lecture given at the New York Public Library as a part of its series "Letters of Transit."

HELEN BAROLINI is the author of *Umbertina,* a novel of the Italian American experience, which will soon be reissued by the Feminist Press. She is also known for her ground-breaking anthology, *The Dream Book: An Anthology of Writing by Italian American Women,* which received an American Book Award. She has published five other books, many stories and essays, and has translated the work of Italian authors. Her most recent book is *Chiaroscuro: Essays of Identity.*

SAUL BELLOW's first novel, *Dangling Man,* was published in 1944. Among his novels since then are *Henderson the Rain King, Humboldt's Gift, More Die of Heartbreak,* and, most recently, *The Actual,* published in 1997. He received the Nobel Prize in literature in 1976. He lives in New England, teaches at Boston University, and is coeditor, with Keith Botsford, of *News from the Republic of Letters.*

JEREMY BERNSTEIN is a professor emeritus in physics at the Stevens Institute of Technology. He was a staff writer for *The New Yorker* from 1963 to 1993. He has published articles on science and travel in most of the major magazines. His latest books are *A Theory for Everything, In the Himalayas,* and *An Introduction to Cosmology.*

SVEN BIRKERTS has published essays and reviews in *Harper's Magazine, The Atlantic Monthly, The New Republic,* the *New York Times Book Review,* and elsewhere. *The Gutenberg Elegies: The Fate of Reading in an Electronic Age,* his fourth book of essays, appeared in 1995. *Readings,* a new collection, will be published in 1999 by Graywolf Press.

J. M. COETZEE is the author of *Waiting for the Barbarians, Foe, Dusklands, The Master of Petersburg, Age of Iron, Life and Times of Michael K.,* and other novels. His collections of essays include *Giving Offense: Essays on Censorship* and *Doubling the Point.* He is a professor in the Department of English at the University of Cape Town in South Africa.

BRIAN DOYLE is the editor of *Portland Magazine* at the University of Portland, Oregon. His essays and poems have appeared in *The American Scholar, Ar Mhuin na Muice, The Atlantic Monthly, Commonweal,* and *Yankee,* among other publications, and he and his father, Jim Doyle, are the authors of *Two Voices,* a book of their essays. A collection of Brian Doyle's essays on Catholic subjects, *Credo,* will be published in 1999.

"Witness" is from ANDRE DUBUS's collection of essays *Meditations from a Movable Chair* (Knopf). Dubus's son, Andre Dubus III, published an essay in *The Best American Essays 1994.*

JOSEPH EPSTEIN is the author of two works of nonfiction, a short story collection, and nine collections of essays, the most recent of which are *Pertinent Players* (1993), *With My Trousers Rolled* (1995), and *Life Sentences* (1997). The guest editor of *The Best American Essays 1993,* he is a frequent contributor to *The New Yorker, Commentary, The New Criterion, Hudson Review,* and other periodicals, and has recently edited *The Norton Book of Personal Essays* (1997). He teaches at Northwestern University.

IAN FRAZIER is the author of two works of nonfiction, *Family* and *Great Plains,* as well as several collections of humorous essays: *Dating Your Mom; Nobody Better, Better Than Nobody;* and *Coyote v. Acme.* His writing has appeared in *The New Yorker, The Atlantic Monthly, Outside,* and many other magazines. The guest editor of *The Best American Essays 1997,* he lives in Missoula, Montana.

WILLIAM H. GASS is the author of ten books of fiction and nonfiction, including *Omensetter's Luck, In the Heart of the Heart of the Country, On*

Being Blue, The World Within the Word, and *Habitations of the Word,* which won the 1986 National Book Critics Circle Award for criticism. He is the David May Distinguished University Professor in the Humanities and director of the International Writers Center at Washington University in St. Louis. He has been the recipient of grants from both the Rockefeller Foundation and the Guggenheim Foundation and has also received the American Academy and Institute of Arts and Letters Award for fiction. His most recent books include a novel, *The Tunnel;* an essay collection, *Finding a Form,* which won the 1996 National Book Critics Circle Award for criticism; and *Cartesian Sonata,* a collection of novellas.

ELIZABETH GRAVER is the author of the short story collection *Have You Seen Me?,* which won the 1991 Drue Heinz Literature Prize, and *Unravelling,* a novel set in nineteenth-century New England. Her stories have appeared in *The Best American Short Stories 1991* and in the 1994 and 1996 editions of *Prize Stories: The O'Henry Awards.* She has received grants from the National Endowment for the Arts and the Guggenheim Foundation and teaches at Boston College.

EDWARD HOAGLAND has published seven collections of essays, most recently *Balancing Acts;* five books of fiction, including *Seven Rivers West;* and two travel books, *Notes from the Century Before: A Journal from British Columbia* and *African Calliope: A Journey to the Sudan,* both of which were reissued in 1995. He also writes criticism and is the editor of the Penguin Nature Classics Series. He is a member of the American Academy of Arts and Letters and has taught at ten colleges, currently at Bennington. His new essay collection, *Tigers and Ice,* will come out next year.

JAMAICA KINCAID is the author of *Annie John, A Small Place,* and *Lucy.* Her first book, *At the Bottom of the River,* received the Morton Dauwen Zabel Award of the American Academy and Institute of Arts and Letters. She was guest editor of *The Best American Essays 1995,* and her most recent books include *An Autobiography of My Mother; My Brother;* and (with Marianna Cook) *Generations of Women.*

WILLIAM MAXWELL was born in Lincoln, Illinois, in 1908. For forty years he was an editor at *The New Yorker.* His novels and story collections, many of which have been recently reissued, include *Bright Center of Heaven, They Came Like Swallows, The Folded Leaf, Time Will Darken It, The Chateau, The Old Man and the Crossing, Over by the River,* and *So Long, See You Tomorrow.* He has also written several books of nonfiction, including *The Writer as Illusionist, Ancestors: A Family History,* and *The Outermost*

Dream: Essays and Reviews. All the Days and Nights: The Collected Stories of William Maxwell appeared in 1995. He lives in New York City.

JOHN MCPHEE, the author of twenty-five books published by Farrar, Straus & Giroux, has been a staff writer for *The New Yorker* since 1965 and a Ferris Professor of Journalism at Princeton University since 1975.

MARY OLIVER is well known as a poet; her volume *American Primitive* received the Pulitzer Prize in poetry in 1983, and *New and Selected Poems* won the National Book Award in 1992. *Blue Pastures* (1994) was her first book of essays. A volume of her poems, *West Wind,* appeared in 1997; this year her handbook on metrical poetry, *Rules for the Dance,* was published. She is currently working on a second book of essays, *Winter Hours.* She is a member of the faculty at Bennington College.

TIM ROBINSON was born in England in 1935. He studied mathematics at Cambridge and worked as a teacher and artist in Istanbul, Vienna, and London. In 1972 he moved to the west of Ireland and began writing and making maps. He now lives in Roundstone, Connemara, where he runs the Folding Landscape Studio with his wife, Máiréad. He is the author of a two-volume survey of the Aran Islands, *Stones of Aran: Pilgrimage* (1986) and *Stones of Aran: Labyrinth* (1995). *Setting Foot on the Shores of Connemara & Other Writings* appeared in 1996.

OLIVER SACKS, M.D., was born in London in 1933 and educated in London, Oxford, and California. He is a professor of neurology at the Albert Einstein College of Medicine and the author of seven books: *Migraine, Awakenings, A Leg to Stand On, The Man Who Mistook His Wife for a Hat, Seeing Voices, An Anthropologist on Mars,* and *The Island of the Colourblind.* He lives on City Island in New York, where he swims and raises cycads and ferns. He is at work on a book about the periodic table, to be published by Knopf in 2000.

LYNNE SHARON SCHWARTZ's most recent book is *Ruined by Reading: A Life in Books.* Her earlier books include the novels *The Fatigue Artist, Disturbances in the Field, Rough Strife* (nominated for a National Book Award and the PEN/Hemingway Award), *Leaving Brooklyn* (nominated for a PEN/Faulkner Award), and *Balancing Acts,* as well as two story collections, *The Melting Pot and Other Subversive Stories* and *Acquainted with the Night.* Her work has been widely anthologized and is collected in *A Lynne Sharon Schwartz Reader: Selected Prose and Poetry.* Though eschewing the academic life, she has nomadically taught fiction writing in many graduate programs, most recently at Washington University in St. Louis. She has just completed a comic novel of manners, called *In the Family Way: Scenes of Frolic and Folly,* and her next project will be a collection of essays.

LOUIS SIMPSON is the author of fourteen books of verse and several books of literary criticism. In 1998 his *Modern Poets of France: A Bilingual Anthology* (Story Line Press) won the Harold Morton Landon Translation Award, given by the Academy of American Poets. His other recent publications are a memoir, *The King My Father's Wreck,* a collection of poems, *There You Are* (both books published by Story Line), and a selection of his poems translated in French, *Nombres et poussière* (Atelier La Feugraie, Paris). He lives in Setauket, New York.

DIANA TRILLING was born in New York City in 1905. She married the distinguished literary critic Lionel Trilling in 1929 and began her own literary career in the 1940s, writing reviews and criticism for *The Nation* and *Partisan Review.* Her books include *Reviewing the Forties, We Must March My Darlings, Mrs. Harris: The Death of the Scarsdale Diet Doctor,* and *The Beginning of the Journey.* She died in October 1996.

JOHN UPDIKE was born in 1932 in Shillington, Pennsylvania. After graduation from Harvard in 1954 and a year at an English art school, he worked for two years for *The New Yorker*'s "Talk of the Town" department. Since 1957 he has lived in Massachusetts as a freelance writer. His most recent book is a novel, *Toward the End of Time.*

JAMES WOOD is a senior editor at *The New Republic,* before which he was the chief literary critic for *The Guardian,* in London. A volume of his essays, *The Broken Estate: Essays on Literature and Belief,* will be published by Random House in 1999.

Notable Essays of 1997

SELECTED BY ROBERT ATWAN